OXFORD IB DIPLOMA PROGRAMME

CAUSES AND EFFECTS OF 20TH-CENTURY WARS

COURSE COMPANION

David M. Smith

OXFORD
UNIVERSITY PRESS

OXFORD
UNIVERSITY PRESS

Great Clarendon Street, Oxford, OX2 6DP, United Kingdom

Oxford University Press is a department of the University of Oxford. It furthers the University's objective of excellence in research, scholarship, and education by publishing worldwide. Oxford is a registered trade mark of Oxford University Press in the UK and in certain other countries

British Library Cataloguing in Publication Data
Data available

978-0-19-831020-4

10 9 8 7 6 5 4

Paper used in the production of this book is a natural, recyclable product made from wood grown in sustainable forests. The manufacturing process conforms to the environmental regulations of the country of origin.

Printed in India by Manipal Technologies Limited

Acknowledgements

p7: VintageCorner/Alamy; p17: Photo12/UIG/Getty Images; p25: Dominique Berretty/Gamma-Rapho/Getty Images; p29: The Print Collector/Alamy; p31: The Print Collector/Alamy; p33: Photos 12/Alamy; p40: Daniel Garcia/AFP/Getty Images; p46: Adrian Brown/Alamy; p47: Ian Macpherson Aviation/Alamy; p51: Adrian Brown/Alamy; p52: Martin Cleaver/Pool/Getty Images; p66: Howard Sochurek/The LIFE Picture Collection/Getty Images; p76: Keystone Pictures USA/Alamy; p77: Keystone Pictures USA/Alamy; p78: Collection Jean-Claude Labbe/Gamma-Rapho/Getty Images; p80: AFP/Getty Images; p92: Interfoto/Alamy; p96: DIZ Muenchen GmbH, Sueddeutsche Zeitung Photo/Alamy; p101(L): Swim Ink 2, LLC/Corbis; p101(C): Iberfoto/Superstock; p101(R): Documenta/Album/Superstock; p107(L): Sueddeutsche Zeitung Photo/Alamy; p107(R): ZUMA Press/Alamy; p110: Lordprice Collection/Alamy; p125: GL Archive/Alamy; p127: DIZ Muenchen GmbH, Sueddeutsche Zeitung Photo/Alamy; p126: Rob Walls/Alamy; p130: Photos 12/Alamy; p133: DIZ Muenchen GmbH, Sueddeutsche Zeitung Photo/Alamy; p134: World History Archive/Alamy; p135: Chronicle/Alamy; p146: Military Images/Alamy; p161: Everett Collection Inc/Alamy; p166: World History Archive/Alamy; p170: Pete Roberts/Alamy; p171: Lordprice Collection/Alamy; p174: Pictorial Press Ltd/Alamy; p177: DIZ Muenchen GmbH, Sueddeutsche Zeitung Photo/Alamy; p181: Prisma Bildagentur AG/Alamy; p184: Everett Collection Inc/Alamy; p188: GL Archive/Alamy; p186(T): DIZ Muenchen GmbH, Sueddeutsche Zeitung Photo/Alamy; p186(B): Hideo Kurihara/Alamy; p193: ITAR-TASS Photo Agency/Alamy; p204: DIZ Muenchen GmbH, Sueddeutsche Zeitung Photo/Alamy; p213: Archive Image/Alamy; p210: Archive Image/Alamy; p215: US Army Photo/Alamy; p216(T): Interfoto/Alamy; p216(B): Archive Image/Alamy; p220(R): Photo Researchers/Alamy; p218: AV8 Collection 2/Alamy; p220(L): Everett Historical/Shutterstock.

Cover illustration by Karolis Strautniekas, Folio Illustration Agency.

Artwork by QBS Learning and OUP.

We are grateful to the authors and publishers for use of extracts from their titles and in particular for the following:

Bernard Fall: *Street Without Joy: The French Debacle in Indo China*, (Harrisburg, 1961), Stackpole Books. Reproduced by permission.

"European World Dead By the Numbers: World Wide Deaths", The National WWII Museum http://www.nationalww2museum. org/learn/education/for-students/ww2-history/ww2-by-the-numbers/world-wide-deaths.html. Reproduced by permission.

Edward Halifax: *Fullness of Days*. (1956) Dodd, Mead and Co., London, UK. http://spartacus-educational.com/PRchamberlain.htm. Reproduced by permission of Lord Charles Halifax.

Paul Kennedy: Table 20: Warship Tonnage of the Powers, 1880-1914," "Table 19: Military and Naval Personnel, 1880-1914," "Table 14: Per Capita Levels of Industrialization, 1880-1938," "Table 15: Iron/Steel Production of the Powers, 1890-1938," "Table 17: Total Industrial Potential of the Powers in Relative Perspective, 1880-1938," "Table 16: Energy Consumption of the Powers, 1890-1938," "Table 23: UK Munitions Production, 1914-1918," and "Table 32: Relative War Potential of the Powers in 1937" from THE RISE AND FALL OF THE GREAT POWERS: ECONOMIC CHANGE AND MILITARY CONFLICT FROM 1500 TO 2000, copyright © 1987 by Paul Kennedy. Reprinted by permission of HarperCollins Publishers Ltd and Random House, an imprint and division of Penguin Random House LLC. All rights reserved. Any third party use of this material, outside of this publication, is prohibited. Interested parties must apply directly to Penguin Random House LLC for permission.

We have made every effort to trace and contact all copyright holders before publication, but if notified of any errors or omissions, the publisher will be happy to rectify these at the earliest opportunity.

Links to third party websites are provided by Oxford in good faith and for information only. Oxford disclaims any responsibility for the materials contained in any third party website referenced in this work.

Course Companion definition

The IB Diploma Programme Course Companions are resource materials designed to support students throughout their two-year Diploma Programme course of study in a particular subject. They will help students gain an understanding of what is expected from the study of an IB Diploma Programme subject while presenting content in a way that illustrates the purpose and aims of the IB. They reflect the philosophy and approach of the IB and encourage a deep understanding of each subject by making connections to wider issues and providing opportunities for critical thinking.

The books mirror the IB philosophy of viewing the curriculum in terms of a whole-course approach; the use of a wide range of resources, international mindedness, the IB learner profile and the IB Diploma Programme core requirements, theory of knowledge, the extended essay, and creativity, activity, service (CAS).

Each book can be used in conjunction with other materials and indeed, students of the IB are required and encouraged to draw conclusions from a variety of resources. Suggestions for additional and further reading are given in each book and suggestions for how to extend research are provided.

In addition, the Course Companions provide advice and guidance on the specific course assessment requirements and on academic honesty protocol. They are distinctive and authoritative without being prescriptive.

IB mission statement

The International Baccalaureate aims to develop inquiring, knowledgable and caring young people who help to create a better and more peaceful world through intercultural understanding and respect.

To this end the IB works with schools, governments and international organizations to develop challenging programmes of international education and rigorous assessment.

These programmes encourage students across the world to become active, compassionate, and lifelong learners who understand that other people, with their differences, can also be right.

The IB learner Profile

The aim of all IB programmes is to develop internationally minded people who, recognizing their common humanity and shared guardianship of the planet, help to create a better and more peaceful world. IB learners strive to be:

Inquirers They develop their natural curiosity. They acquire the skills necessary to conduct inquiry and research and show independence in learning. They actively enjoy learning and this love of learning will be sustained throughout their lives.

Knowledgable They explore concepts, ideas, and issues that have local and global significance. In so doing, they acquire in-depth knowledge and develop understanding across a broad and balanced range of disciplines.

Thinkers They exercise initiative in applying thinking skills critically and creatively to recognize and approach complex problems, and make reasoned, ethical decisions.

Communicators They understand and express ideas and information confidently and creatively in more than one language and in a variety of modes of communication. They work effectively and willingly in collaboration with others.

Principled They act with integrity and honesty, with a strong sense of fairness, justice, and respect for the dignity of the individual, groups, and communities. They take responsibility for their own actions and the consequences that accompany them.

Open-minded They understand and appreciate their own cultures and personal histories, and are open to the perspectives, values, and traditions of other individuals and communities. They are accustomed to seeking and evaluating a range of points of view, and are willing to grow from the experience.

Caring They show empathy, compassion, and respect towards the needs and feelings of others. They have a personal commitment to service, and act to make a positive difference to the lives of others and to the environment.

Risk-takers They approach unfamiliar situations and uncertainty with courage and forethought, and have the independence of spirit to explore new roles, ideas, and strategies. They are brave and articulate in defending their beliefs.

Balanced They understand the importance of intellectual, physical, and emotional balance to achieve personal well-being for themselves and others.

Reflective They give thoughtful consideration to their own learning and experience. They are able to assess and understand their strengths and limitations in order to support their learning and personal development.

A note on academic honesty

It is of vital importance to acknowledge and appropriately credit the owners of information when that information is used in your work. After all, owners of ideas (intellectual property) have property rights. To have an authentic piece of work, it must be based on your individual and original ideas with the work of others fully acknowledged. Therefore, all assignments, written or oral, completed for assessment must use your own language and expression. Where sources are used or referred to, whether in the form of direct quotation or paraphrase, such sources must be appropriately acknowledged.

How do I acknowledge the work of others?

The way that you acknowledge that you have used the ideas of other people is through the use of footnotes and bibliographies.

Footnotes (placed at the bottom of a page) or endnotes (placed at the end of a document) are to be provided when you quote or paraphrase from another document, or closely summarize the information provided in another document. You do not need to provide a footnote for information that is part of a 'body of knowledge'. That is, definitions do not need to be footnoted as they are part of the assumed knowledge.

Bibliographies should include a formal list of the resources that you used in your work. The listing should include all resources, including books, magazines, newspaper articles, Internet-based resources, CDs and works of art. 'Formal' means that you should use one of the several accepted forms of presentation. You must provide full information as to how a reader or viewer of your work can find the same information. A bibliography is compulsory in the extended essay.

What constitutes misconduct?

Misconduct is behaviour that results in, or may result in, you or any student gaining an unfair advantage in one or more assessment component. Misconduct includes plagiarism and collusion.

Plagiarism is defined as the representation of the ideas or work of another person as your own. The following are some of the ways to avoid plagiarism:

- Words and ideas of another person used to support one's arguments must be acknowledged.
- Passages that are quoted verbatim must be enclosed within quotation marks and acknowledged.
- CD-ROMs, email messages, web sites on the Internet, and any other electronic media must be treated in the same way as books and journals.
- The sources of all photographs, maps, illustrations, computer programs, data, graphs, audio-visual, and similar material must be acknowledged if they are not your own work.
- Works of art, whether music, film, dance, theatre arts, or visual arts, and where the creative use of a part of a work takes place, must be acknowledged.

Collusion is defined as supporting misconduct by another student. This includes:

- allowing your work to be copied or submitted for assessment by another student
- duplicating work for different assessment components and/or diploma requirements.

Other forms of misconduct include any action that gives you an unfair advantage or affects the results of another student. Examples include, taking unauthorized material into an examination room, misconduct during an examination, and falsifying a CAS record.

Contents

YOUR GUIDE TO PAPER 2

The information in this book relates to key figures or events but is not prescriptive. For example, any relevant war can be referred to in an answer on *Causes, practices and effects of wars*. While the author has chosen well-known wars in this book, there is also an opportunity to explore your own regional history using the book as a guide as to the necessary concepts to know and to understand.

The aim of this book is to :

- provide in depth knowledge of a world history topic
- introduce key historical concepts
- develop skills by providing tasks and exercises
- introduce different historical perspectives related to key events/personalities.

The content in this book is linked to the six key IB concepts.

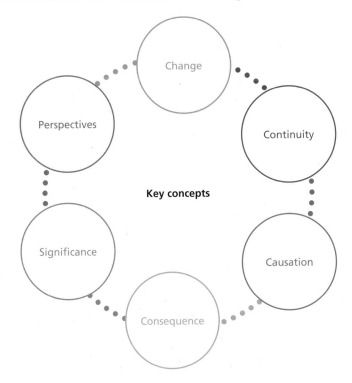

How to use this book

This book contains sections relating to key aspects of *Causes and effects of 20th-century wars* as outlined in the prescribed content section of the IB syllabus, for example, causes, practices and effects of war.

You should use the book in the following ways:

- To gain more detailed knowledge about a significant event or leader
- To gain insight and understanding of different perspectives (explanations) of an historical event

- Use the exercises to increase your understanding and skills, particularly the skill of analysis when contributing to the formulation of an argument

- Consider the exam-style questions at the end of each chapter and think how you would apply your knowledge and understanding in an essay in response to the question.

As you work through the book make sure you develop strategies to help you learn, retaining the information and understanding you have acquired. These may be in the form of timelines (where chronology is important), spider diagrams, cue cards and other methods to suit your individual learning style. It is better to consolidate knowledge and understanding as you go along; this will make revision for the examination easier.

What you will be expected to do

There are 12 world history topics and the course requires you to study two of them. You should learn about a range of factors in the prescribed content relevant to each topic area, as shown in this table for Topic 11: *Causes and effects of 20th-century wars*.

Topic	Prescribed content
Causes of war	• Economic, ideological, political, territorial and other causes • Short- and long-term causes
Practices of war and their impact on the outcome	• Types of war: civil wars; wars between states; guerrilla wars • Technological developments; theatres of war – air, land and sea • The extent of the mobilization of human and economic resources • The influence and/or involvement of foreign powers
Effects of war	• The successes and failures of peace making • Territorial changes • Political repercussions • Economic, social and demographic impact; changes in the role and status of women

Make sure you understand all the terms used under the heading "prescribed content" because these terms will be used to structure examination questions. If you have a clear understanding of all these terms, you will get the focus of your answers right and be able to select appropriate examples.

- If you are studying "The causes and effects of 20th-century wars", an exam question may focus on "political or economic causes", which is in the prescribed content.

- If you are studying Authoritarian States, you may get a question dealing with the topic "Emergence of authoritarian states". When the focus is on the "use of force", this relates to "methods used to establish authoritarian states" in the prescribed content.

- If you are studying the Cold War and the topic area is "Rivalry, mistrust and accord", you may get a question that focuses on "two Cold war crises each chosen from a different region and their impact on the Cold War", as stated in the prescribed content.

The Paper 2 examination is an essay-based examination in which you are expected to answer two questions in 90 minutes in two different topic areas. You **must** choose questions from two different topics. This amounts to 45 minutes per question – not much time for answering what can be rather broad questions on two different subjects. One of the most critical components in succeeding in this examination, therefore, is good time management.

The best ways to improve your essay-writing skills are to read examples of effective, well-structured essays and to practise writing them yourself. In addition to timing, you must understand the skills you need to produce a good answer.

What the exam paper will look like

The will be 24 questions with two questions set for each of the twelve topics. There will be clear headings identifying the topics and the questions will focus on different aspects of the topic as outlined in the prescribed content.

The questions will be "open" questions (with no specific names or events mentioned). This will allow you to apply your knowledge and understanding in response to the question set. Some questions may ask you to refer to events or leaders, "each chosen from a different region".

Preparing for Paper 2

Make sure you understand what the command terms used in essay questions are asking you to do. The most common command terms are:

- **Compare and contrast**
  Identify similarities and differences relating to a specific factor or event

- **Discuss**
  Review a range of arguments

- **Evaluate**
  Weigh up strengths and limitations. In an essay question this is often expressed as "successes and failures"

- **Examine**
  Consider an argument or assumption and make a judgment as to the validity of either

- **To what extent**
  This usually refers to a quotation or a statement, inviting you to agree or disagree with it

Essay skills

Understanding the focus of a question is vital as this is one of the skills and examiner looks for. There are usually two or three **focus words** in a question.

The focus words are identified in the examples below:

Example 1

Evaluate the *significance* of *economic factors* in the *rise to power* of one 20th century authoritarian leader.

The question is asking about the importance of economic issues and crises in the rise to power of an authoritarian leader.

A good answer would be expected to include a range of factors (popularity, threat of force and weakness of existing political system) not just economic factors, before making a judgment on the importance of economic factors in the rise to power of the chosen leader.

Example 2

The *outcome* of Civil war is often *decided* by the *actions of Foreign powers*. To what extent do you agree with this statement with reference to **two** civil wars *each chosen from different regions*.

The question is asking you to consider whether the end of civil wars is usually decided by foreign powers. Again you should consider a range of factors relevant to your chosen examples. It is quite possible that the statement applies to one of them but not the other.

Example 3

Evaluate the *social and economic challenges* facing one newly independent state and how *effectively* they were dealt with.

The question is asking you to do two things – identify social and economic problems and then assess the success and failures of attempts to solve those problems.

The command term tells you what you have to do and the focus words tell you what you have to write about. Make it clear in your answers that you understand both of these and you will show the examiner that "the demands of the question are understood" – a phrase that is used in the markbands for Paper 2.

Markbands

Marks	Level descriptor
0	Answers do not reach a standard described by the descriptors below.
1–3	There is little understanding of the demands of the question. The response is poorly structured or, where there is a recognizable essay structure, there is minimal focus on the task.
	Little knowledge of the world history topic is present.
	The student identifies examples to discuss, but these examples are factually incorrect, irrelevant or vague.
	The response contains little or no critical analysis. The response may consist mostly of generalizations and poorly substantiated assertions.
4–6	The response indicates some understanding of the demands of the question. While there may be an attempt to follow a structured approach, the response lacks clarity and coherence.
	Knowledge of the world history topic is demonstrated, but lacks accuracy and relevance. There is a superficial understanding of historical context.
	The student identifies specific examples to discuss, but these examples are vague or lack relevance.
	There is some limited analysis, but the response is primarily narrative or descriptive in nature rather than analytical.
7–9	The response indicates an understanding of the demands of the question, but these demands are only partially addressed. There is an attempt to follow a structured approach.
	Knowledge of the world history topic is mostly accurate and relevant. Events are generally placed in their historical context.
	The examples that the student chooses to discuss are appropriate and relevant. The response makes links and/or comparisons (as appropriate to the question).
	The response moves beyond description to include some analysis or critical commentary, but this is not sustained.
10–12	The demands of the question are understood and addressed. Responses are generally well structured and organized, although there is some repetition or lack of clarity in places.
	Knowledge of the world history topic is mostly accurate and relevant. Events are placed in their historical context, and there is some understanding of historical concepts.
	The examples that the student chooses to discuss are appropriate and relevant, and are used to support the analysis/evaluation. The response makes effective links and/or comparisons (as appropriate to the question).
	The response contains critical analysis, which is mainly clear and coherent. There is some awareness and evaluation of different perspectives. Most of the main points are substantiated and the response argues to a consistent conclusion.
13–15	Responses are clearly focused, showing a high degree of awareness of the demands and implications of the question. Responses are well structured and effectively organized.
	Knowledge of the world history topic is accurate and relevant. Events are placed in their historical context, and there is a clear understanding of historical concepts.
	The examples that the student chooses to discuss are appropriate and relevant, and are used effectively to support the analysis/evaluation. The response makes effective links and/or comparisons (as appropriate to the question).
	The response contains clear and coherent critical analysis. There is evaluation of different perspectives, and this evaluation is integrated effectively into the answer. All, or nearly all, of the main points are substantiated, and the response argues to a consistent conclusion.

Common weaknesses in exam answers

Many answers demonstrate knowledge often in great detail; these answers tell the story but make little or no analytical comment about the knowledge shown. This is a narrative answer that will not reach higher markbands.

Other answers often consist of statements which have some focus on the question but with limited or inaccurate factual evidence; what examiners often describe as unsubstantiated assertion.

Here are some frequent comments by examiners on answers:

These types of comments mean that the answers do not contain enough evidence to answer the question or support analysis. This is one of the most common weaknesses in exam answers.

Other comments:

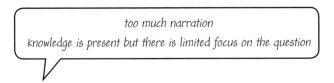

These types of comments mean that the candidates know quite a lot but are not using knowledge to answer the particular question. Answers do not make clear links to the focus of the question.

Writing good essays

Good essays consist of a combination of three elements:

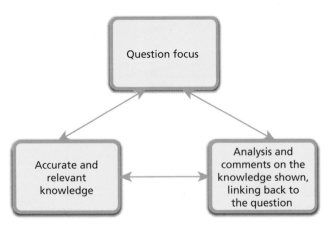

A good essay structure will ensure that you don't miss out key factors, keep your line of argument clear and your focus on the question at all times.

More information on essay skills can be found in the Skills sections throughout this book.

INTRODUCTION

"It is well that war is so terrible or we should grow too fond of it."

Robert E Lee

In the same way that your IB essays should not be narrative in nature this is not a book that simply tells the story of various wars. It is about exploring the nature of these wars, their causes, conduct and consequences. It is about more than simply dissecting warfare and combat to uncover tactics and strategy. It is also about locating war in the larger context of society and the world. As such, the wars discussed in this book need to be examined together and not in isolation. The IB world history topics – as assessed in Paper 2 – are global in nature and require comparison across regions to look for similarities, differences and patterns and this book should be used in that spirit.

The great concepts of history – causation, consequence, continuity, change, perspective and significance – can be expressed, in the same way that we start our historical investigations and extended essays, with questions.

Why do we fight?

Carl Philipp Gottfried von Clausewitz (1780–1831), a Prussian general and philosopher of war, famously wrote that "War is the continuation of diplomacy by other means". This is an enticing simplification of a massively complex human undertaking. It intimates a number of things. Clausewitz seems to be saying that war is a method by which states get something that they want from other states. Certainly there are wars that seem to bear this out. Had the French government been willing to negotiate the independence of Algeria before hostilities broke out, there may not be a chapter in this book on the Algerian War. Even some interpretations of the causes of the First World War can fit into this scheme. Germany, looking for security in the face of perceived Anglo-French economic dominance and encirclement, sought war as a way of achieving this security. Other interpretations of this war, however, stress the idea that none of the powers wanted a war in 1914, but rather stumbled, through a combination of fear, ignorance and diplomatic incompetence, into disaster. While some aspects of the Second World War might fit Clausewitz's maxim, the more ideological aspects of it do not. It may, therefore, explain Germany's invasion of Poland as an attempt to gain valuable "living space" in the east. It does little to shed light on the ideological motives in German foreign policy, such as the invasion of the USSR, which Hitler characterized as a crusade against Bolshevism. Likewise those who interpret Operation Barbarossa as a plan intrinsically linked to Hitler's plan for the annihilation of European Jewry find little explanatory power in Clausewitz.

The fact is that war, like all human endeavours, exists in a cultural context and this context must therefore be important in explaining war. The warrior class has been important in various societies

▲ Carl Philipp Gottfried von Clausewitz (1780–1831), a Prussian general and philosopher of war

throughout history. The Samurai in Japan and the Junker military elite in Prussia occupied an important and prestigious role in their respective societies. In times of war, we therefore see the militarization of society. This is especially true of 20th century wars with their voracious appetite for resources and services. In 1914, a law was passed which saw the German railway system come under the control of the German army in times of war. The opposite trend can also be seen in the 20th century in the civilizing of the military. Countries such as Switzerland, Israel and other states that have instituted mandatory military service ensure that the military occupation is a normal part of civil responsibility in the same way as taxes and voting. The end result of both of these seemingly opposite trends is that using the military to respond to threats, be they natural disasters or aggressive neighbours, is also normalized.

There is a third group of countries that resort to conscription only in times of war and otherwise maintain a relatively small military. The United States, Great Britain, Canada and Australia are among these. In these countries, resorting to the military to address any problem is seen as an extraordinary measure, a sign that all other avenues for resolution have been exhausted. In this sense the resort to war is more in line with Clausewitz, but less in a "next logical step" sense and more in a "failure of normal avenues" sense. Civilian oversight of the military, for instance by ensuring that the position of minister of war is filled by an elected civilian rather than a serving military officer, is one way these countries maintain this cautious approach to the military.

Why do wars continue?

Why do soldiers continue to fight in the face of suffering unimaginable to the civilian? This is different than asking "Why do soldiers go to war?" Certainly at the staff level, the conduct, though not the initiation, of war is the product of their profession, what they train for. The motivations for the average civilian soldier can be as varied as the soldiers themselves. Patriotism, peer pressure, employment and eventually conscription have all propelled potential soldiers to the recruiting office. Indeed this also helps explain why many continue to fight. In the horror of the trenches or the perception of the futility of the US involvement in Vietnam, another explanation is required. Leadership, social cohesion, the end goal and camaraderie have all been used to help explain the human capacity to endure.

Nevertheless, wars do continue despite the suffering of those sent to fight them. Gwynne Dyer has argued, "The internal logic of war has often caused it to grow far bigger in scale than the importance of the issue originally would justify". This certainly holds at least some truth for the First World War. It even sheds light on the seemingly mad proliferation of nuclear weapons. Once one gets over the ludicrousness of being able to destroy all life on earth several times over, the nuclear arms branch of the military can carry with it all sorts of stimulating challenges to which there are reasoned answers, but only if you take that first step into the circle. For those outside the circle it all seems madness.

To what extent does technology determine the course of wars?

The conduct of war has always been influenced by available technology. This being said, there is a complex relationship between technology and warfare. Improvements in material science allowed for the smelting of harder and thus more deadly metals. This same technology, however, had many non-lethal applications that changed the nature of civilization. Likewise supposedly innocuous, non-military discoveries had dramatic military applications. The stirrup increased the effectiveness of mounted archers and swordsmen. The other side of this coin is non-lethal advances developed during wartime. The need to compute artillery trajectories and break enemy codes led to great advances in electro-mechanical computing during the Second World War.

When examining more traditionally lethal military technologies it is important to understand the relationship of offensive to defensive technology. The effectiveness of the trench system as a defensive technology helped stimulate the development of the tank. Hitler's Atlantic Wall forced Allied engineers to develop technology as diverse as the Mulberry Harbour and the amphibious tank. It is also important to differentiate between the actual weapon and its delivery method. It may not matter if the actual weapon is changed; an improvement in the delivery system will increase its lethality. The rocket that sent Sputnik, the first man-made satellite, into orbit was far more threatening than the satellite. Change the trajectory and replace the satellite with a nuclear warhead and the Soviet Union had a nuclear armed intercontinental ballistic missile. Putting poison gas into artillery shells made it far more effective than it had been when it relied on cylinder release and the vagaries of the wind to deliver it to the enemy.

Using human ingenuity to develop more effective and efficient ways to kill other human beings is fraught with ethical questions. Fritz Haber's legacy as an early developer of weaponized chlorine for the German army in the First World War has complicated his Nobel Prize for the Haber-Bosch process, awarded in 1918. Robert Oppenheimer claimed to be forever haunted by his role in the development of the first atomic bomb and urged it not be used on humans. President Truman dismissed him as a "cry-baby scientist". Indeed a number of prominent scientists waged a campaign against the deployment of the atomic bomb. Truman and others used the fact that dropping the bomb was the fastest way to end the war and would therefore end up saving countless, mostly US, lives as a moral argument for dropping the bomb. Even those Japanese, who understood the dropping of the first bomb, were confused about why the second attack was necessary. What are the moral implications of creating technology the sole purpose of which is to kill humans?

The relationship of tactics and strategy to technology is also complex. It has become cliché to say that generals always fight the last war, that is to say strategic thinking always lags behind current circumstances and technology. The only evidence that military thinkers have to go on is past wars. This is, like many aphorisms, an exaggeration. The opening weeks of the First World War played out much as other wars had done – the difference was the scale and it was largely the scale of the losses that persuaded both sides to dig in and take stock. Even to say that the nature of trench warfare was unknown to military leaders in 1914 is to ignore the last months of the US Civil War and the trench works in front of Vicksburg and even earlier in the Peninsular War. John Keegan has argued that the generals of the First World War, far from donkeys leading lions, were constrained by the nature of the war and the offensive and communication technology available to them. Communication did not allow for the effective command and control of the massive formations of men employed during battles such as the Somme or Passchendaele. By the time reliable information reached command several miles behind the front and further orders were sent forward, the situation had changed so radically as to make these commands hopelessly uninformed.

Why do wars end?

Wars end on the whole because one or more of the combatants reason that it is no longer in their interest to continue. At a certain point in the autumn of 1918, German General Ludendorff approached the Kaiser and told him the war was unwinnable and that if Germany and the army were to be saved they must seek an armistice with the Allies. It is in the reasoning that the question becomes complex. The issue of perspective is one complicating factor. From whose perspective was it desirable to continue the First World War past the bloodbaths of 1916? The average *poilu* at Verdun? German arms manufacturers? Was it in the interest of the German family sacrificing butter for guns to continue the Second World War? How did the US State Department's perspective – assessing the aftermath of the Tet Offensive – differ from a Marine besieged at Khe Sanh?

The existence of a legitimate authority to make the decision to end the war is also important. This factored in the US decision not to drop the atomic bomb on either Kyoto or Tokyo. The US wanted to leave enough of the Japanese government intact so that it could surrender.

The reason behind continuing a war is also based on the resources available to pursue it effectively. Should a combatant rationalize that it no longer has the material or human resources to continue the fight it will seek ways to end the war. Such material deficiencies were crippling for the Axis Powers in the last months of the Second World War. But some combatants are willing to endure more suffering than their opponent. At the outset of the Indo-China War, Ho Chi Minh warned the French, "You can kill ten of my men for every one I kill of yours, yet even at those odds you will lose and I will win". This last example highlights another aspect of modern war that became especially evident when the United States fought in South-East Asia. In liberal democracies, wars cannot long continue without public support.

Types of wars

Military history as a subdiscipline of the area of knowledge history has its own knowledge framework, including language and concepts and with this an organizational taxonomy. Although it can be hard to place complex undertakings such as wars into neat categories, imposing some sort of

Class discussion

What factors make wars popular or unpopular with the general public? What role can the media play in this perception?

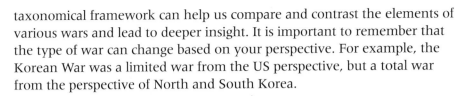

taxonomical framework can help us compare and contrast the elements of various wars and lead to deeper insight. It is important to remember that the type of war can change based on your perspective. For example, the Korean War was a limited war from the US perspective, but a total war from the perspective of North and South Korea.

Total war

This is a war in which one or more combatants commit all of its resources to the war effort. Economic, industrial, natural, material, educational and human resources are mobilized. The term does not generally apply to the geographic scope of a war. For example, the First and Second World Wars were total wars not because they were world wars but because of the resources committed to them. There are a number of implications of total war. When a country commits all of its resources to defeating its enemy, these resources in turn become targets, legitimate in the eyes of the enemy as they are being used to fight. In the 20th century, this has come to mean the targeting, both intentionally and as a result of their proximity to industrial targets, of civilians. Total war also allows for other forms of warfare. Great Britain has always used economic blockade as a key plank in its defensive strategy. Computer or cyber attacks are also becoming part and parcel of warfare. Anything the enemy is using to further its war aims becomes in the minds of some a legitimate target.

Civil war

Civil wars are armed disputes that erupt over often radically different ideas about the direction, governmental system or composition of a country. National fault lines along which these volatile differences develop can be ideological, regional, political, economic or religious. But differences do not in and of themselves cause civil wars. The other key ingredient is the lack of a political system with enough of a monopoly of force or perceived legitimacy to address the competing interests inherent in the divisions. Most established democracies, for example, have models of representation that provide a say in political decisions for differing political and ideological positions, or regional interests. Canada, for example, has a representative democracy that elects legislators from the entire country. This allows these members of parliament to represent the various regional interests in the country. Such democracies are largely able to maintain stability because the citizens see the system as an effective and legitimate method to address competing interests or divisions within the country. When faith in the legitimacy or effectiveness of these democracies is insufficient to maintain stability, governments augment their legitimacy with a monopoly of force, such as the military, police and security organizations to impose order and obedience. Other systems, notably authoritarian forms of government, rely primarily on their monopoly of force to maintain unity amid societal divisions. In short, if a country has a political mechanism either to address the concerns of its factions or to force compliance, divisions will not become civil wars.

Revolutionary war

Revolutionary war is generally a struggle led by a grass roots movement to overthrow what it perceives to be an oppressive authority. That authority can be foreign or domestic. Since this type of war is characterized by its goals, it is conceivable that it will encompass other types of war such as total war or, as in the case of Spain, China and Russia, civil wars. When directed against a foreign occupier, revolutionary war will often involve some level of nationalism and increasingly in the 20th century one or more competing ideologies. Revolutionary wars can spawn from larger conflicts and the opportunity these can present for nationalist movements. The First World War set off the Arab Revolt and insofar as Arab and British interests in the war ran parallel, the defeat of the Ottoman Empire, so too did their military operations, although their overall goals were very different.

When nationalist movements employ terror tactics it complicates matters further, blurring it through the lens of perspective. To the Irish Republican Army (IRA) or the Tamil Tigers in Sri Lanka, they were justified in their terror campaigns against civilians and part of a revolutionary struggle. This characterization of their struggle would be bitterly opposed by British and Sri Lankan officials.

We can distinguish revolutionary war from localized revolts and rebellions perhaps by its scope and duration. We would, therefore, not consider the Bolshevik seizure of power in 1917 as a revolutionary war, while one could argue that the Russian Civil War that followed could be seen as both a civil war and a revolutionary war.

Guerrilla war

For the purposes of this book guerrilla war can be seen more as a tactic employed in war rather than a distinct type of war itself. We see it used in civil wars such as the Chinese Civil War. It formed a major component of revolutionary wars such as the Cuban revolution and is even seen as a component of total war as in the Yugoslav theatre of the Second World War. Mao Zedong, an important theorist of guerrilla war, saw it as a tactic to be used when one is too weak to fight the enemy in a conventional war. For Mao the ultimate military goal of guerrilla struggle is to gain strength and support over time so that the guerrilla force can evolve into a regular, conventional army.

Syllabus overview and assessment

The International Baccalaureate history syllabus is divided into three components – prescribed subjects, world history topics and regional depth studies. The prescribed subjects are document-based case studies. All candidates must study one prescribed subject. The second component of the history syllabus is the world history topics. There are 12 possible topics of which all candidates must study two. The emphasis in these topics is comparative world history and it is therefore important to look at historical examples across different regions of the world. Candidates enrolled in higher level history are also required to study one of the four regional depth studies. All candidates, regardless of whether they are studying higher level or standard level history, are required to complete an historical investigation as their internal assessment.

Both standard and higher level history focus on the following key historical concepts:

- Continuity
- Change

- Cause

- Consequence

- Perspective

- Significance

This book deals with the world history topic "Causes and effects of 20th-century wars" and because it is a comparative world history course these concepts will form the basis of that comparison. Meaningful comparison requires that it be done across elements shared by the two items being compared. Other themes discussed in this book can also form the substance of comparison, which is why the structure of each chapter is consistent. While the above concepts are common to all historical studies, 20th-century warfare has specific themes that will run through each chapter and can also, therefore, form the basis of comparison. These themes include:

- Long-term causes

- Short-term and immediate causes

- Combatants

- Technology and equipment

- Operations

- Effects

When examining these themes it is important to consider not only the military factors, but also social, political and economic dimensions. For example, no examination of the effects of the Second World War would be complete without a discussion of the political aspects of the peace and its impact on the development of the Cold War. Likewise economic factors contributed to the outbreak of the Second World War. The wars set out in the text cover a range of regions – Americas, Europe, Africa and Asia. The First World War and the Second World War are cross-regional wars and can therefore be used to compare dimensions across different regions. For example, if an exam question requires you to compare the use of air power in two wars, each from a different region, the Second World War in Europe and in the Pacific fulfill this requirement.

The world history topics are assessed with Paper 2 of the May or November exams. The exam consists of 24 questions – two on each of the 12 topics. Candidates must answer any two of these questions, provided they are not from the same topic. The format for the answer is an extended essay response and candidates have 90 minutes to answer both questions. Each response is marked out of 15 using pre-set markbands. These markbands are available from your teacher.

Tips for writing a good essay

- Use the five minutes of reading time to consider all the questions relating to the topics you have studied.

- Understand the command terms of the question.

- Unpack the question. Pull out the key terms and be sure to address each in your response.

- Plan each response.

- Include differing perspectives (not necessarily historiography – see below) where applicable.

- Develop a clear thesis statement that addresses the requirements of the question.

- Relate each paragraph back to the thesis/question.

- Be as detailed with historical events as possible.

- Be disciplined with time allocation. The exam is designed to be completed in 90 minutes. This leaves approximately 45 minutes for each response.

- Only use detail that is relevant to your thesis.

- Avoid a narrative response. In other words, do not simply tell a story. Use historical evidence to address the demands of the question. Do not simply write everything you know about the historical events referred to in the question.

Historiography

Historiography refers to the methodology of history and to the accumulated body of historical literature on any given topic. It encompasses schools of historical thought, such as the Annales School, as well as the differing views of historians. Understanding any historical event or period, therefore, requires some knowledge of the historiographical context: what are the major interpretations of the events and what are their relative strengths and weaknesses? That being said, using historiography in your essays is not an end in and of itself. Historiography must serve your argument. If it does not, it has no context and is thus just an exercise in name-dropping. A careful examination of the markbands that are used to grade your essays for Paper 2 and Paper 3 do not mention "historiography". In other words, using historiography is not a requirement of the assessment. Examining "perspectives" is a requirement and this is reflected in the markbands. Discussing relevant historiography is one way to address perspectives, but it is not the only way to do so.

Command terms

Command terms are the parts of a question that tell you the nature of the task. Here are the command terms used in the IB history course:

Command term	Task
Analyse	Break down in order to bring out the essential elements or structure.
Compare	Give an account of the similarities between two (or more) items or situations, referring to both (all) of them throughout.
Contrast	Give an account of the differences between two (or more) items or situations, referring to both (all) of them throughout.
Discuss	Offer a considered and balanced review that includes a range of arguments, factors or hypotheses. Opinions or conclusions should be presented clearly and supported by appropriate evidence.
Evaluate	Make an appraisal by weighing up the strengths and limitations.
Examine	Consider an argument or concept in a way that uncovers the assumptions and interrelationships of the issue.
To what extent	Consider the merits or otherwise of an argument or concept. Opinions and conclusions should be presented clearly and supported with appropriate evidence and sound argument.

> **ATL Thinking skills**
>
> Use each of the command terms in the table to write extended response questions for the material in this chapter. Share your questions with other classmates to answer each other's questions.

Further reading

Black, Jeremy. 2005. "What Wins Wars?" in *Big Questions in History*. Edited by Harriet Swanson, p.143–148. Jonathan Cape. London, UK.

Clausewitz, Carl von. 1976. *On War*. Edited and translated by Michael Howard and Peter Paret. Princeton University Press. Princeton, USA.

Dyer, Gwynne. 2004. *War: The New Edition*. Random House. Canada.

Palaima, Thomas. 2005. "Why Do Wars Begin?" in *Big Questions in History*. Edited by Harriet Swanson, p.129–134. Jonathan Cape. London, UK.

Sun Tsu. 1971 *The Art of War*. Translated by Samuel B. Griffith. Oxford University Press. Oxford, UK.

Townsend, Charles. 2005. *The Oxford History of Modern War*. Oxford University Press. Oxford, UK.

1 THE ALGERIAN WAR: GUERRILLA WAR AND DECOLONIZATION

Global context

The Algerian War 1954–1962, as an example of a 20th-century guerrilla war, highlights many significant historic developments. First, the war was partially a response to the colonial policies of France and as such helps illustrate the relationship between nationalism, imperialism, decolonization and warfare in the 20th century with its profound effects on both Algeria and France. In this section we also examine the strategy and tactics involved in fighting guerrilla wars for both the guerrilla and regular forces, and in so doing explore the brutal nature of this type of warfare for all those involved, including non-combatants.

Timeline

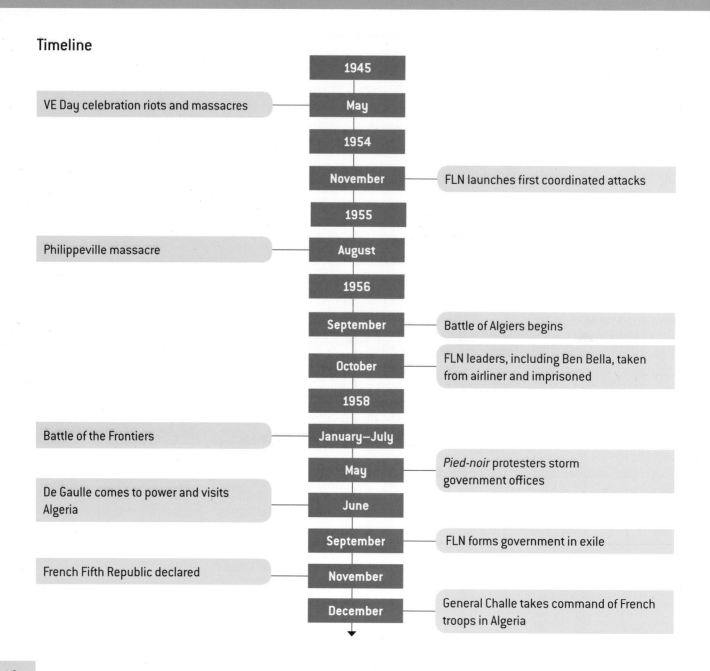

1945	
VE Day celebration riots and massacres — **May**	
1954	
November	FLN launches first coordinated attacks
1955	
Philippeville massacre — **August**	
1956	
September	Battle of Algiers begins
October	FLN leaders, including Ben Bella, taken from airliner and imprisoned
1958	
Battle of the Frontiers — **January–July**	
May	*Pied-noir* protesters storm government offices
De Gaulle comes to power and visits Algeria — **June**	
September	FLN forms government in exile
French Fifth Republic declared — **November**	
December	General Challe takes command of French troops in Algeria

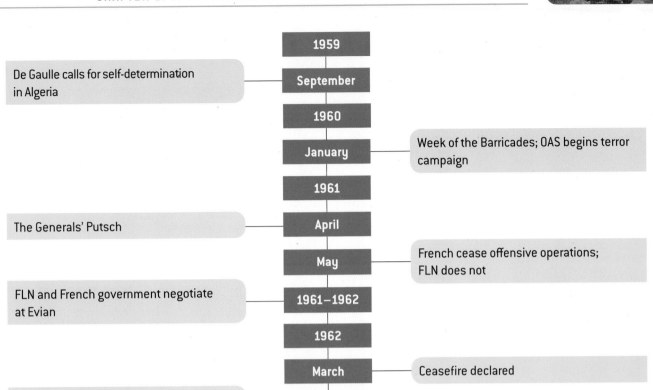

De Gaulle calls for self-determination in Algeria — **1959 September**

1960 January — Week of the Barricades; OAS begins terror campaign

The Generals' Putsch — **1961 April**

May — French cease offensive operations; FLN does not

FLN and French government negotiate at Evian — **1961–1962**

1962 March — Ceasefire declared

France officially recognizes the independence of Algeria — **July**

▲ *Front de Libération Nationale* (FLN) fighters captured by Foreign Legion troops

1.1 Guerrilla war

What is guerrilla warfare?

The term "guerrilla" comes from the Spanish word for "little war" and was originally applied to the Spanish resistance to Napoleon's occupation of Spain in the early 19th century. It generally involves irregular forces involved in an ongoing struggle with an established regular army. Tactical, strategic and political goals are all closely related in most guerrilla movements.

"Irregular" refers to forces that are not widely recognized as belonging to official, full-time, professional armies. Guerrilla soldiers can be farmers or workers one moment and fighters the next. They seldom wear uniforms, nor are they concentrated in any identifiable base. Guerrilla units are generally small and restrict themselves to "hit and run" engagements. As it achieves success, a guerrilla movement may grow in both strength and organization and by the end of the struggle may appear very similar to a regular army. Such was the case in China and Vietnam. Mao Zedong wrote of guerrilla war as a process or continuum, which starts small and in its later phases grows in size and sophistication. The *Front de Libération Nationale (*FLN) fighters in Algeria, however, would not reach the final stages of Mao's model of revolutionary war as the Viet Minh had.

Guerrilla strategy varies depending on the movement's political goals. Many of the late 20th-century guerrilla movements have concentrated on national independence or liberation, generally from European colonial control. In these cases, the overall strategy is one of endurance and nuisance. Guerrilla forces will not engage in the kind of decisive battle that will bring about their demise, but instead harass the enemy until the cost of pursuing the war is no longer worth the benefits and the occupying power withdraws. Relying as they do on the support, coerced or voluntary, of local populations and not depending on formal military training, guerrilla armies enjoy a seemingly limitless supply of potential soldiers. This advantage can be pushed to a logical, although awful, extreme with the conscription of child soldiers. Chief among the weaknesses inherent in guerrilla movements is a difficulty in obtaining an adequate supply of modern weapons. This was often overcome in the second half of the 20th century with the sponsorship of guerrilla movements by larger, wealthier states – rather ironic for those guerrilla forces bent on national liberation.

Guerrilla tactics rely on mobility and stealth. Attacks are generally designed to strike and withdraw before the strength of the conventional forces of the enemy can be brought to bear on the fewer and more lightly armed guerrillas. Because guerrilla forces are often indistinguishable from the general population, the psychological strain on enemy forces can be overwhelming. This, in fact, is one of the key strengths of guerrilla tactics, but can also lead to horrific atrocities on the part of the regular force against civilians suspected of guerrilla activity. Supply and logistics for guerrilla forces are simplified by the small size of the units involved. Many guerrilla units live off what they can take from or are given by the general population. These units will augment any munitions they receive from sponsor states with what they can steal or capture from the occupying forces. The global arms market can furnish weapons to guerrilla forces that can pay and many movements operate various money-making schemes for just this purpose. The Viet Minh, for example, sold both rice and opium grown by Muong tribesmen to obtain funds for weapons. Not really constrained by the law, especially what many considered the law of illegitimate occupying governments, many liberation movements run organized crime rings involving protection and drug operations. Recognizing this fact, many anti-guerrilla tactics involve restricting access to such support, which again can lead to added hardship on non-combatants.

Although forms of guerrilla war have been practised since the 19th century, it seemed to reach a zenith with the victory of Mao's people's army over the Chinese Nationalists in 1949. Ever since Mao so ably mobilized his initially meagre resources to conquer and rule the third largest country in the world, using a well-honed model of revolutionary war, independence movements have been trying to emulate his example. This approach enjoyed success in the period of mid-20th-century **decolonization** – a success that has been difficult to duplicate since. A fine example of the success of guerrilla movements against European colonizers can be found in the Algerian War of Independence often referred to simply as the Algerian War.

decolonization
The global movement in the second half of the 20th century toward independence for territories that had been ruled as colonies of European states. The movement was especially prevalent in South Asia and Africa during this period. Decolonization could be accomplished by either peaceful or violent means.

20th-century guerrilla wars			
War	Guerrillas	Opponents	Result
Chinese Civil War, 1922–1949	Communists	Nationalists	Communists gained more and more support, transforming the war into more of a conventional war. The communists won in 1949.
French Indo-China War, 1945–1954	Viet Minh	France	The Viet Minh forced the French colonial administration to quit the country in 1954.
Vietnam War, 1965–1973	Viet Cong	USA, South Vietnamese army	With the help of regular soldiers from North Vietnam, the Viet Cong were able to force the USA from the country in 1973 and then defeated the South Vietnamese army in 1975.
Algerian War, 1954–1962	FLN	France	After a bloody war, Algeria declared independence in 1962 with the FLN forming the new government.
Afghan Resistance, 1979–1989	Mujahadeen	USSR	With American aid and after 10 years of guerrilla fighting, the Mujahadeen forced the Soviets from Afghanistan. This led to a civil war between Mujahadeen factions.
Indonesian War of Independence, 1945–1949	Republicans	The Netherlands	After four years of negotiation and fighting, the Netherlands recognized the independence of Indonesia.
Mau Mau Uprising (Kenya), 1952–1960	Mau Maus (KCA)	Great Britain	Although intensely violent, the revolt collapsed. Eventually the British administration would recognize an independent Kenya.
Malaysian Insurgency, 1948–1957	MNLA	Britain	The guerrilla campaign was not widely supported and was defeated by the British army. Britain recognized an independent Malaysia of its own accord in 1957.
Cuban Revolution, 1957–1959	26th July Movement	Cuban national army	After a progressively more successful military campaign, Castro's guerrillas were able to force the surrender of the government forces.

1.2 Causes of the Algerian War

Conceptual understanding

Key questions

→ What role did socio-economic conditions play in the causes of the war?

→ What influence did the French defeat in Indo-China have on the outbreak of the Algerian War?

Key concepts

→ Cause

→ Consequence

→ Perspective

Long-term causes

Algeria had become a French colonial possession through a series of military campaigns in the 1830s and 1840s. As France exerted more and more control over the territory, floods of European settlers came to take advantage of cheap land and job opportunities. Successive French governments aimed to assimilate Algeria both administratively and culturally, attempting to make it an integral part of France. As the process of assimilation brought more European technology and investment, it also attracted more settlers throughout the late 19th century. Some natives resisted the assimilation with guerrilla-style attacks on French troops and European settlers. The combination of the military campaigns and the European settlement, with its accompanying European illnesses, meant that by the 1870s the native population of Algeria was declining while the settler population was increasing. Economic inequalities aggravated Muslim discontent with the colonial regime.

By the time the war broke out, 75% of the Muslim population was illiterate in Arabic. Unemployment among the nine million Algerian Muslims ran to over a million people, with twice that number underemployed. Over 90% of the wealth of the country lay in the hands of 10% of the population. These economic inequalities were made worse daily by the high Muslim birth rate. With a birth rate ten times lower, the *pied noirs* feared being overrun by Muslims in the coming years. In many ways, this pattern of colonization, poverty, disenfranchisement and resistance can be seen as both a long-term cause of the Algerian War and the rationale for the guerrilla tactics employed.

> *pied noirs*
> Literally meaning "black feet", it was a term given to French settlers and descendants of French settlers in Algeria.

The first half of the 20th century would expose French society to both a disastrous victory and a humiliating defeat as well as occupation in the two world wars. The social consequence of these wars was reflected in the contradictory impulses of the French government and French society at large. On the one hand, there was a desire to break with the past and reject the values and systems that had brought France to the brink of destruction. But there was also a desire to recapture the glory, influence and power of 19th-century France. These contradictory impulses were evident in French colonial policy in the post-Second World War era. The desire to reject the past was manifest in the granting of independence to Tunisia and Morocco with relatively little friction in the mid-1950s. A longing for the past was seen in the ferocity with which the French tried to maintain control of her Indo-Chinese holdings and in Algeria. In any case, a coherent colonial policy guided by a clear vision was close to impossible in a fractured political scene that saw no less than 20 different governments in the years 1945 to 1954.

The political chaos that typified the **Fourth Republic** reflected a deep economic malaise in the 10 years after liberation. Dependent on Marshall Aid for reconstruction and forced into its strictures – aid that would underpin her eventual economic recovery – France stumbled along in a period of perpetual high inflation, debilitating strikes, plunging exports and sluggish growth, all the while trying to fund an escalating war in Indo-China. She would be faced with another war almost as soon as the other had ended. On the one hand, the potential profits from Algeria were tempting to the French governments; this had to be weighed against the cost, both in money and blood, of keeping it.

Short-term causes

The end of the Second World War can be seen as providing a more immediate cause of the Algerian War, although it preceded the outbreak by nine years. Celebrations marking the surrender of Nazi Germany in May 1945 turned violent when Algerian nationalists staged demonstrations and were in turn confronted by European settlers (*pied noirs*). When the violence subsided some weeks later, 6,000 people – Muslim, *pieds noirs* and French soldiers – were dead.

This event revealed the three sides that would become involved in the Algerian War nine years later: the French government, the *pieds noirs* and Algerian nationalists, of which there were a number of organizations. Although for the most part the French army would be the strong arm of the French government, there were times when it acted as a fourth side, protecting its own interests at the expense of the government's orders and at one point openly revolting against the metropolitan government. The brutality and violence of the 1945 riots anticipated the viciousness of the war to come.

The Algerian nationalist movement was, as many such nationalist movements, fractured by method and goal. The *Union Democratique du Manifeste Algérien* (UDMA) sought negotiated equality and autonomy within a French state. The older strand of nationalism, the Ulema, favoured statehood based on traditional Islamic law. A hybrid of these two visions found expression in the Movement for the Triumph of Democratic Liberties (MTLD) after 1945, which combined a reverence for traditional Islam, a left-wing social agenda and complete independence from France. It was from the MTLD and its militant branch the *Organisation Spécial* (OS) that the FLN, led by Ahmed Ben Bella, would emerge, eventually encompassing most Algerian nationalist aspirations. These aspirations were fuelled by poor economic conditions for Algerian Arabs, income

Fourth Republic
The French government from 1946 to 1958. It was created by a constitution after the Second World War.

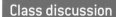

differentials and the accompanying inaccessibility of land ownership. While Arab Muslims made up the majority of non-colonial Algerians, the various Berber ethnicities were also an important group with nationalist aspirations. The need to balance the interests of these two main nationalist groups within the FLN led to the concept of collective leadership that was to guide the organization throughout the war.

Outside influences also played a role in the timing of the outbreak of hostilities in 1954. Mao's example only grew in lustre, having taken control of China in 1949 and, three years later, fighting the United States to a standstill in Korea. It seemed as though anything might be possible. The French defeat at **Dien Bien Phu** and their subsequent withdrawal from Indo-China also seemed to present a historic opportunity for Algerian nationalists. Although there had been guerrilla-style attacks throughout the French occupation of Algeria, the FLN began to plan a marked increase in coordinated attacks shortly after the French military disaster at Dien Bien Phu, even though there were very few similarities between the two causes or situations.

- Unlike the Viet Minh, the FLN did not have any particular ideological orientation.

- While the Viet Minh enjoyed the sponsorship of a major power, China, the FLN had no such aid.

- While Indo-China was geographically remote from France and thus more difficult to support, Algeria was close.

- French law prohibited the use of conscripts in Indo-China, but there were no such restrictions on the use of French conscripts in Algeria.

- Algeria was considered an integral part of Metropolitan France whereas Indo-China had been a colony. The war in Indo-China, therefore, was managed by a combination of military, foreign office and colonial office officials. There were no such bureaucratic inefficiencies in the Algerian War.

Nevertheless, the FLN judged the time to be right and on 1 November 1954 it conducted a number of coordinated bomb attacks across Algeria. This marks the start of the Algerian War.

Class discussion

How are nationalist and economic issues related? Had there been economic prosperity across Algerian society, would there have been a nationalist movement?

Dien Bien Phu

Site of a battle between the Viet Minh and the French army between March and May 1954. This Viet Minh victory drove the French from Indo-China and led to the partition of the country into North and South Vietnam.

1.3 Combatants

The FLN

The FLN and its military wing the *Armée de Libération Nationale* (ALN) organized the country into six military zones – Wilayas. The FLN commanders in each Wilaya were responsible for all FLN activity in the district. This included military operations, but also recruiting, political

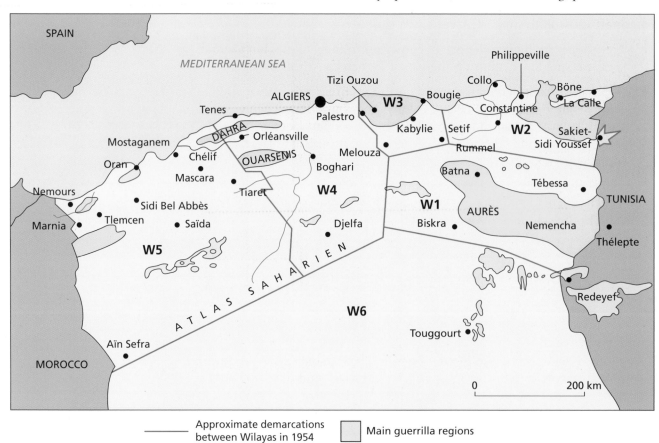

▲ The Algerian War

indoctrination, taxation, assassinations and intimidation. Ethnic and tribal infighting within the Wilayas often limited the fighting effectiveness of these districts, but in the end they proved an effective organizational structure for a guerrilla movement that was flung across a large rugged landscape and was fractured in both composition and at times goals.

The Central Command of the FLN spent a good portion of the war sheltering in neighbouring Tunisia or Morocco. From these safe havens they attempted to coordinate and direct the activities of the Wilayas. For the 1 November 1954 attacks the fighters were divided into four-man cells, each cell ignorant of the operations of other cells. After this, however, each Wilaya combined its fighters into sections, companies, and battalions, the 110-man company being the most common operational unit as the war progressed. The strength of these formations varied dramatically with the fortunes of the FLN. In 1957 they had roughly 15 000 full-time guerrillas and a further 15 000 to 20 000 part-time guerrillas. The FLN maintained troops in the safe havens of Tunisia and Morocco throughout the war and these would leak into Algeria as needed. When French troops sealed the borders with the neighbouring states, the FLN combat strength fell off. With the more aggressive French operations inflicting heavy losses on the FLN, full-time fighters fell to around 8,000 by 1959. The FLN army in Tunisia and Morocco grew fairly continuously, reaching 35 000 by 1962.

▲ ALN soldiers from Wilaya 4, 1962

The French

The French forces in Algeria numbered some 74 000 soldiers at the outset of the war, but this number quickly rose to around 400 000 and stayed constant for the duration of the conflict. The force was a mixed bag. Elite units such as the **legionnaires** and paratroopers were the core of the fighting strength, but the bulk of the French forces were reservists, conscripts and irregular formations of sympathetic Algerians – *harkis*.

> **Class discussion**
>
> What are the advantages and disadvantages of having the FLN leadership located outside Algeria in Tunisia?

> **legionnaires**
> Soldiers in the French Foreign Legion, an elite formation within the French army. The Legion, created in the 1830s, accepts volunteers from foreign states, but also contains substantial numbers of French citizens.

> **harkis**
> Algerian Muslims who fought for the French during the Algerian War.

Class discussion

What may have motivated the *harkis* to fight for the French against the FLN?

Throughout the war the French had difficulty manning its army in Algeria. Conscription was always unpopular, more so during an unpopular war. The size of the troop commitment and the fact that only about 15% of it was made up of professional soldiers made training and leadership crucial and not always available in sufficient quantities. Increasing the length of service for conscripts to 27 months may have increased the size of the force, but it did nothing for its morale or fighting ability and likely decreased it. The sharp divide between the elite units with their attendant arrogance and the rest of the army with its growing disillusion was a constant strain on the morale of the French forces.

Advantages and disadvantages of conscription	
Advantages	**Disadvantages**
Increases the pool from which to draw soldiers	Soldiers may lack motivation
Makes the size of the army predictable	Subjects the military to all the social factions in a country
Can spread the burden of military service across social classes and groups	Can breed resentment in the population as a whole as a form of governmental control and interference
Can integrate the military into society more thoroughly	Military losses are felt throughout the population
Increases civic participation and sense of civic responsibility	Constant turnover of troops can make training expensive
	Requires close cooperation between military and civilian authorities.

Equipment

The FLN

The FLN and her military arm, the ALN, were constantly short of weapons of all kinds. At the outbreak of the war bombs and grenades were assembled at various points throughout Algiers and weapons gathered from a variety of sources – Second World War cast-offs, stolen hunting rifles and the occasional machine gun – about 350 small arms in all. At this stage the FLN lacked both the funds to purchase weapons on the open market and a national sponsor to furnish them with arms. While Nasser made much of Egypt's kinship with Algerian Muslims and sympathy with the FLN's struggle, this did not initially translate into any form of practical aid. Material would, however, begin to flow from Egypt and other sources later in the war, despite French efforts to stop it. These armaments, however, were mostly small arms consequently keeping the size of FLN operations small.

After 1956 the regular units of the Wilayas were fairly well equipped with Second World War-era small arms including light machine guns. Artillery, mortars and even bazookas were virtually unheard of unless captured from French troops. Mass transport too was rare, with most movement limited to animals, small vehicles and the age-old form of troop movement – feet.

The FLN's terrorist activities that concentrated on urban targets in large cities like Algiers required different types of ordinance that were used in the field and these were manufactured in hidden bomb "factories".

Foreign support for guerrillas		
War	Guerrillas	Supporter (s)
Algeria	FLN	Egypt
Vietnam	Viet Minh and Viet Cong	USSR, China
Afghanistan	Mujahadeen	USA
Angola	MPLA	Cuba
Nicaragua, 1974–1979	Sandinistas	Cuba
Nicaragua, 1981–1987	Contras	USA
Pakistan	Mukti Bahni	India

The French

The French units in Algeria were part of a well-equipped modern army and they brought all that this implies to bear on the FLN. Small arms were far more standardized than the early days in Indo-China. The terrain of Algeria allowed for a far more effective use of armour and mechanization than it had in Indo-China. Tanks, half-tracks, weapons carriers and truck transport were widely available to the French forces in Algeria.

The mobility that the French lacked in Indo-China was achieved in Algeria with the help of helicopter transport. While there were some parachute drops, much of the French airborne forces rode into battle in the belly of troop-carrying helicopters. By the end of the war the French had about 120 transport helicopters in Algeria that could shift troops around the country or even around a battlefield to respond to emergent situations. Smaller helicopter gunships could provide ground forces with support as could aircraft such as the T-6 Texan and P-47 Thunderbolts.

1.4 Strategy and tactics

Conceptual understanding

Key questions

→ How did French strategy change over time? Why did it change?

→ How did FLN strategy change over the course of the war?

→ What role did materials play in the strategy of each side?

Key concepts

→ Continuity

→ Change

The FLN

As previously mentioned, a guerrilla movement succeeds if it survives and survival was indeed the goal of the meagrely equipped FLN fighters in the early days of the war. Material concerns always partly dictated overall strategy and tactics as did the guerrilla goal of controlling people more than territory. To that end the FLN sought to demonstrate that the French administration could not effectively administer nor protect the population – both Muslim and *pied noir*. These demonstrations involved ambushing convoys and patrols, attacking small outposts and bombing civilian targets. Terror campaigns targeted suspected sympathizers among the Muslim population and French *pied noir* administrators.

The FLN's non-military strategy tried to create parallel administrations in villages far from the urban centres to marginalize the sympathetic local leaders through whom the French administered Algeria. This effort worked in coordination with the brutal strategy of inflicting terror against European civilians to provoke equally brutal French retaliation, which the FLN leadership believed would further alienate the Muslim population.

The FLN effort never reached the "offensive" stage of Mao's revolutionary model, stuck as it was in the guerrilla phases. As such, the main operational doctrine of the ALN was to avoid a confrontation with larger, better armed French formations.

The French

French forces in Algeria were divided into two main types. Sector forces were comprised mostly of reservists and conscripts and were deployed in countless posts spread out across the country. These posts were to observe and restrict FLN movement and influence in their sector. If the enemy was encountered in strength, the mobile reserve of elite legionnaires and "paras" were flown or trucked in to deal with the threat. This strategy was modified later in the war when airborne forces used their mobility during search and destroy missions.

Taking to heart Mao's famous doctrine that "the guerrilla must move amongst the people as a fish swims in the sea", the French sought to drain that sea. Whole villages – eventually some 600 000 Algerians – were relocated to camps. These abandoned villages and surrounding areas now became "free fire zones" in which the French would fire on anyone found there, reasoning that they had to be guerrillas.

Class discussion

Why do nationalist movements tend to be fractured? How does this affect the post-colonial administration of successor states?

▲ French soldiers work with Algerians. Why was it important to the French to work with Muslim Algerians?

Elaborate defensive lines were designed to cut the flow of men and material from the two neighbouring states of Morocco and Tunisia.

TOK discussion

To what extent did the French learn from their experience in Indo-China? What does this tell us about the degree to which we learn from history?

1.5 Operations

Conceptual understanding

Key questions

→ To what extent was the Morice Line effective?

→ What role did technology play in the French ability to fight the FLN?

→ What was the significance of the Battle of Algiers?

→ What role did terror play in the war?

Key concepts

→ Continuity

→ Change

→ Significance

1955

The attacks of 1 November 1954 targeted 70 police stations, army posts and government buildings. Although these attacks met with some success, they failed to trigger the general uprising that the FLN had hoped for.

Lacking a major sponsor state and the weapons that such a state could supply, the FLN was limited to small actions, the bombings of infrastructure mostly, throughout 1954 and into 1955. The French had no such limitations. The government in Paris made it clear that Algeria was part of France and would remain so. To that end, the French bolstered their military presence in Algeria, sending paratroopers and legionnaires who then conducted a campaign of assassination and retaliation against suspected FLN supporters. This campaign bit deep into the FLN leadership. As in most guerrilla wars, a brutal pattern emerged in Algeria during 1955. FLN attacks would provoke retaliatory attacks by the French army, who would use vicious tactics both to discourage civilian support for the FLN and to obtain information about their activities. In an effort to coerce such support, the FLN would put often brutal pressure on Algerian civilians and terrorize the *pieds noirs*. It was on non-combatants that much of the hardship of this and other guerrilla wars fell.

This was made evident in August 1955 when a unit of FLN guerrillas descended on the city of Philippeville. By the time the guerrillas had left, 123 civilians, Muslim and *pieds noirs*, had been murdered. The retaliation of the French military claimed 1,200 victims by its own estimates, 12 000 by outside estimates. This type of retaliation was an example of the principle of **collective responsibility** adopted by both French and FLN forces throughout the war and designed to discourage support for the enemy. Again, it was the civilians that bore the brunt of it. Because the violence was meted out by both sides and fell on both European

collective responsibility
The practice of holding all members of a population responsible for the actions of a few of its members.

and Algerian populations, the Philippeville massacres and aftermath radicalized the moderates on both sides. *Pied noir* gangs conducted their own terror campaigns against Algerians, who in turn joined the FLN in greater numbers.

1956

The French administration intensified its efforts throughout Algeria during 1956. It moved those suspected of actively supporting the FLN, sometimes whole villages, and imprisoned leaders, while at the same time implementing limited economic reforms to alleviate some grievances. This approach was supplemented by an aggressive military campaign in which legionnaires and paratroops used helicopter transport to move into remote areas and root out FLN fighters, a tactic that the United States would adopt in Vietnam 10 years later. Helicopters, it seemed, allowed anti-guerrilla forces to rely less on infrastructure such as roads and thereby removed a major guerrilla target. In some ways, their use gave to the regular force the mobility previously enjoyed only by the guerrillas.

The FLN continued to be plagued by supply issues, despite receiving some support from Nasser's government in Egypt. By the end of 1956, however, French military strength in Algeria reached 400 000. This coordinated approach dealt a significant blow to the FLN, which lost over half its fighting strength during that year. France was using half a million soldiers to conduct operations against a force of about 30 000 irregular, guerrilla fighters. The question became, as in all occupations, which side could last longer, in terms both of sustaining adequate material support and the will to continue the war.

The Battle of Algiers

In 1956–1957, the FLN moved the war to the cities, most notably to the capital, Algiers. The "Battle of Algiers" was more a series of terror attacks by FLN guerrillas, including women, and reprisals by the French military. By moving the war to the cities, the FLN leadership hoped to gain more international attention and support. The danger in such a move is that it is harder to hide in a city because you need the support of more people. The possibility of betrayal is far greater in the city. The French used this fact against the FLN by terrorizing the population and using torture to extract information, eventually rooting out most FLN fighters in Algiers. As the French military began to rely more on torture, and as this fact became more known in France, French public opinion began to turn against the war.

▲ French officers interrogate an Algerian woman. What difficulties could French soldiers face in obtaining information?

ATL **Thinking skills**

Alan Dershowitz, a legal scholar, has made the argument that the limited use of torture can be necessary in democratic states.

If torture is going to be administered as a last resort in the ticking-bomb case, to save enormous numbers of lives, it ought to be done openly, with accountability, with approval by the president of the United States or by a Supreme Court justice.

Source: Interview with Wolf Blitzer, CNN, 4 March 2003. http://edition.cnn.com/2003/LAW/03/03/cnna.Dershowitz

1 What does Dershowitz mean by a "ticking-bomb case"?

2 Do you agree with Dershowitz? Why or why not?

3 Would Dershowitz advocate a similar use of torture by authoritarian regimes? Why or why not?

4 Does his justification for torture apply to the French in Algeria?

Morice Line
The Morice Line was a fortified barrier between Algeria and Tunisia designed to keep FLN fighters and supplies in Tunisia from getting to Algeria.

The Morice Line and the Battle of the Frontiers

When France granted independence to Morocco and Tunisia in 1956 and 1957, it inadvertently supplied the FLN with a valuable resource – a place to hide. To neutralize this resource, the French military constructed a barrier between Tunisia and Algeria. The **Morice Line**, as it became known, consisted of an electrified fence, reinforced with anti-personnel mines, artillery and 80 000 soldiers patrolling its length. A similar line attempted to insulate Algeria from Morocco. Despite the complexity of the line, the FLN continued to launch attacks from both Tunisian and Moroccan sides of the lines. One such attack led to a French air strike on the Tunisian town of Sakiet. The FLN continued to build up a significant conventional military force behind the Morice Line and, although it never played a significant role in the war itself, it posed a question of whether the Morice Line and the French military force would need to be permanent. Again, France was faced with the question of whether or not Algeria was worth such an ongoing effort.

The presence of sympathetic border countries is a dilemma faced by many counter-insurgency efforts. The Ho Chi Minh trail in Vietnam that ran from North Vietnam to South Vietnam through neighbouring Laos and Cambodia would frustrate the American effort throughout the war and lead to the disastrous invasion of Cambodia in 1971. Even in the early 21st century, such refuge has played a significant role in the conflicts in both Iraq and Afghanistan. Efforts to deal with such support always carry with them the danger of widening the war.

The ALN increased efforts to bring arms across the border from Tunisia. The French forces met these efforts with a series of engagements from January to July 1958 – the Battle of the Frontiers. The ALN were losing around 3,200 men a month early in the battle, the French about 350. By July the ALN had lost about 20 000 and abandoned the attempt to move troops in significant numbers across the border.

Guerrilla campaigns traditionally wed military and political goals. The degree to which the political fate of France was tied to the insurgency in Algeria was clearly illustrated in May 1958. After the fall of the government in Paris and before a new one could be formed, the *pieds noirs* and leading military commanders in Algiers conspired to take control of the civil administration of Algeria. The conspiracy was not restricted to Algeria. An important component of the rebel generals' plan, and what they said would stave off further action on their part, was the political resurrection of Charles de Gaulle. De Gaulle was seen by many as a force of political stability. The army trusted him as a former military man. At that point, the *pieds noirs* trusted him as a leader who believed that Algeria should remain under French control. In France the left and right trusted him as someone who would act on the best interests of France ahead of political squabbling. De Gaulle, however, was himself circumspect about what he believed those interests to be. A new constitution brought about the birth of the French Fifth Republic and with it de Gaulle as president.

▲ French soldiers search for ALN fighters

Technology and war: helicopters

Experiments with vertical take-off and landing aircraft had been ongoing throughout the post-First World War period, but a mass produced model was not available until near the end of the Second World War. As a combat vehicle, the helicopter began to come into its own during the Korean War, providing versatile extraction of wounded soldiers from combat zones. The French believed they saw in the helicopter an answer to one of the chief problems that had plagued them in Indo-China – their inability to transport troops on short notice to remote areas and then to extract them. The helicopter freed the French of their dependence on road systems and meant they could match the guerrilla's mobility and unpredictability. In Algeria this potential was realized. Once ground forces made contact with ALN troops, French airborne troops, generally 20 to a helicopter, could be rapidly deployed, reinforced and evacuated as the situation dictated. By the end of the war, small mobile reconnaissance ground units would track and locate ALN units and call in helicopter troops to engage the enemy. Smaller helicopters armed with machine guns could provide fire support to ground or airborne troops. In 1960 the French forces had 120 helicopters that were moving 21 000 troops in and out of combat each month. The United States army would further develop helicopter warfare in Vietnam.

The Challe Plan

A new French military commander, Maurice Challe, and renewed French initiatives brought FLN forces in Algeria to the brink of destruction throughout 1959. Challe brought a new military strategy to Algeria that was intended to work with the urban renewal projects of the Constantine Plan such as the construction of low-rent housing and the reclamation of 250 000 hectares of land for agriculture. Challe's plan was to concentrate troops in the north of the country and move systematically from the west, where the ALN was comparatively weak, to the east were it was strongest. French forces would capture towns and villages and then from these conduct long-term sweeps through the adjacent countryside. Once this phase of an operation was complete, the swept territory would be secured through the construction of strong points manned by *harkis*. The Challe Plan also called for increased naval

Ho Chi Minh, leader of the Viet Minh forces and later North Vietnam in its struggle against France and the United States, once said:

You can kill ten of my men for every one of yours I kill, but even at these odds, you will lose and I will win.

1 Explain why Ho thought this to be true.

2 What disadvantages are there for guerrilla forces in pursuing a strategy of **attrition**?

3 Is Ho's statement valid for all guerrilla wars? Why or why not?

4 Research two other guerrilla wars, each taken from a different region. Does Ho's claim apply to these conflicts?

attrition
In military terms, the doctrine that seeks to weaken the enemy by depleting and destroying their resources, human and material, to the point that they surrender or otherwise abandon the fight.

Class discussion

Keeping Kissinger's words in mind, what would it have taken for the FLN to "lose"? What about other guerrilla forces in other guerrilla wars?

patrols to intercept weapons shipments. The Challe Plan was largely a success. The ALN fighting units and the territory that they controlled shrank steadily throughout Challe's offensive.

Terror attacks and the Week of the Barricades

Despite its weakness in Algeria, the FLN continued to launch terrorist attacks in France, making the cost of the war more evident to French civilians. Throughout the war there were some 42 000 terrorist attacks in France, claiming 2,800 civilian lives. Such attacks affected de Gaulle, who appears to have seen Challe's victory over the FLN in the field as a temporary success in an endless conflict. De Gaulle was also acutely aware that since 1945 the process of decolonization was accelerating around the world and that, as a result, the age of European colonialism was waning. He decided to put the issue of Algerian independence or self-determination to a referendum, in both France and Algeria. Believing de Gaulle had betrayed them, *pieds noirs* set up barricades in the streets and Challe refused to take action against them. The *pieds noirs* took them down of their own accord a week later. The referendum passed and, to the horror of the French military commanders in Algeria and the *pieds noirs*, de Gaulle set about negotiating the future of an Algerian state.

This development illustrates an important point about guerrilla war in the cause of national independence. Even though the insurgency seemed near defeat, it was the prospect of it flaring up after a period of dormancy that frightened de Gaulle and the rest of France. This was especially threatening given the military presence of the FLN in Tunisia. As Henry Kissinger would later say, "A conventional army loses if it does not win. A guerrilla army wins if it does not lose". De Gaulle understood this and determined that Algeria was not worth the cost. For de Gaulle that cost appeared to be never-ending guerrilla war.

There were still difficult negotiations ahead. Complicating matters was the fact that the FLN did not, in the end, speak for all Algerian nationalists, a fact further complicated by the hundreds of thousands of Algerian Muslims who remained, in varying degrees, loyal to France, including some 60 000 who served in the French military. With the support of the *pieds noirs*, the military staged a short-lived coup in Algiers in 1961, though not it seems with the support of much of the conscripted rank and file of the army. Finally, in 1961, desperate *pieds noirs* and some military officers formed a deadly terrorist organization known as the *Organisation de l'armée secrète* (OAS). The OAS conducted bomb attacks and shootings throughout Algeria and France until 1962, with both Algerian Muslims and the French army as their targets.

1.6 Effects

Conceptual understanding

Key questions

→ What was de Gaulle's reasoning in agreeing to negotiations with the FLN?

→ What were the effects of the war on French society?

→ How did the war affect the *pieds noirs* and the *harkis*?

Key concepts

→ Continuity

→ Change

→ Perspective

As in all wars, the most immediate effect was in the form of casualties. Counting the dead is a difficult and political task in all wars and becomes especially difficult in a guerrilla war. Guerrilla armies seldom keep accurate records of troop strength for security reasons, which makes counting the dead far from easy. It is in the interests of both sides to under-report their own casualties and over-report those of the enemy for morale and propaganda purposes. There can also be propaganda value in over-reporting the civilian casualties caused by the enemy. Counting civilian deaths is likewise a challenge and even more so in a guerrilla conflict when the line between civilian and soldiers is, by definition, blurred. Accurate census data is also necessary and this is not always available.

Algeria, by all accounts, was a brutal and costly conflict. Estimates range from 500 000 to one million deaths. According to their records, the French military experienced 18 000 dead and 53 000 wounded in the years 1954–1962. When the FLN came to power in 1962, it conducted a campaign of retribution against those Muslims who it suspected had remained loyal to the French regime during and after the war. Estimates put the fatalities of this campaign to 150 000.

After the **Evian Accords** ended the fighting in 1962, there was a mass migration of *pieds noirs* and *harkis*. Fear of FLN reprisals forced many to face the choice of "the suitcase or the coffin", as many put it at the time. Close to a million *pieds noirs* fled to France in the wake of the FLN victory, putting a significant strain on French society in terms of housing and social programmes. Some 40 000 *harkis* also fled to France. These refugees were generally segregated from the French population, housed in camps for years, suffering chronic unemployment and poverty. In 2000, unemployment among *harki* descendants ran at 30% while the rate for France as a whole was 9.7%.

The legacy of the Algerian War is ambiguous. For some, it stands as an example of the power of guerrilla war in the cause of national liberation. For others, it stands for the brutality that guerrilla war can engender in both sides.

ATL Thinking skills

Compare and contrast the perspectives below on the effects of the Algerian War.

- FLN
- *pieds-noirs*
- French military
- *Harkis*

Evian Accords

An agreement signed on 18 March 1962 between the French government and the FLN. The agreement established a permanent ceasefire in the Algerian War and the removal of French forces. It guaranteed the religious and property rights of French citizens who remained in an independent Algeria.

Exam-style questions and further reading

Exam-style questions

1   Discuss the role of technology in the outcome of the Algerian War.

2   Evaluate the FLN's use of guerrilla war against the French in Algeria.

3   Examine the use of terror by both sides in the Algerian War.

4   To what extent did socio-economic issues in Algeria cause the war?

5   Evaluate the relative strengths and weaknesses of the combatants in the Algerian War.

Further reading

Evans, Martin. 2011. *Algeria: France's Undeclared War.* Oxford University Press. Oxford, UK.

Horne, Alistair. 1977. *A Savage War of Peace: Algeria 1954–1962.* Viking Press. New York, USA.

Shepard, Todd. 2008. *The Invention of Decolonization: The Algerian War and the Remaking of France.* Cornell University Press. Ithaca, USA.

Understanding the question

An effective essay response starts with a thorough understanding of what the question requires. Paper 2 questions are tricky in that they seem very broad, but they require a specific and detailed response. Here are some steps that you can go through to help make this transition.

Step 1: What are the command terms in the question?

As the name suggests, a command term is what the question requires you to do. You first task is to determine what the command term requires of you.

Command term	Task
Analyse	Break down the topic in order to bring out the essential elements or structure.
Compare	Give an account of the similarities between two (or more) items or situations, referring to both (all) of them throughout. A thematic approach is the best way to tackle these questions: this means that you must first decide on which common components or themes you are going to conduct the comparison. These common components will be used to compare both elements of the question.
Contrast	Give an account of the differences between two (or more) items or situations, referring to both (all) of them throughout. A thematic approach is the best way to tackle these questions: this means that you must first decide on which common components or themes you are going to conduct the contrast. These common components will be used to contrast both elements of the question.
Discuss	Offer a considered and balanced review that includes a range of arguments, factors, or hypotheses. Opinions or conclusions should be presented clearly and supported by appropriate evidence.
Evaluate	Make an appraisal by weighing up the strengths and limitations. Like compare and contrast questions, this command term requires you to identify the criteria against which you are evaluating the subject of the question.
Examine	Consider an argument or concept in a way that uncovers the assumptions and interrelationships of the issue.
To what extent	Consider the merits or otherwise of an argument or concept. This requires you to examine multiple perspectives on the argument or concept. Opinions and conclusions should be presented clearly and supported with appropriate evidence and sound argument.

Step 2: What concepts apply to the question?

This course explores six major historical concepts:

- Continuity
- Cause
- Perspective
- Change
- Consequence
- Significance

Because these concepts are central to the IB history curriculum, it makes sense that they are important components in IB assessment. When you approach an exam question, therefore, you must decide which of these concepts apply to the question. These concepts then form the focus of your response. This means that each paragraph should refer to the concepts you have chosen. You do not need to address all the concepts;

in fact, one or two are usually sufficient. Some of the concepts, such as cause and consequence or continuity and change, tend to go together and can be considered as a pair in some cases.

Step 3: What curriculum topics and content are being assessed?

Each world history topic that you are studying is divided into:

- topics
- prescribed content
- suggested examples.

One way to look at these elements is that "topics" and "prescribed content" are *what* you must learn, whereas "suggested examples" is *how* you learn these. The material in "topics" and "prescribed content" can be named in the question and therefore need to be studied explicitly and referred to as required in your response. For example, in a question on the "causes and effects of 20th-century wars", a question could explicitly refer to the "long- and short-term causes" of a 20th-century war, as this is explicitly stated in the curriculum. You can explore the long- and short-term causes of any 20th-century war you choose.

The important thing is that you understand which topics and prescribed content the question requires.

Step 4: Does the question require discussion of more than one region?

Paper 2 focuses on comparative world history. Questions will often require you to examine events from different regions, as shown on the map in the exam. If you choose one of these questions, be sure to use examples from more than one region and discuss each region in a balanced fashion. You can use more than one region in answering any question, but some questions *require* you to examine more than one region. Remember that the First World War and the Second World War are cross-regional wars and can be used to answer questions requiring wars from different regions. For example, when answering a question on the causes of two wars, each from a different region, it is perfectly acceptable to examine the causes of the Second World War in Europe and the Pacific as your two wars.

Step 5: What wars are you going to use to address the question?

The curriculum guide does not stipulate that you study any specific wars. Rather, it requires that you use any 20th-century wars to study the concepts, topics and prescribed content. This means that the last step in understanding the question is choosing the wars that will best help you examine the question. You need to understand the war(s) as it applies to the previous four steps. Remember, detail and depth are important in IB exams, so choose the examples that you understand in depth and detail.

2 THE FALKLANDS/MALVINAS WAR: THE FAILURE OF DIPLOMACY

Global context

The Falklands/Malvinas conflict came at a time of uncertainty for both combatants. Britain was in the midst of a major economic restructuring spearheaded by Margaret Thatcher's Conservative Party. Deregulation and privatization resulted in high unemployment, social unrest and labour strife. Argentina was ruled by an unpopular military Junta that took as one of its key aims the destruction of left-wing organizations and their supporters. The result was a "dirty war" of terror against its own citizens.

The Cold War began to heat up as it lurched into its last decade. The Soviet invasion of Afghanistan in 1979 had brought *détente* to a halt and the election of Ronald Reagan brought a hard-line anti-communist to power in the United States. Reagan made common cause with Thatcher against communist states around the world. Reagan's foreign policy also seemed a natural fit with the anti-communist stance of Argentina's Junta. The coming conflict would force the US to choose.

Timeline

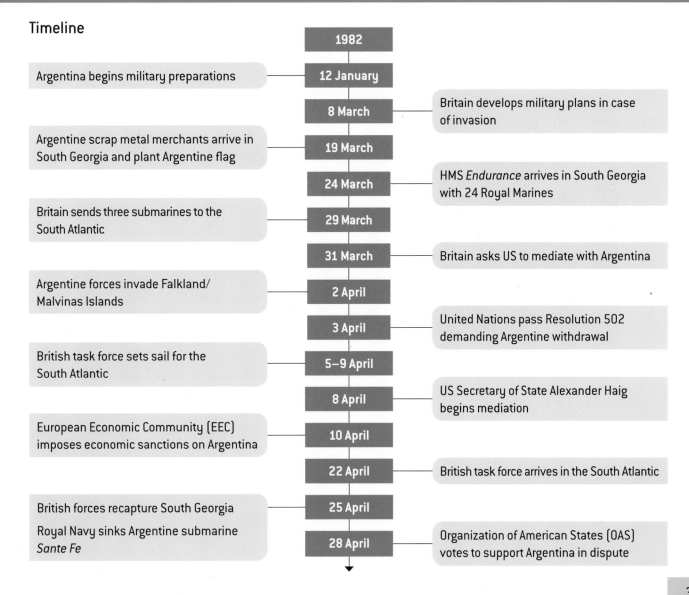

	1982	
Argentina begins military preparations	12 January	
	8 March	Britain develops military plans in case of invasion
Argentine scrap metal merchants arrive in South Georgia and plant Argentine flag	19 March	
	24 March	HMS *Endurance* arrives in South Georgia with 24 Royal Marines
Britain sends three submarines to the South Atlantic	29 March	
	31 March	Britain asks US to mediate with Argentina
Argentine forces invade Falkland/Malvinas Islands	2 April	
	3 April	United Nations pass Resolution 502 demanding Argentine withdrawal
British task force sets sail for the South Atlantic	5–9 April	
	8 April	US Secretary of State Alexander Haig begins mediation
European Economic Community (EEC) imposes economic sanctions on Argentina	10 April	
	22 April	British task force arrives in the South Atlantic
British forces recapture South Georgia	25 April	
Royal Navy sinks Argentine submarine *Sante Fe*	28 April	Organization of American States (OAS) votes to support Argentina in dispute

US formally supports Britain in dispute Britain proclaims Total Exclusion Zone (TEZ)	**30 April**
	1 May — Air war begins
Royal Navy sinks ARA *General Belgrano*	**2 May**
	4 May — Argentine air force sinks HMS *Sheffield*
British forces land on San Carlos Argentine air force sinks HMS *Ardent*	**21 May**
	12–29 May — Battle of Goose Green
Battle of Fitzroy	**8 June**
	11–14 June — Battle of Stanley
Argentina surrenders	**14 June**

▲ The wreckage of an Argentine armoured vehicle destroyed during the Falklands/Malvinas War

2.1 Causes of the Falklands/Malvinas War

Conceptual understanding

Key questions

→ To what extent was both Argentine and British policy toward the Falkland/Malvinas Islands ambiguous?

→ To what extent were the actions of both Argentina and Britain influenced by domestic concerns?

Key concepts

→ Cause

→ Consequence

→ Perspective

Long-term causes

Located in the South Atlantic Ocean some 300 miles (480 km) off the coast of South America, the Falkland/Malvinas Islands are a rocky group of islands, home to about 2,000 people, mostly involved in sheep farming. Historically, France, Spain and Great Britain have occupied the islands, but none with a great deal of enthusiasm, even leaving them unoccupied for a 50-year stretch in the 18th century. When Argentina won her independence from Spain in 1816, she laid claim to the islands, calling them the Malvinas. While the British were not necessarily committed to the occupation of the islands, which they regarded as having negligible strategic or economic value, the British government was not about to have its foreign policy dictated by a fledgling South American republic. A small British force reasserted control over the islands in 1833, from which time they have been continuously occupied by the British, although the Argentines have never relinquished their claims to the territory. It is these events, predating the war by some 150 years, upon which both the Argentines and the British would base their case for war in 1982. There were, however, some more important and immediate background factors that need to be considered.

By 1981, Argentina had been ruled by an increasingly unpopular military **Junta** for five years. The Junta took power in a coup designed to restore order during a time of deep political instability. Ideologically, the Junta was on the far right and as such used its extensive authoritarian power to repress all elements of the left – unions, political parties, intellectuals and eventually anyone who was suspected of criticizing the regime. Some estimates put the victims of this "dirty war" as high as 30 000, collectively known as "the disappeared". This extreme social pressure within Argentina was compounded by a severe economic

Class discussion

Why is civilian occupation an important aspect in a country's claim to a territory?

TOK discussion

What role does history play in a country's claims to territory? What are the strengths and weaknesses of basing claims on history?

Junta

A committee or council that rules a country. The term often applies to military rulers of Latin American countries.

crisis, stemming from crippling foreign debt. The Junta calculated that a quick patriotic war would help galvanize public opinion behind the government.

In terms of broader foreign policy aims, the Junta, and many previous regimes in Argentina, considered that the position of Argentina as a power was dependent on control of the South Atlantic. Geographically, the most important position upon which such control depended was Antarctica. The 1959 **Antarctic Treaty**, which essentially internationalized and demilitarized the Antarctic, meant that Argentina would have to look elsewhere for an anchor in the South Atlantic. As Chile asserted more authority over Tierra del Fuego (a group of islands off the southern tip of South America separated from the mainland by the Straits of Magellan), the Falklands/Malvinas became vital to Argentina's position in the South Atlantic. In 1980, with improving relations with both its northern neighbours and the USA, and its new anti-communist president Ronald Reagan, the time seemed right for a settling of accounts with Britain over the Falklands/Malvinas.

> **Antarctic Treaty**
> A treaty by which the signatories pledge to keep the Antarctic a demilitarized and nuclear weapons-free zone and to cooperate in the promotion of scientific inquiry in the Antarctic.

ATL Research and thinking skills

As we have seen, the Falklands/Malvinas are not the only disputed territories in the world. Choose one of the territories from the list below and answer the following questions.

1 What are the arguments for each side's claim of ownership?

2 What steps have been taken to solve the problem: war, negotiation, third-party arbitration?

3 What is the probability that the situation will escalate into a war? Justify your answer.

- Arunachal Pradesh—India and China
- Cyprus—Greece and Turkey
- Kuril Islands—Japan and Russia
- Ogaden—Somalia and Ethiopia
- Hans Island—Denmark and Canada

Economic instability also played a role in the British decision to go to war. Prime Minister Margaret Thatcher's economic policies, designed to fight inflation through austerity measures that would involve widespread **privatization**, anti-union legislation and higher taxation, caused deep divisions in the country. These policies led to a sharp rise in unemployment in Britain in the years leading up to the Falklands War. Thatcher was a fervent anti-communist and staunch supporter of Ronald Reagan and the United States' approach to the Cold War. While she took a hard line against the USSR, Argentina in the Falklands conflict and Irish Republican Army (IRA) prisoners, she did not support economic sanctions against the Apartheid regime in South Africa. Thatcher's austerity measures, however, meant downsizing the military, which, in turn, necessitated a re-evaluation of what the British could realistically protect with her armed forces. Such a re-evaluation determined that a permanent diplomatic solution to the Falklands question needed to

> **privatization**
> The economic practice of selling government assets to private owners.

be found. The most workable solution appeared to be some form of leaseback, in which the islands would belong to Argentina, but would be administered by Britain. While such a solution seemed to make practical sense, it was unacceptable to some hardliners in the British government and became untenable once representatives of the islands' British citizens were included in the negotiations with the Argentine government.

Britain did not initiate the conflict and, therefore, we cannot say that Thatcher planned to use the war to bolster public support, but domestic concerns did indeed help to dictate Thatcher's response to the crisis. Thatcher's personality must also be considered. As the first woman to lead a large, industrialized western state, she was forging a reputation for an uncompromising and unyielding approach to governance when the war broke out. This approach to criticism and opposition was evident in the British coal strikes and IRA bombings later in her career as Prime Minister. Nothing in her past suggested that Thatcher would back down from a challenge to British **sovereignty** in the Falklands or anywhere else. This, however, is the image of Thatcher that would emerge largely after the conflict, and for many partially because of it.

> **sovereignty**
> The ability of a country to act independently of any outside authority.

Short-term causes

Although negotiations on a Falklands/Malvinas settlement had been attempted at various points in the 20th century, they broke down once again in early 1982. With a deteriorating domestic situation and pressure from hard-line members of the Junta, General Galtieri, the leader of the Junta, decided to force the situation. Galtieri was a member of Argentina's ruling military Junta from 1976 to 1982, leading the Junta from 1981 to 1982. He was a fervent anti-leftist and directed the "dirty war" against left-wing critics of his government. This ideological stance endeared him to the US administration. The bond was not, however, strong enough to entice Reagan to abandon his British ally. Military preparations for taking the Malvinas began in early 1982 amid a great deal of secrecy, suggesting that what Galtieri wanted was not just any solution to the dispute, but a military one. Had he wanted to use the military to pressure the British into a diplomatic solution, it made no sense to hide the preparations. It seems that by 1982, the Junta had decided to force the question by means of military action.

A small dispute involving Argentine scrap metal merchants on another disputed island, South Georgia, gave the Junta the opportunity to go ahead. The Argentine navy seemed to deliberately provoke the British when, in March 1982, they transported the merchants to the island for a second time. They travelled in silence and failed to notify the British government, planting the flag of Argentina, and refusing to leave when asked to do so. The British response was to dispatch the soon to be recalled ice patrol vessel HMS *Endurance* from Stanley, the capital of the Falklands/Malvinas, to evict the Argentines from South Georgia. Instead of confronting a small party, the *Endurance* and the Royal Marines aboard, however, were greeted by a full Argentine occupation force. The British, for their part, made little genuine effort to defuse the

South Georgia incident. This, combined with faulty Argentine military intelligence, suggested to the Argentines that Britain was already preparing to take substantial aggressive action in the South Atlantic, indicating that neither side was acting with anything like a complete picture of the situation or a clear plan of action. Believing, as they did, that a British taskforce was on its way to the South Atlantic, most in the Junta concluded, therefore, that time was of the essence and on 26 March ordered a full invasion of the Falklands/Malvinas to be carried out on 2 April.

It would seem, then, that this conflict was caused by a lack of clarity on both sides. Argentinean goals were unclear from the start. Did they want to occupy and exercise sovereignty over the Malvinas? Did they want to pressure the British government into negotiating an arrangement by which the British government would lease the islands from Argentina? Or did they simply want to inject a sense of urgency into the negotiations? As the planning and operation proceeded, the Junta meandered its way to a goal of further negotiations, but this was pursued with little consistency. It was also unclear on the relationship between military posturing and diplomacy in resolving the situation. Were their military actions designed to bring Britain to the table in order to negotiate a solution, or were these preparations and the war that would follow the actual solution? When this lack of clarity was combined with faulty military intelligence, war became hard to avoid.

The British were likewise unclear in what they wanted from the Falkland Islands. Their response to this uncertainty was to stall for time by not taking the negotiations as seriously as the Argentines did, leaving the impression that they wanted the status quo. When it opted for an ambiguous, though nonetheless military, response to the South Georgia incident in spite of other indications that it was abandoning the South Atlantic militarily, the British government bolstered the Argentine misconception of the situation.

2.2 Combatants

Conceptual understanding

Key questions

→ To what extent were both Britain and Argentina prepared for war?

→ What role did geography play in the relative strengths and weaknesses of each country?

→ What were the relative military strengths of each country?

Key concepts

→ Continuity

→ Change

→ Significance

Great Britain

The Argentine incursion came at a time when, in accordance with Thatcher's downsizing efforts, the Royal Navy was reducing its size, including decommissioning its aircraft carriers and its South Atlantic icebreakers. Nevertheless, within five days of the Argentine invasion, the British military had put together a naval task force and had set sail for the South Atlantic.

The task force consisted of some 28 000 sailors and soldiers. The land forces were divided into two brigades and consisted of army regulars as well as Royal Marines. The Royal Marines formed an important part of Britain's rapid reaction capabilities and were specifically trained in amphibious operations. These forces formed what was essentially a division and as such contained within it all the elements required to carry on operations, including artillery, medical and logistic capabilities.

This task force was a substantial response, consisting of destroyers, frigates, merchant ships, and two aircraft carriers, HMS *Invincible* and HMS *Hermes*, and included civilian passenger liners *Canberra, Uganda* and the *Queen Elizabeth II*, that were pressed into service. In all some 65 ships carried a landing force of 7,000 troops. The 13 000-km voyage would be split in two, with the task force making a supply stop at Ascension Island, an island owned by Britain on which there was an airstrip administered by the United States military. The USA would continue to give practical support to the British throughout the conflict while still trying to find diplomatic solutions, an ambiguous position that confused many and angered the Argentines. Nevertheless as they approached the islands, the British would be limited to carrier-borne aircraft, about 42 of them, roughly one third that of the Argentine air force. Although the

Harrier Jump Jets used by the British were versatile aircraft, combining as they did the ability for both traditional and vertical take-off, they were not as fast as the Argentine Mirage or Super Étendard.

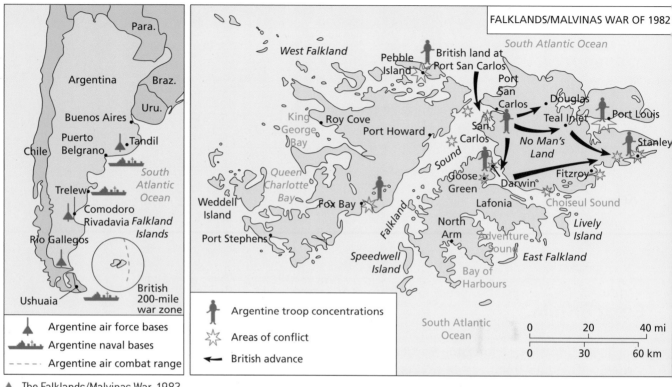

▲ The Falklands/Malvinas War, 1982.

▲ The Royal Navy ship HMS *Ardent* on escort duty during the Falklands/Malvinas War

Argentina

Argentina's navy had the ability to operate in all three major aspects of naval warfare: submarine, surface and air. Although her vessels, including four submarines, were dated, they posed a threat to the British forces. The strength of the Argentine armed forces was its air force. It had around 120 aircraft available for operations against the British task force. The quality of the force was mixed. Its US-made Skyhawks were older and in various states of upkeep. The air force also had French-made Mirage III and Super Étendards, the latter equipped with the deadly Exocet anti-ship missile. Weapons and ammunition were limited as a result of the US arms embargo that US President Carter implemented in 1976 in response to the Junta's "dirty war" against its domestic political opponents.

Class discussion

What difficulties did the location of the islands pose for the British military?

▲ A French-built Mirage III similar to those used by the Argentine air force during the Falklands/Malvinas War

> ## Conceptual understanding
>
> ### Key questions
>
> → To what extent was British strategy determined by geography?
>
> → How did Argentina seek to overcome its military weaknesses?
>
> ### Key concepts
>
> → Continuity
>
> → Perspective

Great Britain

Faithful to British strategy of the previous 400 years, Thatcher's government set up a blockade of the area surrounding the Falkland Islands on 12 April, calling it a Maritime Exclusion Zone (MEZ) to avoid the semantics of the word "blockade", suggesting as it did an act of war. The United States had the same concern during the Cuban Missile Crisis when they used the term "quarantine" instead of "blockade". The MEZ stated that the British would consider any Argentine military vessel within the zone a legitimate target. As the task force approached the islands, the MEZ was changed to a Total Exclusion Zone (TEZ), in which any vessel, military or civilian, found in the 200-mile (320 km) zone without British permission was a legitimate target. The notice also indicated the same for any aircraft, preventing the Argentines from reinforcing from the air. Adequate air cover was the primary concern for the British forces. Operating from aircraft carriers, their effective air strength was limited. Bombing raids on Argentine positions were undertaken by heavy bombers operating from the US base on Ascension Island. This proved difficult, as heavy bombers needed to be refuelled in the air. Elements of the task force directly supporting the invasion would shelter in Falklands Sound and be supported by the rest of the task force further out. Time was of the essence as the task force could not operate for long so far from support.

Land operations would consist of establishing beachheads at San Carlos and then moving against the Argentine forces at Goose Green. The campaign was to come to a conclusion with the capture of Stanley.

Class discussion

What justification could the British use for establishing their Maritime Exclusion Zone?

Argentina

Initial Argentine strategy relied on the hope that the British would not respond in strength and that the South Atlantic winter would make operations too difficult for a British task force. The surprise attack would leave Britain with little option but to negotiate the transfer of the islands.

The growing tensions over the islands in early 1982, however, blunted the surprise. Argentina also assumed that the United States would either advocate for a quick resolution or remain neutral. The Junta then launched the operation months earlier than they had hoped to, allowing the British to avoid the worst of the winter weather. The early start also meant that the Argentine army had not finished mobilizing its reserves.

Once the Junta had committed to full-scale invasion and they realized that the British were responding in force, they settled on a strategy that would rely on their advantages – air power and geographic proximity. The Argentine air force would launch attacks on the British ships at sea and in Falkland Sound. Their numeric superiority would allow them to deploy some of their aircraft as decoys to lure the smaller number of British aircraft away from the ships while others attacked. If the Argentines could prolong the war, the British would be forced to withdraw.

Class discussion

To what extent were Argentine plans based on faulty assumptions? To what degree was this obvious at the time?

Source skills

The British response

Prime Minister Margaret Thatcher's speech to Parliament on the Falklands Crisis, 29 April 1982.

http://www.totalpolitics.com/speeches/war/falklands-war/34258/speech-on-the-conduct-of-the-falklands-war.thtml

". . . the Government has taken every possible step that had a reasonable prospect of helping us to achieve our objectives – the withdrawal of the Argentine forces and the end of their illegal occupation of the islands, the restoration of British administration, and a long-term solution which is acceptable not only to the House but to the inhabitants of the Falkland Islands.

It is the Government's most earnest hope that we can achieve those objectives by a negotiated settlement. We have done everything that we can to encourage Mr. Haig's attempts to find a solution by diplomatic means. I shall have something more to say about that in a moment.

As the House knows, the Government has also taken military measures to strengthen our diplomatic efforts. Mr. Haig's initiative would never have got under way if the British Government had not sent the naval task force to the South Atlantic within four days of Argentina's aggression against the Falkland Islands.

What incentive would there have been for the Argentine Junta to give Mr. Haig's ideas more than the most cursory glance if Britain had not underpinned its search for a diplomatic settlement with the dispatch of the task force? Gentle persuasion will not make the Argentine Government give up what they have seized by force."

Questions:

1   What does Thatcher mean by "every possible step that had a reasonable prospect of helping us to achieve our objectives"?

2   With reference to its origin, purpose and content, discuss the value and limitations of this source for a historian studying British efforts to resolve the Falklands crisis.

3   Using this source and your own knowledge, evaluate the extent to which the British government pursued both diplomatic and military options consistently in resolving the Falklands crisis.

Key questions

→ What role did Argentine air power play in the war?

→ To what extent were the British forces in the South Atlantic vulnerable to air power?

→ To what extent did the Argentines have a viable defence plan for the islands once they occupied them?

Key concepts

→ Cause

→ Consequence

→ Significance

Operation Rosario and its aftermath

The Argentine plan for invasion called for an amphibious landing with tracked landing vehicles. This force was to take the airport and the capital. Commandos were to land at a separate location to seek out the small force of Royal Marines that defended the island and capture the British Governor. In all, some 500 Argentines were to attack the islands. Not wanting to give the impression that they intended a long occupation, much of the invasion force was to be withdrawn, thus paving the way for negotiations. The islands were defended by about 60 Royal Marines whose commander believed the landing would happen at a different location on the island and so the invasion force landed largely unopposed. Once they realized that the British were responding in force, the evacuation order was reversed and the Argentines began reinforcing their positions on the islands.

Thatcher's cabinet was deeply divided over whether or not to go to war. The combination of surprise, economic weakness and a recent report from the Secretary of State for Defence indicating that defending the islands with current resources would be very difficult and recapturing them far more so persuaded most of her cabinet that negotiation was their only recourse. The Prime Minister's mood was galvanized by the First Sea Lord Admiral Sir Henry Leach who assured the Prime Minister he could have a task force ready to sail in 48 hours. Thatcher and the cabinet grasped at the hope that this presented. With Leach's assurance, Thatcher silenced the dissenters in her cabinet and could face Parliament and the public with her decision to retake the islands.

▲ British Royal Marines about to go on patrol during the Falklands/Malvinas War

As soon as the crisis looked like it could easily escalate into a shooting war, diplomatic efforts to stop it erupted with a fury. These efforts centred on three main forums: the United Nations (UN), the Organization of American States (OAS) and a well-meaning but ineffectual mediation effort by the US Secretary of State Alexander Haig. Haig was an army general who had served in Vietnam, held posts in both the Nixon and Ford administrations and as commander of NATO forces. Strangely, it was Argentina that brought the matter before the UN Security Council. Faulty Argentine intelligence believed that a military task force had left for the South Atlantic even before the invasion of the islands as a show of force. Argentina brought this before the Security Council as an act of aggression, seeking a denunciation and the associated justification for her own military plans. The Argentines did not want to show their hand regarding the actual invasion and therefore any approaches to members of the Security Council for support were tentative and ineffectual. The British had no such issues of secrecy and took the initiative, bringing a resolution to the Council on 3 April. Resolution 502/1982, drafted by the British, called for a cessation of hostilities, a withdrawal of Argentine military forces, and a diplomatic solution to be found that respected the principles of the charter of the UN. This last demand, with its emphasis on the principles of the UN, was no diplomatic pandering. The charter emphasizes the principle of self-determination and the British knew that, if left up to the islanders, the Falklands/Malvinas would be forever British. The resolution passed. The British had won the first diplomatic round.

The Latin American states of the OAS generally supported the Argentine cause. The OAS proved a troublesome forum for the USA during the crisis, as she was both a member of NATO with Britain and a member of the OAS with Argentina. This apparent conflict of interests was compounded by the Rio Pact of 1947, the terms of which bound the signatories – most Latin America countries and the United States – to regard an attack on one as an attack on all. By the end of April, Argentina had won a resolution under the Rio Pact, denouncing Britain and calling for a cessation of hostilities. The United States abstained from the vote and, considering the Argentines as the aggressors, ignored the resolution.

Haig's diplomatic mission was in many ways doomed from the start. The position of the United States was not ideal for that of a mediator as it was more closely connected to the British than the Argentines. The consequences of an Argentine failure, in terms of American foreign policy, paled in comparison with the implications for Britain. Dealing with the Junta also proved difficult for Haig. There appeared no clear decision-making process between the three leaders of the Junta – General Galtieri, General Dozo and Admiral Anaya. As Haig's mission came to an unsuccessful end, the USA lined up more clearly with Britain, providing material, logistical and intelligence support.

▲ The Royal Navy ship HMS *Antelope* explodes after being attacked by Argentine aircraft

Class discussion

How did the war affect US influence in the region?

The air war

After easily retaking South Georgia on 25 April, and in the process disabling the Argentine submarine *Santa Fé*, the British force proceeded on to the Falkland Islands. When the task force arrived on 1 May, it wasted no time in launching air attacks on the Argentine defenders, who lost several aircraft. The next day, a Royal Navy submarine torpedoed the Argentine cruiser *Belgrano*, which sank taking 321 sailors with her. Whether or not this action conformed to the British rules of engagement became a source of controversy after the war. For the most part, Argentine naval forces stayed clear of the Royal Navy from that point. The Argentine air force fared better, sinking the destroyer HMS *Sheffield* with a French-made Exocet missile fired from a French-made Super Étendard jet. The Argentine air force would continue to have success against the Royal

Navy ships throughout the war, especially when they moved into close quarters around the islands to support land operations. By 20 May, last attempts at mediation by Peru and the United Nations failed and the effort to retake the Falklands/Malvinas was about to begin.

Operations on the Islands

Sheltering their invasion fleet between the two main islands, the British landed at San Carlos, across the island from the capital, establishing three separate beachheads on 21 May and putting 4,000 men ashore, meeting little resistance. The British achieved surprise through a combination of Argentine missteps and diversionary attacks. Argentine air attacks were repulsed through the day, although at the cost of one British ship sunk and two damaged. Air attacks on the invasion fleet continued for several days, with one long-range, although unsuccessful, attack on the more distant British aircraft carriers. As the British forces began to move inland, the Argentine air force continued to harass the staging area. Nevertheless, the British moved inland.

The first objective, however, was not Stanley. The British command instead opted for a more limited attack on the Argentine garrison at Goose Green and Darwin to further secure the beachhead. The attack began on 27 May and, after two days of fighting, the 500 attackers forced the surrender of the approximately 700 Argentine defenders. After an abortive and costly blunder at Fitzroy, the British forces moved on to surround the capital and in a series of smaller engagements captured high ground surrounding it. From this position of strength, the British forces moved on to Stanley and compelled the eventual surrender of the Argentine garrison and its 12 000 survivors on 14 June 1982.

What were the outcomes of the war?

Capturing and holding the islands from 2 April until 14 June had cost Argentina 746 dead and 1,200 wounded. Almost half of the Argentine dead were lost at sea when the *Belgrano* sank. Recapturing the islands cost Britain 250 dead and 770 casualties, and US$1.19 billion, although this figure does not include the replacement of lost equipment and ships. In many ways, this war had ramifications that reached far beyond these sterile numbers.

Unable to sustain their position in the face of public outrage against both the war and the "dirty war" that it had conducted against its own citizens, the military Junta resigned. The interim president Reynaldo Bignone oversaw the dismantling of the Junta. Political parties that had been driven underground during the dirty war emerged into the light of day and new parties were formed. By 1983 free elections were held that brought Raúl Alfonsín to power at the head of a centre-left government. Alfonsín's government would begin the process of bringing the perpetrators of the dirty war to justice. By 1986, pressure from the military brought this process to a stop.

The war only exacerbated the dismal financial situation in Argentina, a situation that would plague it well into the 21st century. In the immediate post-war period inflation would run as high as 900% while at the same time there was limited growth in the economy. In 1983 President Alfonsín was forced to appeal to the International Monetary Fund (IMF) and would end up having to refinance the country's debt agreements.

Research skills

Use the following table to explore Argentina's economy before and after the war.

	1981	1985
Inflation rate		
Gross national product		
Defence spending		
Unemployment rate		
Possible conclusion:		

While failure meant political defeat for the Junta in Argentina, it meant political advantage for Thatcher's government. She had been in power for three years with little discernible style of leadership, unable to stabilize a faltering economy. Britain's victory in the Falklands/Malvinas radically altered the former. She was from this point seen by the public and the international community as a decisive leader who preferred action to negotiation. Whether this was actually the case is not the point; it was perceived to be the case. Her control over her party and cabinet critics increased. She capitalized on the wave of patriotic sentiment that accompanied the recapture of the islands and parlayed it into an election victory the following year, despite deep divisions within British society and enduring economic woes. Could she have won this election without the Falklands War? It would have been difficult. She would invoke the victory in speeches to Parliament and to the public. It certainly increased the confidence to push ahead with unpopular domestic policies. Despite a general programme of privatization and spending cuts, the conflict insulated the Royal Navy and Royal Air Force from such measures even though they had been marked for drastic reductions before the Argentine invasion.

Having gone to such great lengths and expense to preserve its position in the South Atlantic, Britain had little choice but to reassert her presence there. A new air base was built, garrisoned with some 1,500 troops who were still there on the 25th anniversary of the conflict. With the growing prospect of large offshore oil deposits in the South Atlantic, the British stance in 1982 almost seems prescient. Thirty years after the war the British government spends some £200 million per year on the defence of the islands.

Thinking skills

Thatcher's Secretary of State for Defence John Nott had drafted a report prior to the war that indicated the islands would be very difficult to defend with resources as they then stood. How did the Falkland/Malvinas War change this? What was the British military presence in the islands in 2005? What percentage of the British defence budget was taken up with Falklands' defence?

Exam-style questions and further reading

Exam-style questions

1 To what extent was the Falklands/Malvinas War preventable through negotiation?

2 Examine the role of the United States in the development of the Falklands/Malvinas War.

3 Examine the role of the United Nations in the development of the Falklands/Malvinas War.

4 Examine the relationship between domestic concerns and the causes and consequences of the Falklands/Malvinas War.

5 Compare the role played by air and naval power in the conduct of the Falklands/Malvinas War.

Further reading

Aitken, Jonathan. 2013. *Margaret Thatcher: Power and Personality.* Bloomsbury. New York, USA.

Middlebrook, Martin. 2009. *The Argentine Fight for the Falklands.* Pen and Sword. UK.

Middlebrook, Martin. 2012. *The Falklands War.* Pen and Sword, UK.

Privratsky, Kenneth L. 2015. *Logistics in the Falklands War.* Pen and Sword. UK.

3 THE VIETNAM WAR: REVOLUTIONARY WAR IN INDO-CHINA

Global context

As with the end of the First World War, the end of the Second World War threw the international order into flux. The collapse of the Japanese Empire with its army still in the field made a complex situation even more uncertain. The spectre of an ideological-based world order grew more likely each month in the post-war period. France's place in this new world order was unclear and the status of its former colonies even more so.

The United States, a French ally, was still moderately anti-colonialist, but was struggling with the implications of combining new global forces such as ideology with more traditional global paradigms such as nationalism and imperialism. The instability of the post-war years provided great opportunities for nationalist movements around the world that sought to capitalize on the vulnerable condition of the old imperial powers.

Timeline

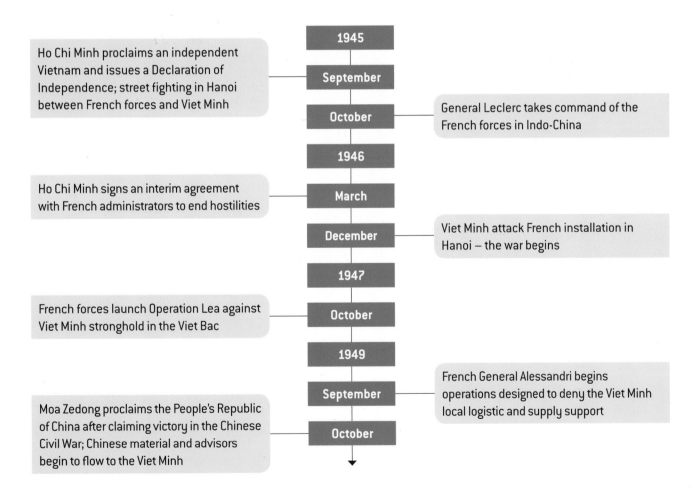

1945

September — Ho Chi Minh proclaims an independent Vietnam and issues a Declaration of Independence; street fighting in Hanoi between French forces and Viet Minh

October — General Leclerc takes command of the French forces in Indo-China

1946

March — Ho Chi Minh signs an interim agreement with French administrators to end hostilities

December — Viet Minh attack French installation in Hanoi – the war begins

1947

October — French forces launch Operation Lea against Viet Minh stronghold in the Viet Bac

1949

September — French General Alessandri begins operations designed to deny the Viet Minh local logistic and supply support

October — Moa Zedong proclaims the People's Republic of China after claiming victory in the Chinese Civil War; Chinese material and advisors begin to flow to the Viet Minh

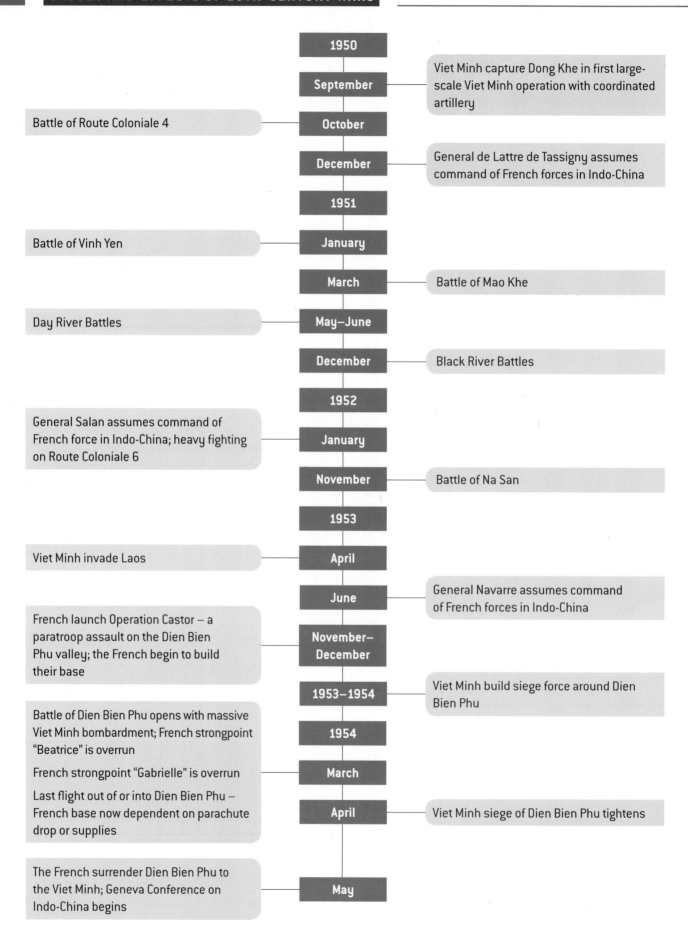

	1950
	September — Viet Minh capture Dong Khe in first large-scale Viet Minh operation with coordinated artillery
Battle of Route Coloniale 4 —	**October**
	December — General de Lattre de Tassigny assumes command of French forces in Indo-China
	1951
Battle of Vinh Yen —	**January**
	March — Battle of Mao Khe
Day River Battles —	**May–June**
	December — Black River Battles
	1952
General Salan assumes command of French force in Indo-China; heavy fighting on Route Coloniale 6 —	**January**
	November — Battle of Na San
	1953
Viet Minh invade Laos —	**April**
	June — General Navarre assumes command of French forces in Indo-China
French launch Operation Castor – a paratroop assault on the Dien Bien Phu valley; the French begin to build their base —	**November–December**
	1953–1954 — Viet Minh build siege force around Dien Bien Phu
Battle of Dien Bien Phu opens with massive Viet Minh bombardment; French strongpoint "Beatrice" is overrun	**1954**
French strongpoint "Gabrielle" is overrun —	**March**
Last flight out of or into Dien Bien Phu – French base now dependent on parachute drop or supplies —	**April** — Viet Minh siege of Dien Bien Phu tightens
The French surrender Dien Bien Phu to the Viet Minh; Geneva Conference on Indo-China begins —	**May**

3.1 Causes of the Vietnam War

Conceptual understanding

Key questions

→ How did Ho Chi Minh combine nationalism and communism in the Viet Minh movement?

→ How did the end of the Second World War in the Pacific affect the beginning of the war?

Key concepts

→ Cause

→ Consequence

→ Continuity

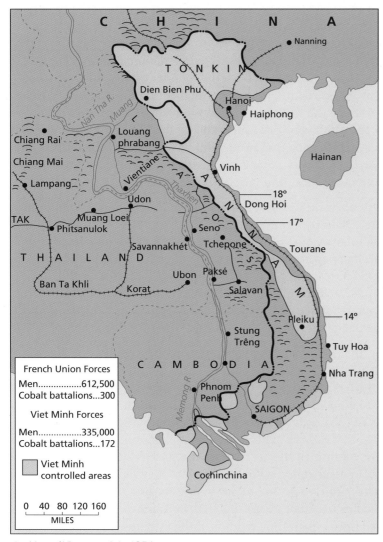

▲ Map of Vietnam, July 1954

Long-term causes

France asserted imperial control over Vietnam over a 30–year period. By 1885 what is now Vietnam had come under centralized French control. Throughout this period and after, various Vietnamese nationalist groups staged armed resistance to French control. The French authorities introduced a programme of westernization. The emphasis on western education and the Roman Catholic Church provided an affront to traditional Vietnamese culture, further aggravating Vietnamese nationalists. An overly complex bureaucracy designed to further this assimilation made for inefficient rule. Meanwhile Vietnamese resources were used to enrich metropolitan France at the expense of the colony. Although there were a number of significant uprisings against French rule in the 19th century, they failed for lack of widespread organization. In this sense Ho Chi Minh and the Viet Minh can be seen as a continuation of this nationalist tradition.

Short-term causes

The first act of the 30-year conflict in what is now Vietnam developed amid a dynamic and confusing international situation emerging from the end of the Second World War. The complex relationship between the victorious superpowers was deteriorating, adding the amorphous element of ideology to traditional power politics in a way unseen before. Defeated empires were adrift in administrative chaos. The pre-war colonizers were trying to reassert colonial authority while nationalist movements were trying to use the flux to establish independent states. In South-East Asia the confusion was compounded by the fact that the Japanese had not been defeated in the field, but rather as a result of the cataclysmic explosions in Hiroshima and Nagasaki. This strange situation left hundreds of thousands of armed Japanese troops still in charge of vast amounts of territory throughout Asia and the Pacific with no real plan for the transfer of power, let alone an idea of to whom that power would be transferred.

Into this gap stepped Ho Chi Minh, leader of the Viet Minh, a Vietnamese nationalist party with communist leadership. From 1941 he had led a small guerrilla force against the Vichy French (who administered the colony for the Japanese) and against the Japanese directly, for which they received American support. As the Japanese withdrew and before the French could send troops, Ho and the Viet Minh entered Hanoi and proclaimed independence on 2 September 1945, issuing a Declaration of Independence deliberately modelled on the American document of 1776.

In the months that followed, Ho juggled the competing interests of his own Viet Minh Party, those of the Chinese Nationalist troops occupying the north of the country and the French occupying the south. Choosing between what he believed the lesser of two evils, Ho agreed to the re-occupation of the north by French troops in exchange for recognition of an independent Vietnam "within the French Union". The French government never ratified the agreement and further negotiations yielded no results. As Ho's frustration rose so did levels of violence between French and Viet Minh troops in and around Haiphong and Hanoi. Open warfare erupted in December with the Viet Minh retreating to their Viet Bac stronghold from which they would conduct the rest of the nine-year struggle against the French.

Class discussion

To what extent was a war between the French and the Vietnamese inevitable given the goals of each side?

Source skills

The Viet Minh

Source A

Ho Chi Minh
Vietnamese *Declaration of Independence,*
2 September 1945

"All men are created equal. They are endowed by their Creator with certain unalienable Rights; among these are Liberty, Life and the pursuit of Happiness." This immortal statement appeared in the Declaration of Independence of the United States of America in 1776. In a broader sense, it means: all the peoples on the earth are equal from birth; all the peoples have a right to live and to be happy and free.

Nevertheless, for more than eighty years, the French imperialists, abusing the standard of Liberty, Equality and Fraternity, have violated our Fatherland and oppressed our fellow-citizens. They have acted contrary to the ideals of humanity and justice. Politically: they have deprived our people of every democratic liberty…

The French have fled, the Japanese have capitulated, Emperor Bao Dai has abdicated. Our people have broken the chains, which for nearly a century have fettered them and have won independence for the Fatherland. Our people at the same time have overthrown the monarchic regime that has reigned supreme for dozens of centuries. In its place has been established the present Democratic Republic…

"The whole Vietnamese people, animated by a common purpose, are determined to fight to the bitter end against any attempt by the French colonialists to reconquer their country."

Source B

Ho Chi Minh to US Intelligence Officer Charles Fenn, 1945. From Pierre Brocheux, *Ho Chi Minh: A Biography*.

"First, you must understand that to gain independence from a great power like France is a formidable task that cannot be achieved without some outside help, not necessarily in things like arms, but in the nature of advice and contracts. One doesn't in fact gain independence by throwing bombs and such. One must gain it through organization, propaganda, training and discipline. One also needs a set of beliefs, a gospel, a practical analysis; you might even say a bible. Marxism-Leninism gave me that framework."

Source C

Viet Minh directives to its soldiers (1948)

1   *Not to do what is likely to damage the land and crops or spoil the houses and belongings of the people.*

2   *Not to insist on buying or borrowing what the people are not willing to sell or lend.*

3   *Never to break our word.*

4   *Not to do or speak what is likely to make people believe that we hold them in contempt.*

5 To help them in their daily work (harvesting, fetching firewood, carrying water, sewing, etc.).

6 In spare time, to tell amusing, simple, and short stories useful to the Resistance, but not to betray secrets.

7 Whenever possible to buy commodities for those who live far from the market.

8 To teach the population the national script and elementary hygiene.

Source D

Ho Chi Minh, July 1952
Ho's Selected Writings

"Army cadres concern themselves solely with military affairs, Government cadres with administrative jobs, Party cadres with Party business. They are like men standing on one leg. It is wrong for a cadre to be acquainted only with one field. He will not be truly proficient because army, mass, government and party work forms a whole which would not be strong and complete should one of its components come to miss."

Questions

1 a To what extent is Ho's contention "Our people have broken the chains, which for nearly a century have fettered them and have won independence for the Fatherland" [Source A] accurate?

   b What message is being conveyed by Source D?

2 With reference to its origin, purpose and content, analyse the values and limitations of Source C for historians studying the methods of the Viet Minh.

3 Compare and contrast what Source A and Source D tell us about Ho's strategy for independence.

4 Using the sources and your own knowledge evaluate the role of ideology in Ho's guerrilla strategy.

In this sense then, the French Indo-China War was among the first of the wars of decolonization that would sweep the world in the post-war era. It would also be among the first, along with the ongoing Chinese Civil War, that would add the Cold War notion of ideology to the mix of motives. In the end though, ideology played a secondary role in the motives of the two main combatants. Ho and the Viet Minh wanted a Vietnam free of foreign control and in the years 1945–1954 this meant ousting the French. For their part the French wanted to reassert their imperial control over South-East Asia and by extension reclaim their pre-war world power status. In a way the French wanted to turn the clock back and the Viet Minh were willing to fight and die in large numbers to prevent that.

3.2 Combatants

Conceptual understanding

Key questions

→ How were the French hampered in the early years of the war?

→ What were the advantages and disadvantages of the Viet Minh structure?

→ How did political considerations affect both the French and the Viet Minh?

→ What role did foreign involvement play for both the French and the Viet Minh?

Key concepts

→ Perspective

→ Significance

The Viet Minh

To say that any part of this war was strictly a guerrilla war is inaccurate and this is well illustrated in the design of the Viet Minh forces. From the late 1940s, the Viet Minh had the ability to conduct local, small-scale guerrilla operations while at the same time maintaining large-unit organization and combat capability. The Viet Minh forces were structured into three components, organized hierarchically. At the bottom were local, part-time guerrilla forces – the Dan Quong or Popular Forces. The Dan Quong were recruited and based in small villages and hamlets. These units were used as porters and maintained transportation routes while providing intelligence on enemy positions and movements as well as on their neighbours. For instance, when regular force units moved through an area, the local Dan Quong force would be required to supply porters to support the movement of the larger force, always on the lookout for abandoned French material that could be scavenged.

In terms of combat, the Dan Quong conducted small force ambushes, sabotaged transport and set booby traps. While these units were local, they were directed from the Viet Minh central command. Distinguish yourself at this level and you were eligible to serve in the next level of Viet Minh military organization, the full-time guerrilla forces that were organized regionally and were better equipped than the local forces. They operated in battalions of up to 1,000 men later in the war. In the years 1946–1950 these units shouldered much of the Viet Minh's military operations using "traditional" guerrilla hit and run tactics. As the regular force grew in size and sophistication, these regional forces were occasionally used in support of large-scale operations.

The highest level of the Viet Minh forces was the regular force. As in most western armies, the Viet Minh regular or main force was organized into divisions, which contained all the elements needed to conduct large-scale operations – intelligence, artillery, supply and eventually armour and air support. Divisions were sub-divided into regiments and battalions. For the majority of the war a Viet Minh division would have a strength of around 10 000 men. It is no coincidence that these larger units such as divisions were formed in the period after 1949 when equipment and expertise began pouring south from Mao's recently conquered China.

Commanding these various components was a command structure centred on a commander-in-chief who controlled the whole military organization through a system that grouped several regions into territories – the so-called **interzone system**. This interzone system was more comprehensive than simply another level of military organization and reflected the Viet Minh philosophy of revolutionary warfare. The interzone managed all aspects of the conflict including elections, assassinations, taxation, recruiting, propaganda and supply.

The total strength of the Viet Minh changed over time. In 1947 Giap, the Viet Minh commander, had about 50 000 regular force troops and about 40 000 popular and regional troops at his disposal. By 1951 this strength had swelled to 110 000 regular force and about 225 000 regional and popular forces. As the war reached its crescendo in 1953, Giap commanded 125 000 regulars, 75 000 regional troops and 250 000 popular force troops.

Viet Minh equipment

Just as with the French, the Viet Minh were armed with a motley assortment of small arms including French, Japanese, Czech and American rifles. When the war broke out in 1946 the Viet Minh had around 60 000 rifles and a few thousand light machine guns as well as some mortars, grenades and about six small artillery pieces. They would continue to use whatever weapons they could lay their hands on, such as Chinese cast-offs including US material captured during the Korean War. Each victory over the French brought new weapons into the Viet Minh arsenal. After 1950 each month brought ever-larger shipments of weapons south from China. Early in 1952, 250 tons of munitions and other supplies reached the Viet Minh's main base area, a territory called the Viet Bac, north-east of Hanoi, each month. By the time the two sides faced off at Dien Bien Phu this number had risen to 4,000 tons per month. As the Korean War wound down this monthly shipment contained large quantities of artillery and recoilless rifles, many of which would prove crucial to the Viet Minh victory at Dien Bien Phu.

Material wasn't the only assistance the Chinese offered their new clients. After 27 years of nearly constant warfare the People's Liberation Army (PLA) had gained a considerable amount of practical military experience and they seemed more than willing to share it. In 1950 the PLA sent 79 officers south to help the Viet Minh with planning and logistics. Although handfuls of Viet Minh fighters had trained at PLA schools since 1946, this increased dramatically after the PLA's victory in 1949. In the period 1952–1953, 10 000 Viet Minh officers and 40 000 soldiers were trained in China.

The French

The French forces in Indo-China suffered political and structural issues every bit as daunting as those faced by the Viet Minh. Political fractures ran deep in post-war France. Retribution for collaborators,

Class discussion

How might the Viet Minh recruit its members?

ideological divisions, economic weakness, and dependence on Marshall Aid made a unified approach to the war in Indo-China impossible. The **Fourth Republic** was plagued by weak coalition governments – 19 in total during the course of this war. The fact that the French Communist Party was a member of some of these governments and a vocal opponent of the war added a level of contradiction and confusion to the situation that made any effective military action close to impossible.

Throughout the war the French forces suffered a chronic shortage of manpower. Yalta had tied a sizable portion of France's post-war army to the French zone of occupation in Germany. Conscripts were legally forbidden from serving in colonial theatres of war. As a result the French Far East Expeditionary Corps was cobbled together from diverse military units from all corners of what was left of the French Empire. Only about 42% of the French forces in this war were born in Metropolitan France. Instead the troops came from France's North African Army and colonial regiments from Africa and Asia. The legendary **French Foreign Legion** provided a reliable professional formation, as did the regular parachute units of the French army. The French attempted to augment these units with locally recruited but French-led auxiliaries – generally local tribesmen who had various reasons for fighting the Viet Minh. These auxiliaries were trained in secret camps by covert western operatives.

Local Vietnamese men could find themselves recruited into French army units or conscripted into the new Vietnamese National Army (VNA), created at the behest of the Americans who wished to see the war "Vietnamized" – presaging Richard Nixon's 1969 policy. The VNA was generally poorly led, poorly equipped and added little to the French war effort. It was the unenviable lot of these soldiers to be caught between the increasingly popular Viet Minh with their system of brutal retaliation for collaborators and the "official" and often equally brutal oppressive force of the French overlords enforcing conscription.

Fourth Republic

The French government from 1946–1958. It was created by a constitution after the Second World War.

French Foreign Legion

This is a formation of the French army founded in 1831, made up of non-French nationals who wish to serve in the French army. Initially the Legion's officers were French, but over time the officer corps contained many nationalities. Likewise many French citizens make up the rank and file of the Legion. The Legion has served in every major French conflict since 1831.

ATL Thinking and research skills

As a condition of continued military and financial aid, the United States insisted that the French turn more and more of the fighting over to the Vietnamese National Army (VNA), a process they called "Vietnamization". President Richard Nixon would use this same goal and name in 1969 as a plan for reducing the United States' military commitment to South Vietnam. The notion of replacing foreign occupying troops with local security forces was to be used in other wars.

Research the events of the following wars and answer the questions that follow.

- Vietnam 1969
- Bay of Pigs 1961
- Yugoslav Civil War 1994
- Iraq 2010
- Afghanistan 2010

1 What foreign forces were involved? What was the level of military commitment at its height?

2 What were the motives of the foreign powers?

3 What were the tasks assigned to the local forces? How were local troops prepared for these tasks?

4 What challenges did the local troops face? What challenges did the foreign troops face?

5 How did the foreign power disengage from the country? How well did the local troops accomplish their security goals?

Class discussion

Why would the Vietnamization of the war be important to the United States government?

At the beginning of the conflict the French forces had a total strength of 115 000. In the last years of the war this had grown to 175 000 (French, Africans, Asian and Foreign Legion). To this could be added 55 000 local auxiliaries and 150 000 VNA troops. Again, it is important to remember that these forces were far from equal in fighting ability. This fact is compounded by the nature of the war, requiring as it did a high degree of mobility, a capability of only a fraction of the French forces.

French equipment

On paper the French had a modern army, but in reality its material situation suffered in much the same way as its personnel situation did. This problem was especially acute in the first years of the war when material was gathered and scavenged form diverse sources. British, American, even German and Japanese equipment found its way into the French war effort. It was not uncommon for French units to be armed with a variety of small arms using non-regulation ammunition. As the United States began to bankroll more and more of the French effort after 1950 – they would eventually spend US$3 billion keeping the French in the field – weapons and equipment became more plentiful and standardized.

The French had about 275 artillery pieces that remained in place and about 250 pieces of mobile artillery. The mobility of the French forces was limited, however, by a road system that was crude at best. On these unreliable roads the French moved their armoured cars and gun carriers. After 1950 they had a steady supply of armoured personnel carriers and some tanks, the effectiveness of which was severely hampered by the topography of the country. Amphibious units were active in the south and used M29C armed amphibious vehicles (Weasels) made in the United States.

The limitations forced upon French mobility by the terrain of Indo-China could have been partially overcome by what later would be known as air mobility using newly developed helicopters. These, however, were severely limited in number and capability and were reserved for medical evacuations in the years 1949–1954. The only other air mobility option available to the French forces was paratroop drops. Throughout the war the French paratroop units were frequently dropped into dangerous situations to rescue other elements of the army and conduct operations against the Viet Minh. In reality, however, this solved only half the mobility issue. Dropping from planes such as a C47 worked well for inserting troops into a combat situation, but airplanes could not be used to extract these same troops when needed in the way that helicopters can. This hard fact condemned paratroopers to grueling and dangerous marches out of remote areas that further limited their effectiveness. The lesson would be learned before France's next war; helicopters would be used to give the French troops in Algeria mobility unknown to those who fought in Indo-China.

▲ French soldiers improvise a raft for a river crossing in 1950. What was the relationship of primitive to new technology during this war?

One nominal advantage that the French enjoyed over their enemy was air power. This air power, however, was seldom sufficient to the task. Fast Bearcat and Hellcat fighter-bombers could strafe and drop underwing mounted bombs, but without any bombsights the accuracy was dubious. Small Morane aircraft made of metal and wood were used for artillery spotting. There were a number of larger level-flight bombers and these could be very useful, but were often hindered by the bad weather, especially in the spring as the Battle of Dien Bien Phu demonstrated. One of the more terrifying weapons employed by the French air services was napalm – jellied petroleum which ignited everything in its path.

Technology and war: paratroopers

Parachute technology existed from the First World War, but in the absence of aircraft that could carry significant numbers of soldiers, the idea of using it to inject troops to places otherwise inaccessible by ground was debatable.

As such aircraft became more plentiful in the inter-war period, military thinkers around the world began to imagine how paratroopers might be used in offensive operations. In the Second World War paratroopers played significant roles in the German invasion of both Belgium and Crete. Allied paratroopers were integral to the invasion of Normandy and Operation Market Garden, the ambitious plan to capture the Rhine Bridges intact.

Paratroop operations had a number of elements that were attractive for military planners.

- An airdrop increased the possibility of surprise, expanding as it did the points of possible attack.

- Transport by aircraft minimized the effect of difficult terrain.

- By landing troops behind the front line, the enemy would be forced to defend in multiple directions.

Paratroop operations also had a number of serious drawbacks.

- The number of aircraft required to transport large numbers of troops often eliminated some of the element of surprise.

- Because paratroopers operated independent of supply lines they would have to jump with all the supplies required to sustain them as a fighting unit. This often limited both the time paratroopers could operate without resupply from the air or a link with ground forces as well as the size of munitions they could use – artillery and armour were often beyond their capability.

- In the brief period between exiting the aircraft and gathering into operational units on the ground, the paratroopers were incredibly vulnerable to enemy fire.

- While paratroopers could be inserted into a combat zone by airplanes, airplanes could not extract them. This was a fact of life brutally evident to French paratroopers operating in Indo-China.

Class discussion

To what extent did the United States support the French war effort with money and material? How and why did this support change over the period 1946–1954?

Technology and war: napalm

Napalm is a jellied form of petroleum used in aerial bombs and flamethrowers. Its name derives from its two principle components: naphthenic and palmitic acids. Developed in 1942, napalm was used in the Second World War and became a standard, if terrifying, element of all modern military arsenals. In Vietnam it was generally used in close support of ground troops. When dropped from aircraft it produces a terrifying and deadly spectacle, incinerating large areas of jungle and any people unfortunate enough to be there. Far from a precision weapon and fairly unpredictable once unleashed, napalm was the cause of many civilian casualties during all phases of the Vietnam War.

> . . . All of a sudden hell opens in front of my eyes. Hell comes from large egg-shaped containers, dropping from the first plane followed by others, eggs from the second and third plane. Immense sheets of flame extending to over one hundred metres, it seems, strike terror in the ranks of my soldiers. This is napalm, the fire that falls from the skies. . .[A] bomb falls behind us and I feel fiery breath touching my whole body. The men are now fleeing and I cannot hold them back. There is no way of holding out under the torrent of fire, which flows in all directions and burns everything in its passage. On all sides flame surrounds us . . . I stop at the platoon commander . . . his eyes are wide with terror. 'What is this? The atomic bomb?' 'No this is napalm.'

> Viet Minh Officer

Bernard Fall, *Street Without Joy: The French Debacle in Indo-China* (Harrisburg, 1961), 39–40 cited in Michael Burleigh, *Small Wars, Faraway Places: Global Insurrection and the Making of the Modern World*, (New York, Viking, 2013) 224.

3.3 Strategy and tactics

The French

Despite generally haphazard and inconsistent supply, the one strategic advantage the French forces enjoyed in the early years of the war was in material. In order to make use of that conventional military advantage, French strategic planning sought to bring about one big engagement in which they would defeat the bulk of the Viet Minh forces, thus forcing an end to the war.

While this may have been a militarily sound plan, it neglected the fact that while waiting for such a decisive battle, the French had to govern their holdings in Indo-China. How could this be done in areas they did not control militarily? The French answer was a direct contradiction of their "big battle" strategy. They built blockhouses and observation posts throughout the country and manned them with locally recruited and colonial troops. On a map these outposts indicated French "control" of the country. In reality these poorly armed detachments were easy targets and played right into the hands of the Viet Minh and created the type of war they wanted in the years 1946–1950. Some of the larger outposts were less vulnerable, but the French could only control the area the light artillery or mortar fire could cover.

A string of three such large posts figured prominently in another aspect of French military strategy in Indo-China – interrupting supply routes from China to the Viet Minh. In 1950 these three outposts would be the site of the first large-scale Viet Minh victory – the Battle of Route Coloniale 4 (RC4). Between these and other such posts the Viet Minh guerrillas moved with relative ease. As the war progressed, this outpost mentality created a situation in which the French controlled large cities and the strong outposts, while the Viet Minh controlled the countryside. Areas surrounding the smaller outposts may have been relatively safe for the French forces during daylight hours, but hazardous in the extreme at night. The French military instinct, one specifically rejected by the Viet

Class discussion

To what extent was the Viet Minh victory at RC4 a result of mistakes made by the French command?

Minh itself, to commit resources to the rescue of trapped and isolated units, also favoured the Viet Minh commitment to a long, drawn-out, attrition-style conflict.

In the end, the French needed to bring the war in Indo-China to a resolution quickly. Their domestic political, economic and social situation could not and would not sustain a protracted war in a far-flung corner of an empire in decline.

The French departed from this strategy only briefly. In 1949 General Alessandri, the French Commander in the Tonkin region, sought to deprive the Viet Minh of the local support that is so crucial to effective guerrilla operations. The Viet Minh depended on local support for rice, recruits and taxes. Using French troops to push Viet Minh forces out of small areas and then using local French recruits to destroy Viet Minh infrastructure and support, General Alessandri sought to deny the Viet Minh these essentials. Gradually this system seemed to work. Unfortunately for the French they lacked the resources to hold these areas against the inevitable re-infiltration by Viet Minh guerrillas over time.

Throughout the conflict the French military strategy was precisely that and nothing more – a military approach. By failing to win local support from the Vietnamese themselves with any sort of reform programme, they were essentially saying to the population that if the French were victorious the Vietnamese could expect much the same misery as they had experienced for the past 100 years. They saw the war as a method of regaining administrative control over territory. The Viet Minh, however, saw the conflict as an integrated political, economic, social and psychological struggle and victory could only be won by concentrating on all these facets.

ATL Thinking and research skills

Research the careers of the following French commanders in Indo-China and complete the following table. Remember, before anything can be evaluated, it must be set against a criterion. Be sure to describe the criterion against which you evaluate each commander.

Commander	Dates in Indo-China	Previous postings	Subsequent postings	Evaluation
Philipe Leclerc de Hauteclocque				
Jean-Étienne Valluy				
Roger Blaizot				
Marcel Carpentier				
Jean de Lattre de Tassigny				
Raoul Salan				
Henri Navarre				

The Viet Minh

Ho and his military commander Vo Nguyen Giap developed a comprehensive and detailed plan for what they envisioned as a long war with the French. The plan was based on the writings of Mao Zedong and adapted by the two men to the Vietnamese situation. In this vision, the war would be won by the effective and integrated deployment of two forms of force – military and non-military.

Non-military power encompassed political, diplomatic, economic, psychological and social influence on the enemy, but also the Vietnamese population and even the enemy civilian population. The primary objective of this aspect of the plan was to gain the support of the Vietnamese people through propaganda, indoctrination and intimidation. With this support the Viet Minh could ensure their army a supply of recruits, food, information and taxes. For example, money gained through direct taxation and the sale of locally grown rice or opium was used to purchase weapons smuggled through neighbouring states.

Of course, for the Viet Minh this non-military effort was focused through the lens of communist ideology, albeit with a strongly nationalistic component. Political pamphlets and tracts were regularly distributed and read to a largely illiterate population. A literacy programme tried to address this issue. The army itself was not immune from ideological propaganda and indoctrination. In fact, Ho and Giap saw the ideological consciousness of each soldier as integral to his or her military effectiveness. To ensure this consciousness, all Viet Minh units had political **commissars** who participated in tactical discussions and operated a system of informants among the ranks. The end result of this was a deeply motivated fighting force, the members of which could each place their individual actions within the context of the broader struggle for independence. Viet Minh soldiers knew exactly what they were fighting for. The same could not be said for French recruits or the US soldiers who would follow them.

The military form of force was to be deployed in three fairly distinct phases. The first phase was based on the assumption that the revolutionary force, in this case the Viet Minh, was weaker than the occupying force. To that end, Giap's main objective was to avoid any direct, large-scale confrontation with the superior firepower of the French. This "guerrilla phase" of the war was characterized by small actions generally carried out by Giap's regional force. Ambushes, assassinations, and booby traps plagued the French forces. While the French occupiers were relatively safe holed up in the larger outposts, others in watch towers and additional small detachments were prey for the very mobile guerrillas who melted away into the countryside after attacks. When the French emerged from their positions to hunt the Viet Minh they were often defeated by the vast overgrown landscape, a landscape their enemy knew very well.

While the Viet Minh's regional force shouldered much of the fighting in the guerrilla phase of the war, Giap steadily built his regular force. This meant recruiting, mostly from the regional forces, training and supplying them. A number of Viet Minh officers were trained in China

Class discussion

What would it be like to be a civilian caught between these two sides during the war?

commissars

Communist political officers. In many communist governments, "commissar" is used to denote rather low-level functionaries up to cabinet "ministers".

at Mao's combat school. Giap stockpiled weapons and food stores in Viet Bac. In this base area Giap and Ho established a strong communication infrastructure and even "factories" that produced small arms, mines and hand grenades.

When Mao's PLA swept the Nationalist Forces from mainland China, it almost instantly transformed the nature of the war in Indo-China. By August 1950 about 80 commanders from the PLA trekked south to advise the Viet Minh. Material also began to flow south. Artillery, ammunition, small arms and anti-aircraft guns were delivered regularly, eventually on a fixed rail link. In short the Chinese supplied everything Giap needed to move to the "mobile" phase of the war.

The mobile war phase mixed guerrilla actions with more conventional large-unit actions and was to be the responsibility of both the Viet Minh's regional and regular forces. Giap moved his large forces around northern territories looking for targets of opportunity. As the Viet Minh's strength and experience grew it ranged over larger tracts of land, seeking to drag French forces along, thereby lengthening supply lines and isolating them. It would then be easier to destroy these isolated formations and outposts. Giap's ability to move division-size units and all the supplies they required, including artillery, over harsh landscape was absolutely crucial to the success of this strategy. It was a capability that the French could never emulate, tied as they were to the crude road system or paratroop operations.

The final phase of revolutionary war according to Giap's plan was a general offensive in which the Viet Minh would wage pitched, conventional battle with the French and sweep them from the country. This phase would broadly correspond to the campaign at Dien Bien Phu.

Class discussion

How is Mao's doctrine reflected in the organizational structure of the Viet Minh? What are the advantages and disadvantages of such an approach?

ᴬᵀᴸ Thinking and research skills

Mao Zedong developed a model of revolutionary war that directly and indirectly affected the thinking of revolutionary leaders from Giap to Castro. For each of the following wars complete the table below, outlining the phases of revolutionary war as adapted by Ho and Giap. Based on this comparison, discuss with a partner the extent to which the model is effective.

War	Guerrilla phase		Protracted/mobile phase		Offensive phase	
	Military activities	Non-military activities	Military activities	Non-military activities	Military activities	Non-military activities
Algeria 1954–1962						
Cuba 1957–1959						
Congo Crisis 1960–1965						
Nicaraguan Revolution 1974–1979						

3.4 Operations

Conceptual understanding

Key questions

→ How well did Viet Minh operations correspond to their strategy?

→ How well did French operations correspond to their strategy?

→ How did the nature of combat in Vietnam change as the war wore on?

Key concepts

→ Continuity

→ Change

1946–1950

When it became evident that it would be war and not negotiation that would determine the fate of Vietnam, the Viet Minh concentrated on moving their regular force out of harm's way. This meant retreating from the French-controlled urban areas such as Hanoi into the wilderness of Viet Bac where they would base their operations in the north for the rest of the war.

After the monsoon subsided in October 1947 the French would try to achieve the knockout punch upon which their strategy depended. In an operation codenamed Lea, 1,000 French paratroopers would attempt to surprise their enemy by dropping virtually right on top of the Viet Minh headquarters area in Viet Bac. Meanwhile a column of motorized infantry would move 225 kilometres up a road to link up with the paratroopers. An amphibious force moving up the Clear River would support these movements. The paratroop drop surprised the Viet Minh and Ho himself narrowly escaped capture. After this initial success, however, the paratroopers became an island, fighting for survival while awaiting the relief column. The armour and trucks moving up the road were making sluggish progress, hampered by constant ambush and road sabotage. The rivers were not navigable by the amphibious forces and they had to finish their journey over land on foot. The Viet Minh forces disengaged and slipped away. While they lost more soldiers than the French, they achieved their goal of avoiding a large-scale battle with the superior French forces. Further French operations in November and December 1947 yielded little lasting impact on Viet Minh fighting ability or territory controlled.

There were no major military efforts by either side in 1948, simply the incessant and frustrating routine of guerrilla war – patrol, pacify, ambush, repeat. Slightly larger Viet Minh regional or regular force units attempting, with varied success, to overrun French outposts, occasionally interrupted this brutal routine. On RC4, the dominant road in the north-east, there were 28 large ambushes in 1948 alone. French General

Class discussion

What does the outcome of Operation Lea indicate about the nature of the war?

Alessandri spent most of 1949 attempting to squeeze the Viet Minh's supply of food by extensive patrol and pacification sweeps, seriously threatening Giap's ability to move and fight.

The major operation of 1950 centred on RC4, a road that connected a series of French outposts guarding the approaches from China. Giap began shelling the outpost at Dong Khe in September. He then unleashed wave after wave of infantry assaults, leveraging his 8:1 advantage in men. This attack coincided with French efforts to push a large column up RC4 to execute a planned evacuation of one of the outposts. This effort of moving a cumbersome column up a narrow road dominated by the enemy yielded the same results as it had two years previously. Meanwhile the column evacuating the fort groped hopelessly through the jungle. The column bogged down on RC4 was ordered through the jungle to link up with the evacuees. Once all the French troops were isolated in the dense vegetation, the Viet Minh hunted down and destroyed the French forces. When the last survivors stumbled out of the jungle they numbered only 600 men. Officially the French listed 6,000 casualties, 4,800 of them dead or missing. This stunning Viet Minh victory at the Battle of Route Coloniale 4 tempted Giap and Ho to think that perhaps the time was ripe to move to the last phase of their revolutionary war model. The battles of 1950 would prove them wrong.

1950–1954

Flush with new weapons and supplies from China, Giap and Ho decided to take the fight to the French in the lowland Tonkin Delta area surrounding Hanoi. This was to be the "great counteroffensive" that would, according to the model, sweep the French from Vietnam. By the end of 1950 the French had a new commander – General Jean de Lattre de Tassigny – a demanding, aggressive and experienced soldier.

Giap and de Lattre clashed first at Vinh Yen in January of 1951. Vicious fighting and de Lattre's reliance on French air power repulsed human wave assaults by the Viet Minh forcing Giap to retreat, but not until after suffering over 5,000 casualties. Undeterred, Giap tried to establish a foothold in the Delta again at the end of March. The French threw the Viet Minh back with the help of a naval bombardment from destroyers and air support, leaving 1,500 Viet Minh casualties. In May the Viet Minh had one more go at the French defences in the Delta. They attacked at several points along the Day River, but not before the rains started. The wet weather favoured the defenders and after three weeks of brutal fighting the Viet Minh retired, leaving their 9,000 dead behind. These three battles seem to suggest that Giap and his forces were not yet ready for the final phase of the revolutionary war model and that while they may have controlled the countryside, French air power and heavy ordinance ruled closer to the urban centres.

Understanding that the Viet Minh relied on, and were very good at, movement, de Lattre sought to restrict that movement by building a line of pillboxes, blockhouses and strong points throughout the north – 1,200 in total, inevitably dubbed the De Lattre Line. De Lattre tried to tempt

Giap into battle again in 1951, but the Viet Minh general would have none of it, emerging from the jungle to attack only when the situation suited him. Much of 1952 thereafter took on the typical form of the war, the French patrolling to establish secure areas and the Viet Minh massing weapons and men for coming engagements while their regional force carried out guerrilla actions. By 1952 Giap had around 110 000 regular force soldiers at his disposal and an ever-increasing amount of modern weapons supplied by the Chinese.

Seeking to break the frustrating monotony of a Viet Minh-controlled countryside, the French established a significant base in the hinterland where their material advantage of artillery and air support could count outside the lowland areas. They established such a base at Na San complete with 10 000 troops, artillery, a ring of outer defences and an airstrip. Giap attacked Na San in November and, after heavy fighting, was repulsed. Both sides took lessons from this encounter, some more useful than others. The French took heart in this new scheme of large remote posts that could be supplied by air, thereby liberating them from the crude and dangerous road system. Giap learned that he needed to prepare the battlefield more thoroughly if he wanted to overrun such a base. He needed more accurate intelligence on French troop strength. The Viet Minh had to take and hold the surrounding high ground for observation and the placement of his own artillery – artillery that he could use to eliminate the vital airfield upon which the entire French "air-ground base" concept depended. Supplies had to be stockpiled for a long siege – he would be patient and not try to overrun the base and its outer defences too early in the operation. That operation would come in the spring of 1954 at Dien Bien Phu.

Dien Bien Phu

Most discussions of the fateful struggle at Dien Bien Phu seem to waver between praise for the resourcefulness and skill of the Viet Minh and the need to find a Frenchman to blame. As in all aspects of history the truth lies somewhere in-between. What is not in dispute is that between March and May 1954 in a remote valley in Vietnam the Viet Minh faced off against the French in the final battle of the war.

Early in the war it had been the French who sought a large, definitive engagement. By 1954 it was Ho and Giap who looked for such a fight. Peace negotiations where set to begin in Geneva in May 1954 and a decisive victory over a sizable French force would allow Ho to negotiate from a position of strength. As the battles of 1951 had demonstrated, this battle had to take place in a region in which the French naval, air and armour superiority counted for little. General Navarre, the French commander, seemed to oblige, picking the remote base at Dien Bien Phu to make his stand. Although his thinking seemed to change over time, Navarre's logic seemed to suggest that this was a sound method of deterring any intentions Giap had of invading neighbouring Laos. A strong base, resupplied by air, could also be used to stage large-scale sorties into territory that had long been denied to the French by the Viet Minh command of jungle mobility.

▲ French soldiers at Dien Bien Phu. What role did artillery play in the Viet Minh victory?

When the battle commenced on 13 March 1954 the Viet Minh attackers outnumbered the French defenders by a factor of about 5:1. This numeric superiority was the product of a long period of preparation. After the French re-occupied the base in November of 1953, Giap began to methodically "prepare the battlefield" using supply lines that depended on 1,000 trucks and over a quarter of a million porters. Food and ammunition were carried into the combat base and cached along the route of the march for the infantry. Hundreds of thousands of artillery, mortar and rocket shells were packed in the valley and then up the steep slopes of the surrounding highlands to service the guns dug into the hillsides. Those guns themselves had to be dragged up the steep jungle trails. French attempts to discover and interrupt this supply effort using its air power proved fruitless. As much energy was put into camouflaging the supply lines as carrying the material along them. In all, it was a massive human undertaking to supply the 40 000 combat troops that Giap would deploy against the French dug into the valley floor.

French supply depended on the fragile air link with Hanoi. The French base at Dien Bien Phu had an airstrip, but this became an important and easy artillery target for the Viet Minh gunners dug into the hills and was unusable for the large supply effort for which it was designed later in the siege. Whatever the defenders needed would then have to drift in to their positions by parachute. As often as not, however, the ammunition and food drifted in to the Viet Minh positions, more frequently as the French defensive perimeter shrank. The loss of the airstrip also meant that the wounded could not be evacuated, creating scenes of unimaginable suffering late in the battle.

▲ French defences at Dien Bien Phu. In what ways did the battle resemble earlier conflicts? What elements were new?

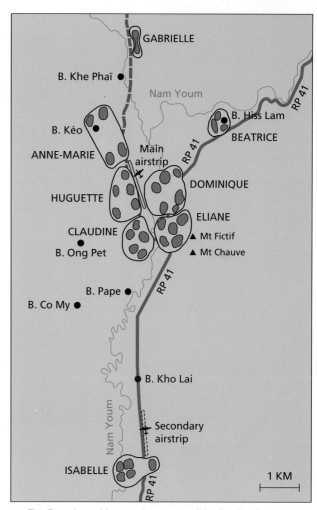

▲ The French positions at the outset of the Battle of Dien Bien Phu

French preparations were as sloppy as the Viet Minh's were thorough. The French position at Dien Bien Phu consisted of an outer perimeter of hilltop bases, Gabrielle, Beatrice, Anne-Marie and Isabelle, Huguette, Claudine, Dominique and Eliane, surrounding a central position centred on the ruins of the village. The defensive theory was that these positions could support each other with interlocking artillery fire. The outer positions were further designed to break or blunt Viet Minh assaults before they got to the central position. A reserve was kept in the central position that could be used to counter-attack any position in peril.

While the plan may have been sound, its execution was inept. The fortifications on the hills and in the central position were not built strong enough to withstand the Viet Minh artillery, lacking sufficient wood and steel reinforcement. What local timber was available was quickly used up, stripping much of the base of cover and camouflage. Viet Minh spotters in the surrounding hills could easily identify important targets. Inadequate drainage turned the French defences into a soupy mess once the rains began. The southern position, Isabelle, was too far away for its artillery to support anything but the central position and too far from that for timely infantry support. Isabelle would fight as an island, isolated from the central position for much of the battle. Artillery itself was inadequate in numbers and poorly placed and managed. They could not take out Giap's well-concealed guns while they themselves were easy targets. Two days into the battle the Viet Minh gunners had obliterated two of the three major French artillery positions, after which the French artillery commander committed suicide.

French preparations seemed to be based on a woeful and negligent underestimation of their opponents. Everything that Giap did seemed a surprise to the defenders. These surprises included:

- amassing large amounts of heavy artillery on the hills overlooking their positions

- being able to support and supply these guns for weeks on end

- concealing the guns so effectively as to make them invulnerable to the French gunners

- concentrating attacks on the outlying posts before assaulting the main camp

- having sufficient anti-aircraft guns to severely limit the use of French air power

- having the engineering capability to tunnel and trench ever closer to the French positions, slowly strangling them after over-running their outer fire bases.

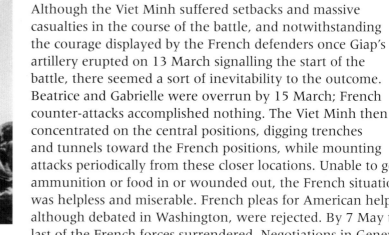

Although the Viet Minh suffered setbacks and massive casualties in the course of the battle, and notwithstanding the courage displayed by the French defenders once Giap's artillery erupted on 13 March signalling the start of the battle, there seemed a sort of inevitability to the outcome. Beatrice and Gabrielle were overrun by 15 March; French counter-attacks accomplished nothing. The Viet Minh then concentrated on the central positions, digging trenches and tunnels toward the French positions, while mounting attacks periodically from these closer locations. Unable to get ammunition or food in or wounded out, the French situation was helpless and miserable. French pleas for American help, although debated in Washington, were rejected. By 7 May the last of the French forces surrendered. Negotiations in Geneva commenced the next day.

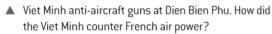

▲ Viet Minh anti-aircraft guns at Dien Bien Phu. How did the Viet Minh counter French air power?

Class discussion

Why did the United States not intervene to aid the French at Dien Bien Phu?

ATL Thinking skills

For each time period analyse the nature of combat according to the categories given. What can be said about the degree to which the nature of combat stayed the same throughout the war and the degree to which it changed (continuity and change)?

	1946–1950	1950–1952	1952–1954
Forces involved			
Strategy/tactics			
Equipment			
Leadership			

3.5 Effects of the Vietnam War

Conceptual understanding

Key questions

→ What was the significance of the French defeat for other wars of decolonization?

→ How did the French defeat affect the Cold War strategy of the United States?

Key concepts

→ Consequence

→ Perspective

The complete and stunning collapse of the French in Indo-China had come at a huge human cost – over 80 000 of the French forces were killed and over 200 000 wounded. Some estimates put the Viet Minh dead at over 300 000.

Ho achieved his goal of negotiating from a position of strength in Geneva, a strength that frightened both the United States and even his Chinese sponsors. The negotiations, however, fell short of giving him the united, independent country for which they had been fighting for nine years. Instead the country was partitioned at the **17th parallel**, thereby ensuring a resumption of the conflict at some later date, albeit with a different enemy. The South was placed under the control of Ngo Dinh Diem and the Emperor Bao Dai. The North became a communist state under the leadership of Ho.

17th parallel
This is the demarcation line between North and South Vietnam decided upon at the Geneva peace conference.

Close to one million Vietnamese fled the North in the wake of the Geneva Conference. While many Viet Minh fighters in the South returned to the North, many stayed behind as political and military operatives who would form the basis of the Viet Cong that would continue the fight against the Diem regime and its US sponsor. Unification elections were to be held in the years after the Geneva meetings, but these never came to pass. Instead, Diem used his anti-communist stance to secure US support, which he then used to consolidate his position within South Vietnam against his opponents, both communist and non-communist. Diem's anti-Buddhist policies did little to ingratiate him to the population – he was never a popular leader. Having lost its French surrogate, the US sought to shore up its presence in the region by establishing the South East Asia Treaty Organization (SEATO) to guard South Vietnam, Cambodia and Laos from the spread of communism.

The French dismantled their administration in a speedy and orderly fashion, transferring control to Diem's government. The defeat at Dien Bien Phu had effectively shrunk France's colonial holdings to North Africa and sapped its will to fight for other colonial holdings such as Morocco and Tunisia, both of which negotiated independence shortly

TOK discussion

How might the defeat in Indo-China affect the French national self-image? How might this have affected future decisions about their empire? How might this defeat be viewed in light of past French military history?

after the French withdrawal from Indo-China. The noted difference was Algeria. Dien Bien Phu illustrated to the world in general – and Algerian nationalists in particular – what could be achieved with a determined guerrilla campaign and a willingness to suffer. For the French, having lost Indo-China by war and Tunisia and Morocco at the negotiating table seemed to strengthen their resolve when it came time to fight for Algeria.

▲ Vietnamese General Giap briefs his officers during the siege of Dien Bien Phu

Exam-style questions and further reading

Exam-style questions

1 Evaluate the French defence of Dien Bien Phu.

2 Compare and contrast the military strength of the Viet Minh and the French forces in Indo-China from 1946–1954.

3 What role did air power play in the war in Indo-China?

4 To what extent was the war in Indo-China from 1946–1954 a guerrilla war?

5 Discuss the reasons for the French defeat in Indo-China.

Further reading

Duiker, William J. 2012. *Ho Chi Minh: A Life*. Hachette Books. New York, USA.

Fall, Bernard. 1964. *Street Without Joy*. Stackpole Books. Harrisburg, USA.

Karnow, Stanley. 1983. *Vietnam: A History*. Viking Press. New York, USA.

McDonald, Peter. 1993. *Giap*. W. W. Norton. New York, USA.

Windrow, Martin. 2004. *The Last Valley; Dien Bien Phu and the French Defeat in Vietnam*. Weidenfeld and Nicolson. London, UK.

Structuring your essay

There is any number of ways to structure an essay. All sound essay structures, however, have certain elements and form. An essay can be broken down into three basic parts: an introduction, a body, and a conclusion. We discuss the introduction and conclusion in more detail in a separate Skills section (see page 149).

Planning your essay

In time-sensitive exercises like the IB history exams, planning is usually one of the first elements that suffers. Regardless of the time pressure, you should take a little time to sketch out a brief outline for your essay. What is your thesis? What evidence will you use to support it? How will you order your evidence? Where will you deal with your qualifier or any counter-evidence?

Answering these questions, however briefly, before you start will help you use your time efficiently and keep you focused on the task. It will also ensure that you remember to get all your ideas into the essay.

Writing body paragraphs

Your body paragraphs consist of three separate elements:

1 **Topic sentence:** This is essentially the argument or part of an argument with which the paragraph is concerned. An argument is generally something that on the surface is not necessarily correct. For example, the statement "The French forces at Dien Bien Phu fought effectively for the majority of the siege" can be argued either in the affirmative or in the negative.

2 **Supporting evidence:** These sentences are detailed historic "facts" that support the argument you made in the topic sentence.

3 **Coordinating/transition sentence:** This is the last sentence (or sentences) of the paragraph. This is where you make the link between the material in the paragraph and the thesis, explaining how the paragraph supports the thesis. It is in these sentences that you demonstrate how your argument and evidence relate to the question and in which you carry out the command terms.

For example:

Question: Examine the role of technology in one 20th-century war.

Thesis: Although superior strategy played a role in the Allied victory in the Second World War, technology also played a vital role in Allied land, sea, and air operations.

Sample paragraph

Technology improved the Allied ability to find and sink German U-Boats during the Battle of the Atlantic. Phosphorous star shells improved the night vision of escort vessels allowing them to attack surfaced submarines at night. The Hedgehog depth charge system allowed for a higher and more accurate rate of fire when attacking submerged submarines. The development of the absolute altimeter improved the accuracy of airborne attacks on submarines. By the end of the war the death rate of German submariners was 75 per cent. Technological improvements allowed vital supplies to move from North America to Europe.

Argumentative topic sentence related to the thesis and question
Detailed historical facts that support the topic sentence
Concluding sentence linking back to thesis and elaborating on how the preceding material supports the thesis

Reminders for structuring your essay:

- Support your assertions with detailed historical evidence.

- Relate each paragraph back to the thesis and question.

- Order your arguments and evidence from least convincing to most convincing.

- Avoid being overly narrative.

- When writing a compare and contrast paper use an integrated approach rather than an end-on approach.

- Balance your paragraphs as best you can. You should not have one massive paragraph and several short paragraphs.

- Only use material that is relevant to your thesis. Just because you studied it and know it, does not mean it should go in your essay. Stay focused on the question and your thesis.

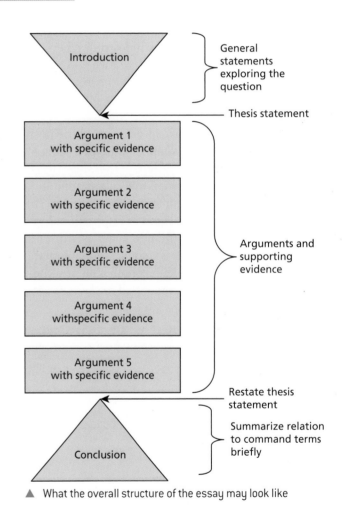

▲ What the overall structure of the essay may look like

83

4 THE SPANISH CIVIL WAR: IDEOLOGY AND CONFLICT IN THE 20TH CENTURY

Global context

The Spanish Civil War was far from being the first or last civil war. So why does it loom so large in 20th-century history? Much of its significance derives from its global context. Ideologically, economically and politically the 1930s were a turbulent time like few others in modern history. Economically the Great Depression had laid waste to all the industrialized economies in the world. Those, like France and Britain, had already been savaged by the First World War. The economic powerhouse of the United States was laid low by record high unemployment and drought. The dislocation of the post-war years and the depression helped bring a new ideology to the international stage. Fascism eschewed international cooperation in favour of confrontation and self-sufficiency. This uncooperative trend in international relations was not limited to the new regimes. Most industrialized powers took to economic and diplomatic isolation as a cure for their economic ills at some point in their history. Britain had raised isolationism to an art form in the 19th century.

What was new was the new ideological landscape of the post-First World War world. Three of the most powerful countries in the world were controlled by ideologies that the world had never seen before and, more importantly, that the other powers had never dealt with before. In many ways the 1930s was an unlucky confluence of forces. Some economically depressed states, including the US, Britain and France, were tempted into isolationism at the exact time a new, expansionist ideology was taking hold in other states such as Italy and Germany. Countries on both sides of this divide were reluctant to engage with – or were outright hostile toward – the third dominant ideologically based state, the Soviet Union.

All of these coincidences and contradictions were played out in the Spanish Civil War. Economic depression, isolationism, interventionism, ideological conflict, and the changing balance of power in Europe all played a role in the tragedy that became the Spanish Civil War.

Timeline

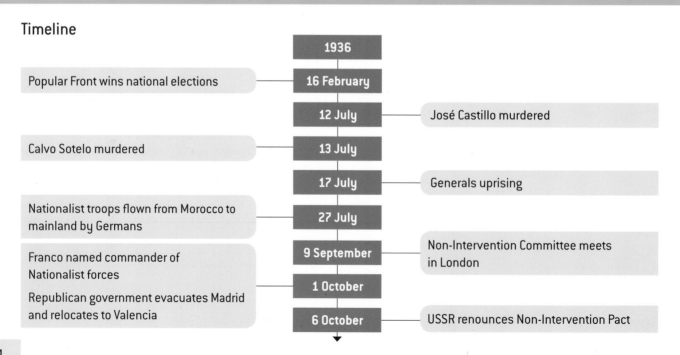

	1936	
Popular Front wins national elections	16 February	
	12 July	José Castillo murdered
Calvo Sotelo murdered	13 July	
	17 July	Generals uprising
Nationalist troops flown from Morocco to mainland by Germans	27 July	
	9 September	Non-Intervention Committee meets in London
Franco named commander of Nationalist forces	1 October	
Republican government evacuates Madrid and relocates to Valencia		
	6 October	USSR renounces Non-Intervention Pact

9 October	Popular Army formed
7 November	Nationalists begin assault on Madrid
8 November	International Brigades arrive in Madrid
22 December	Italian "volunteers" arrive in Spain
1937	
February	Battle of Jarama
8–18 March	Battle of Guadalajara
26 April	Guernica bombed
3–8 May	May Days (fighting between POUM/CNT and PSUC/UGT militias) in Barcelona
17 May	Juan Negrin replaces Francisco Largo Caballero as Prime Minister of the Republic
14 December	Republican government evacuates Valencia and relocates in Barcelona
1938	
24 July	Republican forces begin Ebro offensive
16 November	End of Ebro campaign
1938	
26 January	Barcelona falls to the Nationalists
1 April	Franco declares war ended

4.1 Causes of the Spanish Civil War

Long-term causes: a fragmented country

Divisions cut across Spain in just about every conceivable direction. Regionalism and even localism fractured the country and often trumped loyalty to Spain as a whole. Basques, Catalans, Galicians and many other groups had cultural, linguistic, historic and economic differences that often precluded any form of national cooperation. While parts of Spain were economically strong and reasonably dynamic, other areas were backward in terms of industrial and agricultural production methods. In some regions, agriculture was dominated by small, peasant landholders, while others were dominated by vast estates.

These divisions were reflected in the myriad of political organizations, parties and ideologies that took root across Spain throughout the 50 years prior to the Civil War. As in many countries, the traditional conservative triad of landowners, church and army anchored the political right in Spain. Land ownership across the country was concentrated in relatively few families. Half of the land in Spain was owned by a mere 50 000 individuals. The Catholic Church, though rocked by the forces of secularism in the 19th century, still had a great deal of influence in Spanish society, especially in education. At the other end of the political spectrum, regionalism again influenced the formation of political and ideological movements. In industrial areas, such as Barcelona and other parts of Catalonia, a form of anarchism that was based on trade union principles became popular. This **anarcho-syndicalism** advocated decentralized, worker control of factories, as well as the other stock and trade of unions – shorter working weeks, higher wages and better working conditions. If anarcho-syndicalism was largely an urban phenomenon, its country cousin was a more traditional anarchism. This movement, strong in poor, rural areas such as Andalusia, sought a revolution leading to a vague combination of land redistribution, decentralized authority and freedom from taxes.

anarcho-syndicalism
A political doctrine that advocates replacing central governments with decentralized, worker-controlled committees loosely based on a trade union model. Found in numerous countries such as France and Italy, it achieved its greatest mainstream success in the *Confederación Nacional del Trabajo* (CNT) in Spain.

This revolution was to come about by an equally vague combination of spontaneous action and the creative potential of the masses.

Anarchism was not the only left-wing ideology plying its trade in 1930s Spain. Variants of Marxism and socialism had been struggling for support from the late 19th century. But even the Marxists were fractured. Stalinists feuded with Trotskyites. Socialists argued with trade unionists. By the time of the Civil War, these different views had produced a dizzying array of organizations and political parties.

Short-term causes: the failure of the Second Republic and the Popular Front

By April 1931, popular support for the monarchy had been completely eroded. When the army withdrew its support of Alfonso XIII, he slunk into exile and general elections in June of that year brought a coalition of centre-left parties to power, led by Manuel Azaña. The new government wasted no time in enacting sweeping agricultural, labour and anti-clerical legislation. New laws protected tenants from eviction, encouraged collectives and cooperatives, and officially split church and state. The new government would recognize civil marriages and divorces. In order to reduce the influence of the army, the new government forcibly retired many officers, granting them full pensions. While such changes made some members of the political left happy, they did not go far enough for those on the extreme left. The conservative right was, of course, furious. Not only did the reforms succeed in alienating the right, they left the majority of ordinary people dissatisfied as they made little more than a dent in the widespread poverty of rural Spain.

There was a great deal of opposition to Azaña's government. The Civil Guard, a form of national police force, rose in rebellion in August 1932 under General Sanjurjo. While the revolt was easily put down – in part with the cooperation of the CNT, the largest anarcho-syndicalist organization – it illustrated the degree of opposition that the government faced. Sanjurjo's rising also demonstrated the limits of the Republic's monopoly of force and legitimacy. While middle-class liberals supported the Republic, the radical left and the conservative right were not convinced. Strikes and disturbances continued throughout 1933. The elections of November 1933 reflected the unstable nature of Spanish politics, bringing a right-wing coalition to power. This new government was immediately denounced by the left, setting off a new wave of unrest. Neither the left nor the right seemed to have enough faith in the democratic decision-making process to trust it to their political rivals.

The suspicions of the left were, perhaps, well founded. The new government immediately began to reverse or ignore Azaña's reforms. The strikes and disturbances reached a crescendo with a short-lived declaration of autonomy by Catalonia and a far more serious revolt in the region of Asturias, crushed by hardened Spanish troops from Morocco. To some on the Spanish left, this revolt was an attempt to avoid the fate of the German left who had failed to resist the rise of the Nazis two years earlier and who were – by the time of the Asturias revolt – defunct. To others, it was confirmation that the radical left in Spain had abandoned the constitution and could not be trusted to govern. Both interpretations indicate a

Second Republic
The system of government that governed Spain from the abdication of Alfonso XIII in 1931 until the end of the Spanish Civil War.

Popular Front
A political strategy of electoral cooperation between left-wing parties designed to prevent vote splitting and thus defeat right-wing parties. The strategy was especially popular in response to the rise of Fascist and other right-wing parties during the 1930s. Popular Front governments were formed in France and Spain during this period.

profound lack of faith in the democratic system upon which the Republic rested. Either interpretation seemed to point to political differences so entrenched that no democratic process could reconcile them.

Spanish political parties 1936–1939					
Left		**Centre**		**Right**	
Confederación Nacional del Trabajo (CNT)	Anarcho-syndicalist union	Partido Nacionalista Vasco (PNV)	Basque Nationalist party	Carlists	King–church party
Federación Anarquista Ibérica (FAI)	Militant anarchists	Unión Militar Republicana Antifascista (UMRA)	Anti-fascist army officers' organization	Confederación Española de Derechas Autónomas (CEDA)	Right-wing coalition
Partido Comunista de España (PCE)	Spanish communist party	Partido Sindicalista (PS)	Syndicalist party	Falange	Spanish fascist party
Partido Obrero de Unificación Marxista (POUM)	Marxist–socialist workers' party	Unión Republicana (UR)	Moderate Republican party	Bloque Nacional	Anti-parliamentary party
Partido Socialista Obrero Español (PSOE)	Spanish socialist party	Izquierda Republicana (IR)	Moderate Republican party	Renovación Española	Monarchist party
Unión General de Trabajadores (UGT)	Socialist trade union			Unión Militar Española (UME)	Fascist army officers' organization
Partit Socialista Unificat de Catalunya (PSUC)	Catalonian socialist party				

Comintern

A short form for Communist International, an organization that originated in the Bolshevik seizure of power in Russia. Its mission was to coordinate and promote the spread of revolutionary Marxist-Leninism throughout the world. Although it contained representatives from many countries, it was largely directed from Moscow and eventually became little more than a tool of Soviet foreign policy.

Immediate causes: the Popular Front and the Generals' uprising

As was perhaps predictable, in 1936 the pendulum of Spanish electoral politics swung back to the left. The Spanish left had embraced an electoral strategy encouraged by the **Comintern** and practised in France, known as the Popular Front. This strategy took the lesson of the Nazi rise in Germany, where infighting among left-wing parties had allowed the Nazis to elect candidates across the country, and aimed to prevent it from happening in other western democracies. Azaña and Indalecio Prieto, a leader of the Spanish Socialist Party

(PSOE) proposed electoral cooperation between various left-wing parties to avoid vote splitting against the relatively more unified right-wing parties.

In the Spanish elections of 1936, in order to concentrate the moderate Republican and more radical left-wing vote, the left-wing parties cooperated organizationally and, for the most part, did not run candidates against each other. While this type of electoral cooperation was not new in Spain, the political developments both at home and in other parts of Europe gave it an urgency particular to the 1930s. It was essentially a defensive strategy, designed to stop the extreme right from taking power legitimately, as Hitler had done.

The parties that participated still had deep political and ideological differences and the cooperation did not go beyond electoral tactics. There was no agreement to cooperate beyond the election, thus proving to be a short-term solution to the problem of a united right. Their electoral platform was a centre-left combination of those proposed by Azaña in previous elections. The anarchists, while not cooperating in any traditional sense of the word, no longer directly encouraged their members not to vote. The parties were able to agree on what they didn't want, but seldom on policies that they did want. In that sense, the Popular Front was born out of a lack of faith in the democratic system, its members not trusting that democracy, traditionally practised, could preserve freedom in Spain.

When the electoral dust had settled, Azaña's Popular Front had carried the day. Predictably, Gil Robles, leader of the right-wing *Confederación Española de Derechas Autónomas* (CEDA) raised the alarm of an impending communist takeover even though there were no Marxists on the cabinet. Nevertheless, the alarm intensified when Azaña was elevated to the post of President in April 1936, despite no real escalation of collectivist policy.

Understanding the threat to the Republic posed by the army, Azaña sought to divide and isolate the most vocally obstinate of the military leadership. General Moda was transferred to a remote post while Generals Goded and Franco were moved away from their bases of support. This did not stop the three rebels from plotting and organizing a military rising. Mola made contact with other right-wing groups, seeking support. The Falange and the Carlists were both persuaded to support the Generals in their scheme. The fact that Azaña's government had not been able to bring civil peace and stability in the face of labour strikes and street fighting between rival parties persuaded some in the army, specifically a rebellious cadre of junior officers, that drastic action was required.

The assassination of a Calvo Sotelo, a right-wing monarchist politician on 13 July 1936, provided the pretext for the general's military insurrection. Despite planning, the insurrection did not go smoothly right from the outset. The garrison in Morocco rose ahead of schedule and had to wait for Franco to arrive before proceeding further.

Class discussion

What makes a government legitimate in the eyes of the citizens? What can a government do to increase its legitimacy?

The Republican government in Madrid, after ignoring warnings of a rebellion, did not act sufficiently fast enough to crush the revolt in its infancy. Once the scope of the crisis became clear, it also hesitated in arming the *Unión General de Trabajadores* (UGT), the *Confederación Nacional del Trabajo* (CNT) and other left-wing organizations who had sufficient manpower but insufficient firepower to resist the rebellious elements of the army. The Republic depended on the action and thus the loyalty of the Civil Guard throughout the country to stave off the rebellion and as such their actions were often the determining factor. In some cases, in Oviedo for instance, the Guard sided with the rebels and thus the city fell to the Nationalists. On the other hand in Barcelona, the industrial and cultural centre of Catalonia, the Guards fought for the Republic and with the help of the local anarcho-syndicalist militia defeated the rebels, led by General Goded himself. Barcelona thus saved would become a centre of Republican resistance throughout the Civil War.

On the local level, quick action could determine whether the revolt was successful or not. If the local workers' organizations could obtain weapons and if they acted against the local garrison with confidence, most soldiers would submit to the authority of the Republic. If the rising, however, was allowed to gain momentum, army units would round up local political leaders, execute them and bring the town under the control of the Nationalists.

Events in Madrid illustrate the dilemma facing the Republican government. When 2,500 rebels barricaded themselves in the local garrison on 19 July, the government had very limited manpower with which to storm the garrison. Loyal officers argued for the arming of the various local party militias. By doing so, however, the government would be giving up its monopoly of force on which all strong central governments rely in times of discord. The point was moot in any event as it was really the only option for dislodging the rebels. The militia was armed and the barracks stormed. Madrid remained in government control. The price for this victory, however, was the empowering and arming of a variety of political parties. The eventual divisions and disagreements between these parties, on whose armed militias the Republic would depend throughout the war, would also seriously impair the fighting effectiveness of the Republican side.

This pattern produced a patchwork of rebel and loyalist holdings early in the insurrection. The rebels held the Andalucian coast, including the city of Seville, and large areas of north central Spain. In the capital, Madrid, the government maintained control, benefitting from the poor organization and hesitation of the rebels. The east of the country also remained loyal. In the anarcho-syndicalist stronghold of Barcelona, the CNT in conjunction with the *Federación Anarquista Ibérica* (FAI), with the help of loyal civil guards, fought a running battle through the streets against the 12 000 soldiers of the local garrison. As the tide turned in favour of the loyalists, General Goded himself, by then a prisoner of the government, urged the rebels to surrender. From that point, Barcelona would be the heart of loyalist Spain. The pattern, however, was clear; the government retained control only where it would accept the help of non-governmental

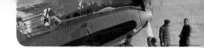

organizations or in places where they army was too poorly organized to establish control. As a form of central control, even over its own forces, the government was weak.

ATL Communication and social skills

Choose from one of the following three groups: "Left" parties, "Centre" parties and "Right" parties. Draft a set of policies that you would enact if you were to form the Spanish government in 1936. Be sure to have policies for each of the following categories:

- Agriculture/land policies
- Industrial policies (hours of work, factory ownership, etc.)
- Education
- Social/cultural policies, including policies on religion

Present your policies to the rest of the class.

Spanish Civil War, July 1936

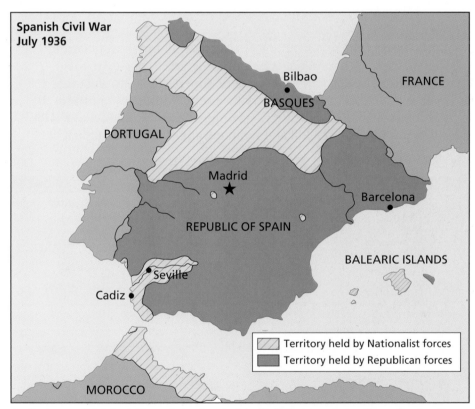

Spanish Civil War
July 1936

FRANCE

Bilbao
BASQUES

PORTUGAL

Madrid

Barcelona

REPUBLIC OF SPAIN

BALEARIC ISLANDS

Seville
Cadiz

Territory held by Nationalist forces
Territory held by Republican forces

MOROCCO

▲ Spain was divided quickly on the outbreak of the Civil War between loyalist and nationalist forces. What factors might have affected which side would establish control of a region in July 1936 before any major engagements had been fought?

4.2 Combatants

Conceptual understanding

Key questions

→ What were the relative strengths and weaknesses of each side at the outset of the war?

→ Which side had the advantage in terms of international support? Why?

→ To what extent did ideology play a role within each army?

Key concepts

→ Continuity

→ Change

→ Perspective

At the start of the war in July 1936, the overall forces were fairly well matched in numbers. As the war progressed, however, the Nationalists steadily gained in numeric superiority, outnumbering their opponent across the country by a third within 18 months of the start of the war. From the very beginning, however, there was a large difference in training, skill and weapons, the Nationalists having the distinct advantage.

▲ A Republican soldier keeps watch. To what extent were the Republican forces made up of professional soldiers? What role did this play in the outcome of the war?

The Republicans

The Republican forces comprised the elements of the military that remained loyal to the government, as well as various militias associated with working-class organizations such as *Partido Obrero de Unificación Marxista* (POUM), CNT and FAI. These militias managed to arm themselves with weapons they had stockpiled over the turbulent years before the Civil War and with those they managed to seize from the army. The government was reluctant to arm them but, faced with the growing crisis, it eventually began to supply them with weapons. Although brave and enthusiastic, the volunteer members of the various militias lacked military training and leadership. Ideological, political and strategic differences made coordination between the militias very difficult, a fact that was exploited by the Nationalists.

Command was a chaotic and fragmented process in the Republican forces. Gaining consensus on strategic and tactical decisions was very difficult on the local level and close to impossible on a national scale. Rival committees developed contradictory operational plans, initiating endless rounds of compromise and negotiation. Even overall goals were confused and at times contradictory. There were those in Asturias and Catalonia, for example, who prioritized regional independence over victory against the Nationalists. Anarchists throughout the Republic believed that social revolution was an integral part of the Civil War. Countless cities, towns and factories were run by local workers' committees. Social policy was debated at the same time as military strategy. Moderate liberals, however, thought that this was folly, diverting energy and attention from what they perceived as the overarching goal of winning the war.

Ideological difference was perhaps one of the most dangerous divisions within the Republican forces. The Communist *Partit Socialista Unificat de Catalunya* (PSUC), taking direction from the Comintern and thus Moscow, sought to eliminate the anti-Stalinist Marxist POUM even though both were ostensibly fighting for the Republic. A series of escalating actions by the PSUC removed POUM members from a number of committees in Barcelona, culminating with open fighting in the streets of Barcelona in May 1937. The May Days pitted the POUM/CNT against the PSUC/UGT militias. After three days of fighting over 500 militia members lay dead and the POUM leadership was depleted. Largo Caballero's government could not survive the split and he resigned as a result. All of this was a serious distraction from the business of fighting the Nationalists as such infighting made unified and effective military action impossible.

Localism also hampered sound military planning. In Asturias, local miner militias fought a long, hard struggle to regain the city of Oviedo, when, albeit in hindsight, their numbers could have been more effectively deployed in the defence – or relief – of far more important military objectives, Madrid for example.

Prime Minister Caballero moved to address the increasingly haphazard system of militias in September of 1936 when he reorganized the Republican forces into a more traditional hierarchical structure. The units of this new Popular Army would have political officers to ensure that the soldiers remained ideologically "correct". The number of these commissars, who were Spanish communists, increased steadily throughout the war. Soviet officers played important roles as advisors and, as the war went on, conduits for Stalinist ideology. This reorganization did help the command and control of the elements that were drawn into the Popular Army, but did little to coordinate the efforts of the CNT/FAI militias which, true to their ideological commitments, refused to submit to the central authority of Caballero's government. The rift widened when Negrin came to power and further expanded as he become ever more dependent on communist support.

Much of the Republican arsenal came from the USSR including rifles, machine guns and artillery. Spanish-made rifles were also produced and used while the manufacturing facilities remained in Republican hands. The Soviets set up factories where weapons were assembled. As the pre-war Spanish army had little armour, Republican tanks and aircraft were Soviet models. The Soviet-built Tupelov SB-2 medium bomber was the fastest of its class and generally an excellent aircraft. The Polikarpov I-16 was a sturdy fighter. Although on paper it was outmatched by the German Messerschmitt Bf 109, in the right hands and in sufficient numbers "the bug" was a sound combat aircraft. The Soviet tanks were well armed and manoeuvrable, generally comparable to the German tanks used by the Nationalists.

The Nationalists

The Nationalists were made up of the military units that had rebelled in July 1936, augmented by volunteers from right-wing organizations such as the Falange and the Carlists. By introducing conscription in the areas they controlled, the Nationalists were able to increase their overall numbers, including Falange and Carlist militias, to approaching 300 000 men at any one time. By the end of the war, the Nationalists would have mobilized just over a million men. The Nationalists were supported by the Catholic Church in Spain and by other conservative elements such as landowners who were frightened by Republican land seizures and collectivization. These components coalesced under General Franco, who emerged as both the military and eventually the political leader of the Nationalist forces.

The fighting ability of the Nationalist forces was somewhat more uniform than that of the Republicans. This changed somewhat when conscription was introduced. Nevertheless the elite Moroccan troops often proved decisive in a number of engagements, especially in the north. The Nationalists also benefitted from a more unified command that only strengthened as the war progressed.

The Nationalists benefitted from the weapons supplied by Germany and Italy. The quality of these weapons was well matched by the Soviet weapons. Aircraft such as the Messerschmitt Bf 109 fighter and the Junkers Ju 87 Stuka dive bomber were generally superior to their counterparts in the Republican air force. Germany sent its early model Panzers to fight with the Nationalists. Although later models of this tank would be excellent fighting vehicles, the Panzer I was outgunned by the Soviet BT series tanks used by the Republicans.

The International Brigades

The western democracies, such as the USA and Britain, officially adopted policies of non-intervention and unofficially hoped for a Nationalist victory, frightened as they were of the spread of communism. Such policies were often at odds with popular opinion in these countries, which saw the war more in terms of the defence of democracy against authoritarian fascism. Non-intervention policies not only stopped official aid to the Republicans, but made it illegal for volunteers to travel to Spain and fight for the Republican cause. This prohibition, however, did not stop some 30 000 people, mostly workers and intellectuals, from smuggling themselves into Spain and enlisting in one of the numerous International Brigades.

The Brigades represented countries from all over the world, including the USA, Britain, France and Canada, but were generally organized by national communist organizations and coordinated by the Comintern, confirming for many Nationalist sympathizers that this was a battle against the spread of Soviet-dominated communism to western Europe, an interpretation that Franco publicly held until his death in 1975. The Comintern operated a recruiting centre in Paris and from here the volunteers were smuggled into Spain to attend a rudimentary training facility, again operated by the Comintern. There were seven Brigades, each divided into battalions based on nationality, such as the Mackenzie-Papineau Battalion from Canada. By 1938 the Republican government decided to disband the Brigades and fold the remaining volunteers into the Republican Army.

The extent to which the Brigades were an effective fighting force continues to be debated. While they fought in most of the major campaigns of the war, the Brigades were never numerically significant and suffered heavy losses. Their presence, on the other hand, was an important morale booster at crucial times such as during the siege of Madrid. While certainly not a long-term solution to the manpower issues facing the Republicans, nor in any way a counter to the heavy support that the Nationalists received, the Brigades did buy time for the Republican Army in several key battles.

> **Class discussion**
>
> Why would civilians from all over the world travel to Spain to fight for the Republicans?

Overseas support

German support

Franco sought aid from Hitler as early as 25 July 1936, a request that the German leader was more than happy to grant. Twenty German transport planes were immediately dispatched to Franco, then still in North Africa, to carry troops to the mainland. Publicly, Hitler maintained that he too wanted to stop the spread of communism in Europe. It later became evident that German foreign policy could benefit from Spain's instability, situated as she was on France's southern border. Furthermore, a Nationalist victory could give Germany access to Spanish natural resources, especially those necessary for arms production.

Throughout the course of the war, Germany supplied the Nationalists with artillery, small arms, tanks and vehicles. The most significant material contribution, however, was in aircraft. The German Luftwaffe (air force) formed the Condor Legion to fight in Spain. This consisted of fighter planes, transport planes and bombers, as well as the personnel to maintain and operate them. The Condor Legion provided the Nationalists with a distinct advantage, as the Republican forces had no air force to match it. The operations of the Condor Legion against Republican cities and towns, with the resultant civilian casualties, as in the Basque city of Guernica, presaged the widespread bombing of civilian targets during the Second World War. In all, around 12 000 German personnel served in Spain, fluctuating at any one time between 5,000 and 10 000 men. This contribution was to prove vital to the Nationalists' victories, especially as the fighting wore on into 1937 and 1938.

Italian support

Italian Prime Minister Benito Mussolini had had his hand in Spanish politics from before the Civil War, financially supporting the monarchists. At the outbreak of the war, he pledged further aid, both material and personnel. By November 1936, Mussolini had reached a secret agreement with Franco, by which the Italian dictator would receive Spanish support in case of a war with France in return for a sizeable increase in aid to the Nationalist army. The Italian army in Spain, the *Corpo Truppe Volontaire* (CTV), would number close to 70 000 men and included militia volunteers as well as regular army units, 700 aircraft and 900 tanks. These Italian formations fought throughout the war, contributing in a number of important battles such as Guadalajara.

Soviet support

Stalin did not enjoy the geographic advantage that Hitler and Mussolini had in supplying their Spanish allies. He was also torn between a desire to lead the forces of world socialism and a distrust of the socialist and anarchist elements in Spain. Domestic concerns, Five-Year Plans and the purges also occupied Stalin's energy. Nevertheless, by October 1936, Soviet material was arriving in Spain to bolster the Republican forces. Unlike the Germans and Italians, who allowed the Nationalists to purchase material on credit, the Republicans had to pay for Soviet aid with Spain's gold reserves. Most of the Republican tanks and planes came from the USSR. The Soviets also played an important organizational role. Much of the recruiting and control of the International Brigades, including political commissars responsible for the ideological development of the Brigades, was handled by Soviet personnel. This influence combined with the broader ideological divisions within the Republican forces to create tension and outright conflict between militias ostensibly on the same side, and this at times hindered the war effort.

The western democracies and non-intervention

In evaluating the response of the western democracies to the Spanish Civil War it is important to remember that it was governed by their own domestic and foreign policy goals more than any altruistic support for either side in the war. Although the Popular Front government in France might be thought to be a natural ally of their counterpart in Spain, it proceeded very cautiously in offering any support, largely because of the desire of its ally, Britain, to avoid confrontation with Italy and its own fear of provoking a resurgent Germany. In a misguided attempt to limit German and Italian aid to the Nationalists, the French Popular Front Prime Minister, Leon Blum, suggested a binding agreement

▲ German pilots confer before a mission. To what extent did the German Condor Legion affect the outcome of the civil war?

Class discussion

What are some arguments for and against German, Italian and Soviet intervention in the Spanish Civil War?

TOK discussion

To what extent is intervention in foreign conflicts an ethical issue?

between nations that they remain out of Spanish affairs. The result was the creation of the Non-Intervention Committee, which effectively barred the sale of arms to either side in the Civil War, a stipulation that was upheld by Britain and France and ignored by Germany, Italy and the Soviet Union. The result was to force the Republicans to rely even more heavily on the support of the Russians, exactly what the British wanted to avoid. The US also refused to sell arms to the Republicans, Roosevelt's hands being tied by the **Neutrality Acts**. This, however, did not stop American oil companies selling oil on long-term credit to the Nationalists, as oil was not included in the Neutrality Acts. In the final analysis, non-intervention severely damaged the Republican war effort but had no real effect on the Nationalist forces.

Foreign intervention in the Spanish Civil War					
Country	**Association**	**Personnel**	**Aircraft**	**Artillery**	**Armour**
Germany	Nationalists	17 000	600	1000	200
Italy	Nationalists	75 000	660	1000	150
USSR	Republicans	3000	1000	1550	900
International Brigades					
United Kingdom	Republicans	2000			
France	Republicans	10 000	300**		
USA	Republicans	2800			
Canada	Republicans	1000			
Czechoslovakia	Republicans	1000			
Poland	Republicans	5000			
Hungary	Republicans	1000			
Yugoslavia	Republicans	1500			
Germany/Austria*	Republicans	5000			
Italy*	Republicans	3350			

* Although the German and Italian governments officially supported the Nationalists, the brigades were formed by volunteers who chose to fight for the Republicans out of principle or ideology.

** Purchased from French government before non-intervention agreement

Neutrality Acts

A number of laws passed in the US Congress sought to establish the US as an officially neutral country. The first act, the Provisional Neutrality Act of 1935, was intended to expire in six months and prohibited American citizens from trading war materials with belligerents involved in a war. Subsequent Neutrality Acts of 1936, 1937, and 1939 expanded and extended the 1935 law to include credit and loans. The acts did not, however, include the sale of oil.

Thinking and communication skills
ATL

Choose either the Republican or Nationalist side. Write and deliver a speech persuading foreign powers to intervene in the war on your side. Be sure to include ideological considerations in your speech. Use any audio or visual materials you can to enhance your plea.

4.3 Operations

The early days of the insurrection saw the rebels take control of only one major city – Seville. All major industrial centres were in the government's hands. The Nationalists' best troops remained stranded in Morocco when the Spanish navy, which the generals had anticipated would carry the elite Moroccan army to the mainland, remained loyal to the government. Logistical support for the uprising came from unlikely corners. The British Royal Navy at Gibraltar helped relay messages for the rebels and when the Spanish naval ships that were to transport the troops from North Africa to the Spanish mainland refused to join the revolt, Hitler ordered German transport planes to take up the slack and transport the Moroccan regulars to the mainland, marking the beginning of increasing international intervention in Spain. These Moroccan troops were the most experienced in the Spanish army and would prove vital to the early survival and eventual success of the Nationalist cause.

After the initial uprising of the generals, it became evident that there would be no quick end to the rebellion. Citizens on both sides took the opportunity afforded by the control of their respective sides to settle old scores with any number of political or even personal enemies. This led to a pattern of violent retribution whenever one side conquered new territory, further increasing the suffering of non-combatants. Republican targets were generally Falange members and Catholic clergy, while the Nationalists sought out anarchists, communists and trade union members. Both sides eventually used sham legality in the form of tribunals to lend an air of legitimacy to the violence. Fame was no protection from the vigilante violence – Nationalist militia in Granada executed the poet Frederico García Lorca early in the war.

Throughout most of the war, the Republican forces were generally on the defensive. They managed to stop a Nationalist offensive towards Bilbao, the Basque capital, in September 1936 and repulse the first of several attacks on Madrid in November of that year. After failing to conquer the capital city, Franco's forces laid siege to it. The resistance

of Madrid would continue for three years and became the emotive rallying point for the Republic, immortalized in the words of Delores Ibarruri, known as *La Pasionaria*, *"No Passaran*!" (They shall not pass!)

Franco's army was bolstered in 1937 by the arrival of more Italian and German troops and materials. He used this increase to launch two more attacks on Madrid, both of which failed. The isolated Basque region was also a target of the Nationalists early in the year, leading to one of the most notorious atrocities of the war. The Basque region would hold out against Nationalist offensives until June 1937, when its capital, Bilbao, fell. As the year progressed, the Republican forces gained more battle experience, fighting more effectively and launching offensives of their own, but these improvements were undermined by tension between the various left-wing parties of the Republic. In Barcelona, in May 1937, tension broke into open warfare pitting communists against anarchists. Clearly a concentrated and organized military effort against the Nationalists could not be pursued while the Republicans were shooting at each other.

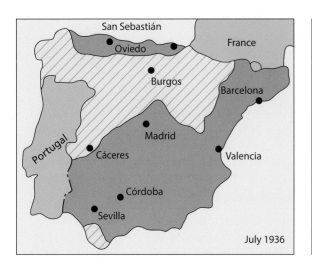

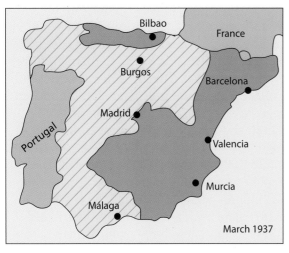
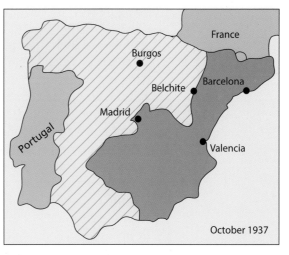

▲ Republican and Nationalist held territory, July 1936–October 1937

Bilbao and the north

In March 1937 the Nationalists captured the Basque region in the north of Spain and its major industrial centre of Bilbao. The Basque region was geographically isolated from the other Republican-held territory and could therefore not be reinforced. Command and control also proved difficult. This had both ideological and practical causes. Basque commanders, reflecting the fiercely independent personality of the Basques, ignored orders from Madrid and conducted the campaign as they saw fit. From March to June the Nationalist forces pushed the defending Basques back to the city of Bilbao. Enjoying command of the skies over the region, the Nationalists had a distinct advantage. The Republicans' air force could have challenged this command, but it was unwilling to risk its aircraft flying over Nationalist-held territory on its way to the Basque region. The defences around Bilbao were antiquated and undermanned, easily reduced by a combination of aerial bombardment and artillery fire. By 10 June the defences were collapsing and the defenders abandoned the city to the Nationalists.

Guernica

By not contesting the Nationalist control of the skies over the Basque region in the north of Spain, the Republicans – by default – allowed the German Condor Legion to conduct a terror bombing campaign against Basque cities and towns. On 26 April the German Condor Legion launched an air attack on the Basque city of Guernica. The city was essentially undefended although it did dominate two important roads that led to Bilbao. The decision to bomb the city was taken by Franco and carried out by the German commander Wolfram von Richthofen, cousin of the famous First World War flying ace Manfred von Richthofen known as the Red Baron.

The German bombers flew side by side, carpet bombing the city for two and a half hours. Because April 26 was a market day, the population of the city swelled past its usual population of 5,000. Civilians fleeing into the fields beyond the city were machine gunned from above. Although some argue that Guernica was targeted for military purposes, the orthodox view is that this was a deliberate targeting of civilians designed to create terror and break their will to resist, a tactic the German air force would later rely on in the Second World War. The armaments factory and the bridge, the only two military targets of note, were left untouched by the carpet bombing. However, terror bombing formed no formal part of Luftwaffe doctrine in 1937 and the Nationalist press concocted an elaborate propaganda story of the Basques destroying their own city to explain the atrocity – an indication that terror was not the goal. The reality probably lies somewhere in between these two views. The Germans and their Spanish partners saw military value in levelling the city and the machine gunning of the fleeing civilians was a result of decisions made by operational commanders on the spot. There is also some debate as to how many civilians were killed in the bombing, with numbers ranging from 300 to 1,700. Pablo Picasso immortalized the horror of that day in his massive painting *Guernica*, a work the artist would not allow to be hung in Spain until it was again a democratic republic.

Source skills

What is evidence?

The Spanish Civil War was characterized by a bewildering range of propaganda produced by all sides. One of the most distinctive genres of this propaganda was the use of artistic posters to convey political messages. Look at the following posters from the Spanish Civil War and answer the questions.

▲ (From left to right) **1** L'industria Textil de Cara a la Guerra. Poster, 1937. A pro-union poster for the UGT (Unión General de Trabajadores). **2** "And you, what have you done for victory?" Poster issued by the UGT and the PSOE (Spanish Socialist Party). **3** Spanish Civil War poster, c. 1937. "The farmer, too, is contributing to the war effort." Poster issued by the UGT and CNT (the anarcho-syndicalist union).

Questions

1 What messages are conveyed by these posters?

2 Does the use of highly emotional language and expressive effects reinforce the propaganda value of these posters?

3 Of what significance are these posters to historians studying the Spanish Civil War?

4 Choose an organization involved in the Spanish Civil War and create a poster to support their cause.

Madrid

Franco's forces were unable to dislodge the Republicans from the capital during the war. Starting in November 1936, the Nationalists tried to wrench the city from the Republicans. The International Brigades, anarchist forces and the Republican army combined forces to hurl the Nationalists back again and again between November 1936 and January 1937. From that point, however, Franco seemed satisfied to lay siege to the capital despite the fact that the resistance of Madrid was an important rallying point for the Republican forces.

Jarama

In another effort to cut Madrid off from the rest of the Republican-held territory, specifically from Valencia and the relocated central government there, the Nationalists launched a major offensive across the Jarama River in February 1937. Initially outnumbered, the Republicans were hard pressed and gave ground against Nationalist artillery, tanks and infantry. The German Condor Legion including tanks fought alongside Nationalist forces. In total the attacking force was close to 40 000 strong. Understanding the gravity of the situation, Republicans rushed reinforcements, including elements of the International Brigades – Abraham Lincoln Brigade from the US and the British Brigade – air power and Soviet tanks. They counter-attacked on 14 February and were able to stop the Nationalist advance. By the end of February movement had ceased and both sides fortified their position. The Nationalist goal of cutting the link between Madrid and Valencia had been thwarted, but the Republicans were unable to throw the Nationalists back across the Jarama River. The battle was costly to both sides, each losing between 6,000 and 20 000 men.

Guadalajara

The Battle of Guadalajara followed a similar pattern to Jarama. In fact, the battles were intended to support each other, but delays meant that they were essentially independent actions. Like Jarama the goal was to cut off Madrid. In this case the attacking force was approximately 50 000 Italian "volunteers" from the CTV supported by tanks. The Italians did not coordinate the tank attack well and without air cover the tanks proved ineffective against established defences. Again the Republicans were able to use air cover more effectively as the battle continued. Initially, as at Jarama, the outnumbered Republican forces gave way. Once reinforcements arrived a Republican counter-attack crushed the Italian left flank. The routed Italians left 6,000 casualties and a great deal of equipment for the Republicans as they fled.

The Ebro offensive

The Ebro offensive was the last major military operation of the war. It was also the longest, lasting from the end of July to mid-November 1938. With sound preparation and the element of surprise, the Republicans gained ground early in the battle. The Republican advance reached the city of Gandesa, its primary objective, but after fierce fighting and huge losses the Popular Army and the International Brigades were unable to occupy the city. The Ebro front settled into a bloody stalemate. The Nationalists used their superiority in air power and artillery to hammer the Republicans, who in turn were ordered to hold at all costs. The result was a war of attrition that decimated the Popular Army, keeping it in a weak defensive position for the rest of the war. In the end each side lost about 60 000 casualties, losses that the Nationalists could weather, but the Republicans could not.

Class discussion

Why would Negrin, the Republican Prime Minister, use his army on costly offensives rather than building strong defensive positions?

Why the Republicans lost

As the war progressed, the Republicans saw a constant erosion of the territory they controlled. By October 1937, they had been reduced to a large territory to the south and east of Madrid and a much smaller piece of land surrounding Barcelona. The Republicans tried to reconnect these two areas of control with the Ebro offensive from July to November 1938, but were unsuccessful. Early in 1939, the last of the Republican strongholds fell, leaving just Madrid and Valencia, which continued to resist. Despite Republican control of the capital, in February 1939 France and Britain officially recognized the Franco regime as the legitimate government of Spain. The last of the Republican defenders surrendered on 2 April 1939. The Spanish Civil War was over.

The Republicans lost for several reasons. Lack of effective central command and control, political infighting, and insufficient arms and materials all played a role in their downfall. Anarchists fought with communists and Marxist/Trotskyists fought with Stalinists. The weaknesses inherent in their military capability forced the Republicans into a predominantly defensive posture from which victory was impossible. Although they did attempt offensives, primarily in 1937, these were often costly and ineffective. For their part, the Nationalists were able to make effective use of the foreign aid they received, most notably the air power of the German Condor Legion. The use of Moroccan regular soldiers gave the Nationalists efficient fighting capability from the beginning of the war, whereas the Republican militias and other forces had to gain valuable experience at the expense of territory.

Aftermath and significance of the war

The immediate cost of the war was devastating. An estimated 500 000 people died between July 1936 and April 1939. Of these deaths, the vast majority were of non-combatants. Over 500 000 Republican supporters fled the ideological purge that followed the Nationalist victory, settling in

France, South and Central America. The physical destruction would take decades to recover from, a fact exacerbated by the pre-war lack of development.

In terms of its broader impact, the Spanish Civil War has been described as a "dress rehearsal" for the Second World War. It is true that the images of this war would become commonplace half a decade later. Carpet bombing of civilians, violent ideological reprisals linked to military operations and the integrated use of air power, armour and infantry made their debut in Spain. Symbolically, the war was a clarion call for the international left to confront the threat posed by expansionary fascism, a fact Spain realized three years before the democracies of the West.

The Nationalist victory strategically weakened the western democracies in the region. Britain's position at Gibraltar and thus in the Mediterranean was threatened by a German and Italian ally. France now had a fascist state on two of her major borders. Germany had secured preferential mining rights in Spain and Spanish troops made a nominal appearance on the Axis side of the Eastern Front during the Second World War.

The war was cast in different roles depending on one's own political perspective. To the intelligentsia of the West, the war was often characterized as a struggle between the forces of repression on the one side and freedom on the other. For the working classes of the world, it was about landed/industrial interest versus workers and unions. Industrialists, the Texas Oil Company, for example, saw the war as a struggle against expansionary communism and the particular brand of economic and proprietary authoritarianism that comes with it. In this way, the views and interpretations of the war reflected the internal divisions within both the Republican and Nationalist sides and help explain how the war captivated the imagination of the world in the late 1930s. The war figures prominently in the works of writers and artists such as André Malraux, Ernest Hemmingway, George Orwell, Dorothy Parker, Paul Robeson and Woody Guthrie.

Strategically, the war brought fascism to both of France's major borders and gave the fascists direct access to the Atlantic, so vital to Britain's interests. In the event, Franco's reluctance to wholeheartedly throw his lot in with Hitler and Mussolini spared the Grand Alliance of the Second World War the reality of dealing with Spain as a declared enemy. This can be attributed to some key differences in fascism as practised by Franco, Mussolini and Hitler. For his part, Franco's regime was able to survive into the 1970s by a mixture of broad right-wing support and repressive authoritarian tactics.

Art and literature inspired by the Spanish Civil War
Ernest Hemingway, *For Whom the Bell Tolls* (book)
George Orwell, *Homage to Catalonia* (book)
Pablo Picasso, *Guernica* (painting)
Woody Guthrie, "Jarama Valley" (song)
Ken Loach, *Land and Freedom* (film)
Guillermo del Toro, *Pan's Labyrinth* (film)
The Clash, "Spanish Bombs" (song)
Herbert Read, "Bombing Casualties: Spain" (poem)
The Lowest of the Low, "Letter from Bilbao" (song)

TOK discussion

The British, French and US governments did not come to the aid of the Republicans in their fight against fascism in Spain. Within six months of the end of the Spanish Civil War, France and Britain were at war with the Axis Powers and two and half years later the US would follow suit. How might the events of the Second World War have changed the interpretation of the Spanish Civil War in these countries?

Exam-style questions

1 Examine the role of ideology as a cause of the Spanish Civil War.

2 Evaluate the significance of foreign intervention in the Spanish Civil War.

3 Examine the reasons for the Republican defeat in the Spanish Civil War.

4 Evaluate the effectiveness of the International Brigades to the outcome of the Spanish Civil War.

5 Compare and contrast the Republican forces and the Nationalist forces at the beginning of the war.

Further reading

Beevor, Antony. 1980. *The Spanish Civil War*. Orbis. London, UK.

Preston, Paul. 2007. *The Spanish Civil War: Reaction, Revolution and Revenge*. W.W. Norton & Co. New York, USA.

Radosh, Ronald and Habeck, Mary (eds). 2001. *Spain Betrayed: The Soviet Union in the Spanish Civil War*. Yale University Press. New Haven, USA.

Rhodes, Richard. 2015. *Hell and Good Company: The Spanish Civil War and the World it Made*. Simon and Schuster. Toronto, Canada.

Thomas, Hugh. 2013. *The Spanish Civil War (4th rev. ed.)*. Penguin. New York, USA.

5 THE FIRST WORLD WAR: TOTAL WAR

Global context

Some historians have referred to the 19th century as the "Long 19th Century", seeing the years 1789–1914 as a more meaningful period than the more arbitrary 1800–1900. Indeed the dominant forces in European history during this period, specifically nationalism, industrialization, militarism, science, and imperialism, can be seen as reaching a zenith of sorts in the years leading up to 1914. Europeans, on the whole, considered themselves the principal society to which all others should aspire. Yet while these forces held within them the promise of widespread material prosperity and "progress" they also held the potential for conflict and disparity. It was this latter course that Europe took in 1914. As one of the great watersheds in history, the First World War produced social, political, and economic change of enormous scope and proportions. It is, however, important to not let the sheer scope and scale of the change blind us to significant elements of continuity between the pre-1914 and post-1918 world.

Timeline

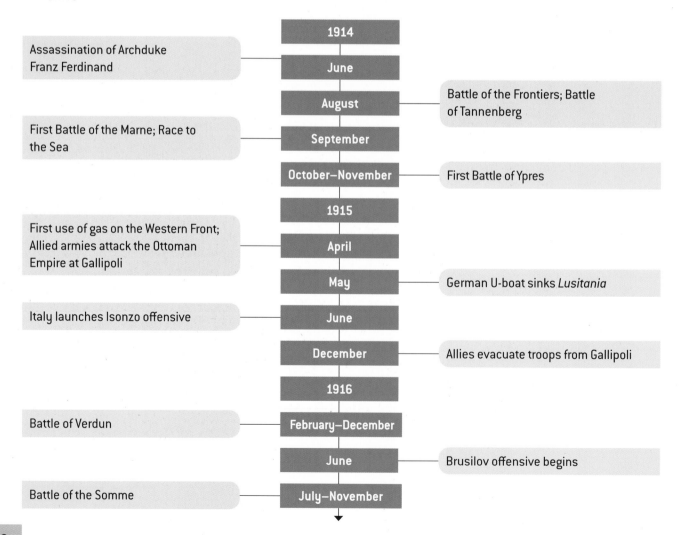

	1914	
Assassination of Archduke Franz Ferdinand	June	
	August	Battle of the Frontiers; Battle of Tannenberg
First Battle of the Marne; Race to the Sea	September	
	October–November	First Battle of Ypres
	1915	
First use of gas on the Western Front; Allied armies attack the Ottoman Empire at Gallipoli	April	
	May	German U-boat sinks *Lusitania*
Italy launches Isonzo offensive	June	
	December	Allies evacuate troops from Gallipoli
	1916	
Battle of Verdun	February–December	
	June	Brusilov offensive begins
Battle of the Somme	July–November	

1917

February — Germany resumes unrestricted submarine warfare; US receives copy of Zimmermann Telegram

Tsar Nicholas II abdicates — **March**

April — French Neville offensive; Canadians capture Vimy Ridge; Elements of the French army mutiny

First US troops land in France — **June**

July — Battle of Passchendaele begins

1918

Wilson introduces the "14 Points" — **January**

March — Soviets sign Treaty of Brest-Litovsk with Germany; Germany launches Spring offensives

Allies launch Amiens offensive — **August**

October — Ottoman Empire concludes separate peace with Allies

Kaiser Wilhelm II abdicates; Allies and Germany sign armistice — **November**

Gavrilo PRINCIP

▲ Arch Duke Franz Ferdinand (left) and his assassin Gavrilo Princip (right)

5.1 Causes of the First World War

Conceptual understanding

Key questions

→ To what extent was the war preventable?

→ How did the causes of the war influence the nature of the war?

→ What is the relative responsibility of each of the European powers for the outbreak of the war?

Key concepts

→ Cause

→ Consequence

→ Perspective

It has become a cliché to speak of the causes of the First World War, known as the Great War, as a "powder keg" (long-term causes) ignited by a "spark" (immediate cause). While clichés can be trite and boring, they also encapsulate an essential truth. Whatever metaphor you choose, the causes of the First World War can be broken down into a number of trends that developed through the end of the 19th century and the beginning of the 20th century, leading up to the fateful events of July 1914, often called the July Crisis.

These causes did not work in isolation, however. They were interconnected. **Militarism** was dependent on industrial capacity. Colonial possessions required larger militaries. It is in this interconnectedness that we can begin to seek the causes of the war itself, as well as the scope of the war as it unfolded.

militarism

A political, diplomatic and social emphasis on military matters. Evidence of militarism often includes increased military spending, development of military technology, a general support for the goals and plans of a nation's military and the influence of military leaders on political decisions.

Long-term causes

It is important to think about what we mean when we say "cause". What we refer to as long-term causes are, in the strict sense, not causes – they did not make the First World War inevitable. Instead, in history, we must talk in terms of probabilities. What follows is a set of developments that made war more likely. These developments fuelled the suspicion, fear and tension between the European powers. Further, they increased the probability of a big war. The trend towards larger militaries, industrial capacity and empires limited the likelihood of a short, limited, regional war involving two, maybe three, countries.

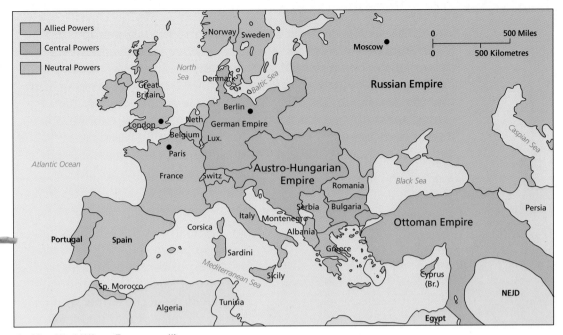

▲ First World War – European alliances

Militarism

Broadly speaking, we can talk about militarism as an overall societal emphasis on the military. The trend towards massive armies and navies at the end of the 19th century can be highlighted in two ways. On the one hand there are the precise, technical aspects that appeal to many military historians – warship tonnage, troop concentration and military expenditure. On the other hand, we should consider those aspects that appeal to the social historian – the relation of the military to the wider society.

It is certainly true that at the turn of the last century, the militaries of the major European powers were the largest in history. Paradoxically, most statesmen, if not generals, believed that this could help avoid a war. This early idea of **deterrence** held that the larger a country's military, the less likely other countries would be to attack. This might have been true if the size of militaries had remained static. The big problem was that they were growing. If a country was worried that a rival state's army was growing faster than its own, the temptation was to attack the rival pre-emptively before the differential was too great. In short, use your army before you lost it.

Regardless, the fact remains that the military forces that the European powers had at their disposal in 1914 were immense. There were approximately 200 army **divisions** in Europe in 1914 including reserves (part-time soldiers called up in the event of war). These massive armies were fed by varying degrees of conscription in all European powers with the exception of Great Britain (introduced in 1916). Men of military age were required to serve from two to six years. In fact, the terms of service were increasing. France passed the

deterrence
Actions or polices designed to discourage an attack by making the consequences of the attack prohibitive.

division
A military unit of around 12 000–18 000 men. Divisions were designed to contain within them all elements necessary to fight an engagement – infantry, artillery, medical and logistic services, command, and communication and intelligence.

▲ The HMS *Dreadnought* was revolutionary in all aspects: design, speed, armament, materials and production methods.

Three Year Law in 1913, increasing mandatory military service from two to three years. By all accounts, the Russian army was the largest in the world. The tsar's standing army numbered about 1.3 million and some claimed it could mobilize a further five million reservists. While these figures alone were enough to give pause to any would-be attackers, more alarming was the fact they were growing.

As impressive as the numbers may seem on paper, the reality reflected a dangerous contradiction. In the case of Russia, the likelihood that all of these conscripts would report for duty as required was wishful thinking and if they had it would have created an even bigger problem. The combination of poor infrastructure, massive distance between military depots and poor military organization meant that the most the Russian army could reliably call into service was about one-fifth of the able-bodied men of military age. This deceptive picture was a double-edged sword. To her rivals, inclined as they were to focus on the strength of other states, Russia was an imposing behemoth. To Russian military planners, aware of the deficiencies in their military apparatus, the theoretical or even actual size of the army meant that mobilization must be undertaken before any potential enemy could mobilize. This was to have ominous ramifications in July 1914.

Militarism was evident not only in the size of armies and navies, but also in the technology used by these forces. By 1914, modern industrial methods meant that the great armament foundries of Krupp and Skoda were producing artillery that could hurl a one-tonne explosive projectile up to 10 miles (16 kilometres). Machine guns could theoretically fire 400 to 600 rounds per minute. In practice, each machine gun was the equivalent of 80 rifles.

The Anglo-German naval race was perhaps one of the starkest illustrations of militarism. When the British Royal Navy launched the revolutionary HMS *Dreadnought* in December 1906, it instantly made every battleship then afloat, including British ships, obsolete. If a country was to have a modern navy after 1906, it had to spend money on **Dreadnoughts**. When this was coupled with Germany's desire for a navy to rival the Royal Navy, as expressed in the Second Naval Law of 1900, it created an arms race that would see the size of these navies increase by a combined 197% between 1900 and 1914.

Dreadnought
A class of battleship first developed in the UK with the class name coming from the prototype for this type of ship, the HMS *Dreadnought*. It was faster and more heavily armed than any battleships that existed at the time. It immediately made every battleship afloat obsolete and became the standard against which all new ships were measured.

Warship tonnage of the powers, 1880–1914					
	1880	**1890**	**1900**	**1910**	**1914**
Britain	650 000	679 000	1 065 000	2 174 000	2 714 000
France	271 000	319 000	499 000	725 000	900 000
Russia	200 000	180 000	383 000	401 000	679 000
United States	169 000	240 000	333 000	824 000	985 000
Italy	100 000	242 000	245 000	327 000	498 000
Germany	88 000	190 000	285 000	964 000	1 305 000
Austria-Hungary	60 000	66 000	87 000	210 000	372 000
Japan	15 000	41 000	187 000	496 000	700 000

Source: Kennedy, Paul. 1988. *Rise and Fall of the Great Powers: Economic and Military Conflict from 1500 to 2000*. London, UK. Fontana Press. P. 261.

Large or even growing militaries do not cause wars. They do, however, engender suspicion and fear in rival states. When this suspicion is coupled with economic rivalry, imperialism and nationalism, it makes war more likely. Further, it makes a large, massively destructive war more likely.

Military and naval personnel, 1880–1914					
	1880	**1890**	**1900**	**1910**	**1914**
Russia	791 000	677 000	1 162 000	1 285 000	1 352 000
France	543 000	542 000	715 000	769 000	910 000
Germany	426 000	504 000	524 000	694 000	891 000
Britain	367 000	420 000	624 000	571 000	532 000
Austria-Hungary	246 000	346 000	385 000	425 000	444 000
Italy	216 000	284 000	255 000	322 000	345 000
Japan	71 000	84 000	234 000	271 000	306 000
United States	34 000	39 000	96 000	127 000	164 000

Source: Kennedy, Paul. 1988. *Rise and Fall of the Great Powers: Economic and Military Conflict from 1500 to 2000*. London, UK. Fontana Press. P. 261.

Industrialization

Some historians have contended that by 1900 economic power equated to military power. Others contend that, while there is a strong relationship between these two concepts, the matter of what constituted a Great Power was more complex. What is not generally disputed is the massive increase in industrial output in the second half of the 19th century. The revolution in production that had taken root in England a century before had, by 1870, spread to the rest of Europe and across the Atlantic. By all measures, Europe was far more industrialized in 1914 than it had been in 1880; this industrialization would help determine the nature of the war to come as the first total war of the 20th century.

Of course, increasing industrial output does not cause war any more than large armies do. There are, however, certain consequences of this increase in manufacturing that played a role in making a general European war more likely. Among these consequences is the fact that the increase was not uniform among the powers. For example, while iron and steel production had increased in the United States by approximately 242% between 1890 and 1913, it had actually decreased in Britain. More to the point for the British, Germany's steel production had increased by approximately 329% in the same period. In absolute terms, in 1913, France was woefully behind all the powers except Austria-Hungary. These disparities helped create competitive economic tension between the powers, which in turn increased diplomatic and political tension.

In order to feed these massive industrial machines, the powers needed access to resources, which in turn created a **neo-mercantilist** mindset complemented by the drive for colonies in the second half of the 19th century. This thirst had been momentarily slaked by the "scramble for Africa" but by 1900 that well had gone dry. The European powers had claimed all of Africa, with a few small exceptions. Sources of raw materials, not to mention markets, had either to be wrung from existing holdings or wrestled, forcibly or diplomatically, from another power.

Not only had industrial output increased, so had trade. By 1913 the total of German exports was equal to that of Britain and in the lucrative American market the Germans significantly outsold the British. To protect and to increase this trade, the Germans needed a modern, powerful navy. It did not take long for the powers to harness their huge industrial potential once the war began. By 1914 France was producing 200 000 artillery shells a day. Even the backward Russian factory system was manufacturing 4.5 million artillery shells in 1916, a tenfold increase on the previous year. The connection between economic rivalry and military rivalry was evident.

> **neo-mercantilism**
> An economic doctrine that emphasizes the need to decrease imports by moving toward self-sufficiency. This move often requires an increase in colonial holdings to supply raw materials and provide markets for finished goods.

The alliance system

If these great, interlocking alliances caused large-scale wars, then NATO and the Warsaw Pact would have brought the Cold War to a disastrous end long before the communist states of Eastern Europe were dissolved at the end of the 1980s. Similar to the Cold War, Europe in 1914 was split into two rival, albeit smaller, alliances. These two alliances were connected by a secondary set of treaties, agreements and alliances to countries around the globe.

After Bismarck had finished forging the German Empire by means of "blood and iron" in 1871, he sought to preserve it by carefully shielding her from war. His method was to create an intricate set of alliances as part of a policy of deterrence. The Dual Alliance between Germany and Austria-Hungary, established in 1879, was a major part of that shield. Within three years, the addition of Italy turned the Dual Alliance into the Triple Alliance, with each state pledging military support in the event that either of the other two became embroiled in a war against two or more opponents. To this Bismarck added the Reinsurance Treaty with Russia in 1887. The cumulative effect of these agreements was, as Bismarck had intended, to isolate France from the rest of Europe, something French diplomats were going to have to work hard to undo.

This work was made easier when Bismarck refused to approve German loans to Russia in 1887 and the post-Bismarckian foreign office elected not to renew the Reinsurance Treaty in 1890. Now Russia, too, was isolated. Between 1890 and 1894, France nurtured a closer relationship with tsarist Russia – offering loans totalling £400 million and coordinating military planning. This new friendship culminated in the Franco-Russian Alliance, formalized in 1894. The Tsar pledged that Russia would attack Germany if Germany ever attacked France or aided Italy in attacking France. France agreed to do likewise if the Kaiser's forces ever attacked Russia or helped Austria-Hungary do the same. The German nightmare of a two-front war was now a distinct possibility.

While France and Russia saw isolation as a dangerous condition, Britain traditionally reveled in it. She emerged from her "splendid isolation" when it suited her and retreated behind her watery ramparts when it was prudent. British statesmen eschewed the rigidity of formal alliances. The diplomatic world, however, had changed by the turn of the century. Britain had been battered by her victory in the South African War. The naval race with Germany was pressuring her treasury. Tensions with France in Africa had nearly erupted into war. The time seemed right to begin a tentative emergence from isolation. First came an alliance with Japan and then a rapprochement with France. The Entente Cordiale of 1904 was the result. By this agreement, Britain and France agreed to settle differences in Africa as well as a number of smaller disputes around the world. Significantly, however, the Entente Cordiale contained no military commitments, preserving Britain's free hand, or so the British thought, in the affairs of continental Europe. By 1907 the British had settled old differences with the Russian Empire and the Entente Cordiale metamorphosed into the Triple Entente. It was a less rigid agreement than the Triple Alliance as the British refused to agree to any binding military action.

Each of these alliance systems was complicated by other agreements made by the powers, some of which were public and some secret. Two notable examples involved Britain and Russia. Britain's alliance with Japan has already been noted, but she was also linked to the largest empire on earth. Even the so-called independent "white dominions" of Canada, Australia and New Zealand were automatically committed to war should Britain declare war on another county. This almost guaranteed that were Britain to support one of her Entente partners militarily, the result would be a global war. On top of this, since 1839 Britain had guaranteed Belgium's perpetual neutrality. For her part, Russia had interests in the Balkans, which helped draw her into an alliance with Serbia, further complicating the web of treaties and agreements in the period 1900–1914.

The net result of this interlocking, secretive and fairly rigid set of alliances was to increase the tension and suspicion between the great powers. While not causing the war, it made it more likely and ensured that it would be large in scope. The complex system was also arduous to maintain, requiring very subtle diplomacy, or what historians Robert Roswell Palmer and Joel Colton have called "the most Olympian of statesmanship". No such level of statesmanship was forthcoming in the summer of 1914.

nation
A nation is a group of people who share a number of commonalities generally including language, culture, historic development and territory.

imperialism
A set of actions and policies by which one national group dominates another national group or its territory.

nationalism
An emotional attachment to a group and a desire for it to be politically independent.

Weltpolitik
The foreign policy adopted by Germany at the end of the 19th century by which she sought to assert her influence around the world.

Imperialism/nationalism

It is important to keep in mind that a **nation** is, at its heart, a group of people. In many ways, therefore, **imperialism** and **nationalism** are two sides of the same coin. The imperialism of one nation state will generally aggravate the nationalist feelings of those it dominates.

Imperial tensions between the European powers became dangerously high in the second half of the 19th century, in large measure because of what has become known as the "scramble for Africa". Until 1850, the European exploration and subsequent exploitation of Africa had largely been limited to the coastal areas. By the 1870s, however, entrepreneurial explorers such as Henry Stanley had begun to awaken to the economic potential of the African interior, touching off a race by European states to claim their own colonies in Africa. The potential of this "scramble" to bring far-flung powers into conflict should be obvious. It certainly was to Bismarck. Despite his disdain for overseas colonies, Bismarck hosted a conference in Berlin in 1885 to hammer out the rules for claiming and exploiting Africa in hopes that these rules would stave off disagreements over ownership. Just as he had no interest in Germany acquiring her own colonies, he did not want disputes between other powers in some distant African land to jeopardize his new Germany by dragging her into a European war.

Despite his efforts, and in some ways because of his efforts, the European powers would come dangerously close to war over African questions after Bismarck's retirement in 1890. Part of the problem lay in Bismarck's desire to stay out of the colony game, the result of which was what the new Kaiser, Wilhelm II, thought was an insulting under-representation of Germany on the world stage. Young Wilhelm demanded that Germany get her "place in the sun" and developed a brash, provocative and ultimately dangerous **Weltpolitik** (world policy) to achieve it. The result of this ill-conceived policy became evident in 1905. During a state visit to French-controlled Morocco, Wilhelm boldly proclaimed that the status of Morocco should be re-evaluated at an international conference. Unfortunately for the Kaiser, this conference, held at Algeciras the following year, upheld French claims to the territory. While the Kaiser had wished to assert German authority, and in the process drive a wedge between the Anglo-French entente, he served only to strengthen the entente and make the rest of Europe wary of German motives and methods on the world stage. The Kaiser travelled to the Moroccan port of Agadir in 1911 to once again pressure France by calling into question her imperial claims. Britain unequivocally supported her ally. Wilhelm came away from Algeciras and the Agadir Crisis feeling that Germany was becoming dangerously isolated and victimized.

The Balkans

The role that nationalism played in the growing international tensions at the turn of the century is best demonstrated in the Balkans. This region was populated by a number of ethnic groups broadly referred to as Slavs and centred in the small independent nation state of Serbia. Political domination in the region had traditionally been split between two rival empires, the Austro-Hungarian and the Ottoman. By the end of the 19th century, the crumbling influence and power of the Ottoman Empire, coupled with Austria-Hungary's desire to retrench and expand her influence in the region, made this a very unstable part of the European political system. The flux in the region reawakened in Russia age-old Balkan aspirations. Growing numbers of radical pan-Slavic nationalists living under the Habsburgs were convinced that their future lay not in a federated Austria-Hungary, but rather in a Greater Serbia or Yugoslavia. With Serbia's ambition to become the leader of a pan-Slavic state added to this frightening situation, the region was becoming dangerously volatile.

When Italy tried to wrest Tripoli from the Ottomans by force in 1911, Serbia saw an opportunity to profit from the sultan's divided attention and resources. Forming the Balkan League with Bulgaria, Montenegro and Greece, she went to war with Turkey. The profit was Albania and Macedonia, with the lion's share going to Bulgaria, a grievance Serbia quickly addressed by defeating Bulgaria in the Second Balkan War in 1913. This time Serbian designs on Albania, and the consequent access to the sea, was thwarted by international intervention, spearheaded by Austria-Hungary. Russia, though a supporter of Serbian claims, backed down when faced with Austrian resolve, just as she had done when the Austrians annexed Bosnia, a Slavic territory, in 1908. The result was the creation of the Independent Kingdom of Albania. The sum total of this confusing ten months of war and negotiation was an Austro-Hungarian Empire determined to stop pan-Slavic nationalist claims, an emboldened Serbia determined to further pan-Slavic nationalist schemes and a twice-humiliated Russian Empire determined to reassert her authority.

It is important to read these background causes together. The massive size of European militaries was made possible by the prodigious increase in European industrial production, fed by raw materials garnered from global empires. The expansion of empires, partially necessitated by the hunger for resources, angered countries such as Germany and Austria-Hungary who wanted to expand their holdings, while simultaneously increasing the anxiety of those at whose expense this expansion would have to occur – countries such as Britain, France, Russia and Serbia, not to mention countless African and Asian peoples, who are often overlooked in this European drama, a drama that was shortly to become a global tragedy.

Short-term causes

The July Crisis

When asked what caused the First World War, people with even the most rudimentary historical knowledge will likely reply that it had something to do with the shooting of a member of the Austrian royal family. As we have seen, however, this is woefully inadequate in explaining an event with the scale and scope of the First World War. Indeed, when Archduke Franz Ferdinand, heir to the Habsburg throne, and his wife Sophie were shot while visiting Sarajevo on 28 June 1914, they were not particularly unique in their fate. The Archduke was but one of eight heads of state that were assassinated in the years 1881–1914, two of them being Habsburgs. No, it was not the assassination itself that sparked the war. Rather, it was an inability to manage the ensuing crisis in the light of the long-term causes outlined above that tumbled the European powers into four years of disaster.

Political assassinations, 1881–1914	
1881	Alexander II of Russia, Emperor of all the Russias
1894	Marie François Sadi Carnot, President of France
1895	Stefan Stombolov, Prime Minister of Bulgaria
1897	Antonio Cánovas del Castillo, Prime Minister of Spain
1898	Empress Elisabeth of Austria
1900	King Umberto I of Italy
1901	William McKinley, President of the United States
1903	King Aleksander of Serbia
1904	Nikolai Bobrikov, Governor-general of England
1908	King Carlos I of Portugal
1908	Luiz Filipe, Crown Prince of Portugal
1911	Peter Stolypin, Prime Minister of Russia
1912	José Canalejas, Prime Minister of Spain
1913	King George I of Greece
1914	Archduke Franz Ferdinand of Austria

Certain members of the Serbian military supported the Bosnian terrorist group "Union of Death", commonly known as the Black Hand, although it appears that this support did not extend throughout the Serbian government. Nevertheless, Austrian officials, specifically the chief of the general staff, Conrad Hotzendorff, and the chancellor, Leopold von Berchtold, wished to seize the opportunity afforded by the assassination to crush South-Slav nationalism once and for all. This would mean war with Serbia. After a pledge of unlimited support from Germany, her only European ally, in the so-called **Blank Cheque**, the Austrians formulated their ultimatum to the Serbs. The exact nature and intent of the Blank Cheque has for years been debated, as has the authorship of the ultimatum itself. It would seem that the terms of the ultimatum were designed to be impossible to accept, offering as it did affront to many aspects of Serb sovereignty.

Blank Cheque

A pledge of unconditional support given by Kaiser Wilhelm II of Germany to Franz Joseph in July 1914. The pledge was in reference to Austria-Hungary's dispute with Serbia and Russia.

Nevertheless, the Serbs capitulated to most of the demands, so much so that the Kaiser believed that with the Serb response "every reason for war drops away". Perhaps he was more surprised than many when Austria-Hungary went to war against Serbia within hours of this response on 28 July 1914.

The Russians viewed the size of the Austrian mobilization as a direct threat to their frontiers. To this was added the memory of the two previous Balkan humiliations. The Tsar ordered partial mobilization against Austria on the night of 29 July.

Understanding the alliance obligations that Germany owed to Austria, the Russian War Minister, Vladimir Sukhomlinov, persuaded the Tsar to change the order to full mobilization along the entire length of Russia's western frontier. As an increasing sense of panic gripped the Kaiser, he demanded that his cousin, the Tsar, cease all military preparation. When this was not forthcoming, Wilhelm ordered the full mobilization of the German army, a mobilization that, as part of the Schlieffen Plan, was directed against France, through neutral Belgium.

Some historians believed that the Germans were clinging to the hope that Britain would stay out of the looming conflict. Others thought that this was never a serious possibility. For his part, the British Foreign Secretary, Edward Grey, did nothing to dispel this notion, reserving Britain's freedom of action until the very last moment. When the German army crossed into Belgium on 3 August 1914, Britain's treaty obligations brought her and her empire into what was now a world war.

War plans

The opening days of the First World War have often been referred to as "war by timetable". Indeed, the act of mobilizing millions of soldiers required a level of coordination unprecedented in 1914. So vital was the railroad system to this endeavour that the German government had taken sole control of the entire German railroad system by the 1880s. The fact was that all the major European powers had to move millions of men to positions on their frontiers, so as to be able to carry out war plans of varying degrees of complexity.

The most famous of these plans was the Schlieffen Plan, named after its creator, Alfred von Schlieffen, chief of the German general staff from 1891 to 1905. In that time he conceived a plan that was designed to deal with the Bismarckian nightmare of a two-front war, against France in the west and Russia in the east. The plan called for a massive concentration of German arms in the west against France. This force, composed of seven armies, would sweep through Luxembourg and Belgium into northern France in a great arc that would conquer Paris within 41 days of mobilization. Meanwhile, Russian forces would be held at bay by a combination of Austro-Hungarian armies and Russia's own sluggish mobilization. The Schlieffen Plan was itself an immediate cause of the war, in that it depended upon Germany mobilizing first. In case of a threat by Russia, as happened in July 1914, Germany's entire grand strategy required the Kaiser to start a war with France.

At first glance it would seem that the German general staff also had a hand in the preparation of the French war plan. France's Plan XVII called for a massing of French armies on their eastern frontier, away from the main thrust of the German army. These troops would then rush gallantly eastwards, regaining at once the honour of the French army and the territories of Alsace and Lorraine. Whereas the Schlieffen Plan was built on meticulous timetabling and organization, Plan XVII rested on the ideas of **élan vitale** and the offensive spirit, prompting Russian mobilization and the coordinated assistance of the British army.

> **ATL** **Thinking skills**
>
> Historian John Keegan has said the Schlieffen Plan was "pregnant with dangerous uncertainty". Think about all the things that might go wrong with the Schlieffen Plan. How might the Germans have accounted for these possibilities?

> *élan vitale*
> In the context of French military doctrine in 1914, *élan vitale* was the preference of attack at the expense of prudent defence. Deficiencies in sound planning and tactical considerations could be overcome with sufficient enthusiasm and vigour.

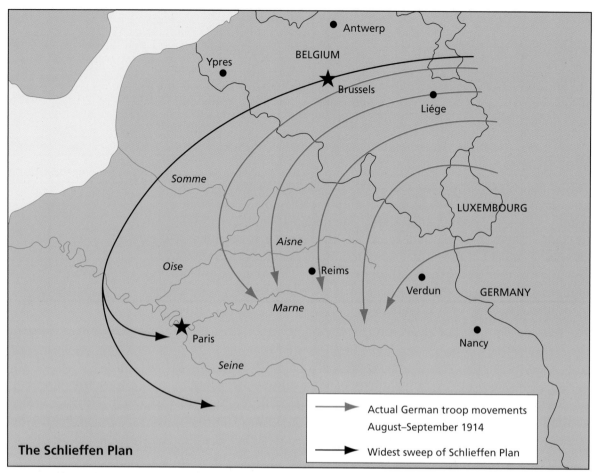

The Schlieffen Plan

Legend:
→ Actual German troop movements August–September 1914
→ Widest sweep of Schlieffen Plan

▲ Schlieffen's original plan called for the capture of Paris within 41 days of mobilization. How did Moltke's decision to wheel the first army in front of Paris, rather than around it, change the nature of the entire war?

ATL Thinking skills

Read the views of the following historians regarding how the First World War began.

Sidney Bradshaw Fay. 1928. *The Origins of the World War*. New York, NY, USA. The Macmillan Company.	Fay was writing in response to the finding of the Paris Peace Conference that Germany was solely responsible for the outbreak of the war. Fay maintained that it was a complex assortment of causes, notably imperialism, militarism and alliances that pushed Europe into war. No one country plotted an aggressive war and many, including Britain and Germany, made genuine, although unskilled, efforts at mediating the July Crisis. In some ways, Fay and those who agreed with him are part of the larger movement that wanted to reintroduce Germany to the community of nations in the spirit of the Locarno Treaty of 1925.
Fritz Fischer. 1976. *German Aims in the First World War*. New York, NY, USA. W.W. Norton.	In the wake of the Second World War, German historian Fritz Fischer re-evaluated his country's role in causing the First World War. In contrast to Fay, Fischer found that Germany sought an aggressive war of expansion in 1914. Germany was surrounded by hostile countries and her economy, culture and influence was in decline. A successful war of expansion would solve these problems and was therefore plotted and encouraged in the years 1912–1914. The July Crisis was deliberately managed to this end. Fischer maintained that these attitudes and desires were not held solely by a maleficent and deluded leadership. After examining a broad cross section of German society in 1914, Fischer concluded that these attitudes and aims had broad support from business interests, academics and all political parties in Germany. It is not difficult to understand why this was a contentious position in post-Second World War Germany.

Eric Hobsbawm. 1989. *The Age of Empire*. New York, NY, USA. Vintage.	Writing in the Marxist historical tradition, Eric Hobsbawm does not find the causes of the war in any one country or person, but rather in the system of industrial capitalism that dominated the economics of western Europe. Hobsbawm argues that industrial capitalism's insatiable hunger for resources and markets fuelled the New Imperialism of the 19th century. While this need was temporarily slaked by the "scramble for Africa", it soon brought European countries into conflict. Further, within industrial powers, this competition required a close partnership between the government and arms producers, for whom peacetime profits had to be maintained. These profits were required so that the industry would be around for the next war, a war in which strength would be measured not in military strength alone, but also in industrial capacity. By arguing a systemic cause of the war, Hobsbawm and other Marxist historians bring a degree of inevitability to the war. Regardless of who led the countries, or which countries were involved, they believe the system would have caused a war eventually.
Niall Ferguson. 1999. *The Pity of War*. New York, NY, USA. Basic Books.	Niall Ferguson, like Fischer, blames one country in particular. For Ferguson, rather than Germany, responsibility rests with the actions, and in some cases inaction, of Britain. Ferguson believes that Fay was wrong, that anti-militarism was rising in Europe by 1914, secret diplomacy had solved many disputes, and that Germany and Britain were more than capable of settling their differences. Rather, he maintains that British political and military leaders had planned to intervene in a European conflict from 1905 and in fact would have violated Belgian neutrality themselves had Germany not done it first. Further, he maintains that Britain misinterpreted German intentions, seeing them as Napoleonic rather than as essentially defensive. These leaders misled the British Parliament into a declaration of war.
John Stoessinger. 1999. *Why Nations Go To War*. 11th ed. New York, NY, USA. Basic Books.	John Stoessinger finds liability for the war largely in the personal failings of those trying to manage the July Crisis. He believes that each of the leaders acted out of an over-inflated sense of both their own country's weakness and their enemy's strength. Further, the supreme leaders in Austria-Hungary and Germany failed to exercise sufficient control over their subordinates, who actively conspired to provoke at least a regional war if not a general European war. Once the "iron dice" were cast, none of the leaders had the nerve to order a halt to the mobilization, even though this was a completely viable option. Had different personalities been in positions of authority in July 1914, there may have never been a war.

1   Which historian has the most convincing thesis? Why?

2   Add your own row to the table. What do you believe caused the war? How might it have been avoided?

3   How might the era in which each of the above historians was writing have affected their views? Why is it important for students of history to understand the context in which historians write?

5.2 Combatants

Conceptual understanding

Key questions

→ What were the comparative strengths and weaknesses of the Allied Powers and the Central Powers?

→ What effect would the entry of the United States and exit of Russia have on this relationship?

Key concepts

→ Cause

→ Consequence

Central Powers 1914

Of a population of 115 million the Central Powers could muster 146 army divisions in 1914, some 1.4 million troops. The German army had an advanced system of command and control, which made for a flexible and efficient movement of troops. This efficiency was enhanced by the fact that the Central Powers also enjoyed geographic adjacency and internal lines of communication, allowing them to move troops between its two fronts and engage in combined military operations. By the end of the war Germany had mobilized 11 million men while Austria-Hungary had mobilized 7.8 million, Turkey 2.9 million and Bulgaria 1.2 million.

The German High Seas Fleet had 14 Dreadnoughts and 22 older battleships. This fleet had technologically advanced artillery fire control and communications. They were able to concentrate this naval force in the North Sea given Germany's relatively fewer colonial defence responsibilities.

Allied Powers 1914

France, Russia and Britain had a combined population of 265 million in 1914. Both Russia and France had a conscript army, while Britain's was a volunteer force in 1914. Together these powers could put foward 212 army divisions, some 2.8 million men in the field. This number was, however, hindered by equipment of poor quality and insufficient quantities in the case of the Russian army.

Communications, command and control were likewise antiquated in the Tsar's army. While the French army was large and relatively well equipped, it was geographically separated from her Russian ally and could thus not concentrate nor coordinate their forces and operations. The size of the British army would swell during war, but it remained small in the early months of the war. Likewise its colonial possessions and dominions would contribute greatly to the size of her fighting force as the war dragged on. In 1914, however, they could contribute little.

For example the Canadian army was a mere 6,000 soldiers in August 1914, but by 1918 it had sent 500 000 men overseas. By the time of the armistice the Allied Powers had mobilized a total of 42 million men, 12 million of them Russian, 8.4 million of them French, 8.9 million of them from Britain and her empire, and 5.6 million from Italy.

The US army in 1917 was a small affair by European standards. The military potential of the United States was, however, enormous. In April 1917 the army stood at about 200 000 men including the National Guard. The Selective Service Act of 1917 introduced conscription, dramatically increasing the size of the army. In the 19 short months that the United States was a combatant in the First World War it mobilized 4.3 million men.

The United States had a world-class navy at the outset of the war, with 10 Dreadnoughts and 23 older battleships. The Naval Expansion Act of 1916 intended to double this over the course of a number of years.

The British Royal Navy, maintaining her modified two-power policy, had a massive fleet at her disposal. She had 20 Dreadnoughts and 39 older battleships. She also, however, had a much larger empire to patrol and not being self-sufficient in food or industrial powers was dependent on safe shipping lanes. Britain was able to take advantage of her alliance with France, who agreed to patrol British interests in the Mediterranean, so that Britain could concentrate her naval forces in the North Sea.

ATL Thinking skills

Look at the data in these tables.

Per capita levels of industrialization, 1880–1938 (Relative to Britain in 1900)						
	1880	1900	1913	1928	1938	Ranking
1 Great Britain	87	[100]	115	122	157	2
2 United States	38	69	126	182	167	1
3 France	28	39	59	82	73	4
4 Germany	25	52	85	128	144	3
5 Italy	12	17	26	44	61	5
6 Austria	15	23	32	–	–	
7 Russia	10	15	20	20	38	7
8 Japan	9	12	20	30	51	6

Iron and steel production of the powers, 1890–1938 (Millions of tonnes; pig-iron production for 1890, steel thereafter)							
	1890	1900	1910	1913	1920	1930	1938
United States	9.3	10.3	26.5	31.8	42.3	41.3	28.8
Great Britain	8.0	5.0	6.5	7.7	9.2	7.4	10.5
Germany	4.1	6.3	13.6	17.6	7.6	11.3	23.2
France	1.9	1.5	3.4	4.6	2.7	9.4	6.1
Austria-Hungary	0.97	1.1	2.1	2.6	–	–	–
Russia	0.95	2.2	3.5	4.8	0.06	5.7	18.0
Japan	0.02	–	0.16	0.25	0.84	2.3	7.0
Italy	0.01	0.00	0.73	0.93	0.73	1.7	2.3

Total industrial potential of the powers, 1880–1938 (Relative to Britain in 1900)

	1880	1900	1913	1928	1938
Great Britain	73.3	[100]	127.2	135	181
United States	46.9	127.8	298.1	533	528
Germany	27.4	71.2	137.7	158	214
France	25.1	36.8	57.3	82	74
Russia	24.5	47.5	76.6	72	152
Austria-Hungary	14	25.6	40.7	–	–
Italy	8.1	13.6	22.5	37	46
Japan	7.6	13	25.1	45	88

Energy consumption of the powers, 1890–1938 (in millions of metric tonnes of coal equivalent)

	1890	1900	1910	1913	1920	1930	1938
United States	147	248	483	541	694	762	697
Great Britain	145	171	185	195	212	184	196
Germany	71	112	158	187	159	177	228
France	36	47.9	55	62.5	65	97.5	84
Austria-Hungary	19.7	29	40	49.4	–	–	–
Russia	10.9	30	41	54	14.3	65	177
Japan	4.6	4.6	15.4	23	34	55.8	96.5
Italy	4.5	5	9.6	11	14.3	24	27.8

Source: Kennedy, Paul. 1988. *Rise and Fall of the Great Powers: Economic and Military Conflict from 1500 to 2000*. London, UK. Fontana Press.

1   Using the information in the tables above, rank the countries according to how powerful they were in 1914. What criteria are you using? What is your definition of power in this context? What happens to your ranking if you take into consideration the information in the tables on page 111?

2   What conclusions can you draw about the relationship between the information and a country's ability to conduct a war?

3   Compare and contrast each country's pre-war and post-war figures. What conclusions can we draw from the comparison? How did this affect your "power ranking"?

Key questions

→ How did the war change from one of movement to a trench-bound stalemate?

→ What was the relationship of offensive technology to defensive technology on the Western Front?

→ To what extent did technology break the stalemate?

Key concepts

→ Continuity

→ Change

→ Significance

Opening moves

As the month of July 1914 came to a close, so too ended what little hope for peace remained in Europe. Germany threw the infamous "iron dice" by declaring war on Russia on 1 August 1914. Regardless of whether the war was or was not at this point a foregone conclusion, the leaders felt that they were reacting rather than acting and as such embraced what they thought was out of their control. To the Kaiser the sword had been forced into Germany's hand. From that point the machinery of the alliance system, perceived national self-interest, and mobilization operated as suspected, if not intended, and the powers of Europe tumbled into war.

Timeline

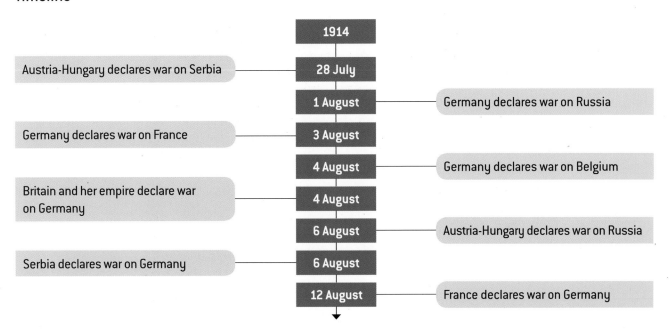

	1914	
Austria-Hungary declares war on Serbia	28 July	
	1 August	Germany declares war on Russia
Germany declares war on France	3 August	
	4 August	Germany declares war on Belgium
Britain and her empire declare war on Germany	4 August	
	6 August	Austria-Hungary declares war on Russia
Serbia declares war on Germany	6 August	
	12 August	France declares war on Germany

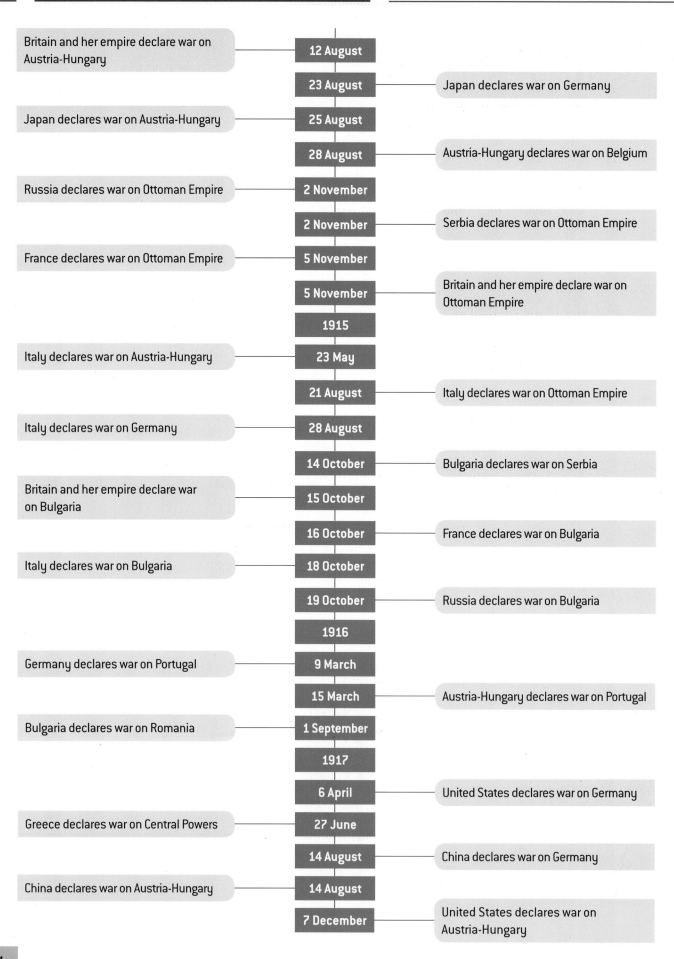

Britain and her empire declare war on Austria-Hungary	**12 August**
	23 August — Japan declares war on Germany
Japan declares war on Austria-Hungary	**25 August**
	28 August — Austria-Hungary declares war on Belgium
Russia declares war on Ottoman Empire	**2 November**
	2 November — Serbia declares war on Ottoman Empire
France declares war on Ottoman Empire	**5 November**
	5 November — Britain and her empire declare war on Ottoman Empire
	1915
Italy declares war on Austria-Hungary	**23 May**
	21 August — Italy declares war on Ottoman Empire
Italy declares war on Germany	**28 August**
	14 October — Bulgaria declares war on Serbia
Britain and her empire declare war on Bulgaria	**15 October**
	16 October — France declares war on Bulgaria
Italy declares war on Bulgaria	**18 October**
	19 October — Russia declares war on Bulgaria
	1916
Germany declares war on Portugal	**9 March**
	15 March — Austria-Hungary declares war on Portugal
Bulgaria declares war on Romania	**1 September**
	1917
	6 April — United States declares war on Germany
Greece declares war on Central Powers	**27 June**
	14 August — China declares war on Germany
China declares war on Austria-Hungary	**14 August**
	7 December — United States declares war on Austria-Hungary

Armies from all the major powers began to move toward each other. Railways made the initial part of this process more efficient than in past wars, but mass transport soon reached its limits and the men and horses detrained and finished the trek on foot. The bulk of the French forces rushed east to the frontier of Alsace-Lorraine. The British Expeditionary Force (BEF) disembarked in France and headed south-east, toward the Belgian frontier. For their part, over a million German soldiers moved west, executing the beginning of the Schlieffen Plan that would, if the plan worked, bring them to Paris 41 days later. Because these massive formations of men and animals were moving much as armies had for millennia – on foot – it would be two weeks before they would be in a position to engage each other in the first of the major battles of the war.

Belgium

The right wing of the German army, according to the plan, would swing through Belgium en route to Paris. The Belgians, for their part, would defend themselves as best as they could. While its army was small by the standards of the major powers, Belgium had invested heavily in a string of frontier fortifications that were imposing by any standards. These forts, designed to withstand the largest guns in existence at the time they were built, were concentrated around the city of Liège and commanded the most accessible route through Belgium from Germany.

The German Second Army consisting of over 300 000 men advanced on the forts, 12 in total manned by only 70 000 men. The Germans took the city, with the help of bomb-dropping Zeppelins – one of the first uses of aerial bombardment in history. In order to neutralize the surrounding forts, however, the Germans would use massive siege howitzers including the "Big Bertha", a 420 millimetre gun that hurled a 770 kilogram shell 12 kilometres. Within 11 days of the initial attack, the Germans had captured the forts, leaving the rest of Belgium open to the sweep of the Schlieffen Plan.

▲ One of the biggest guns of the war, the "Big Bertha" could hurl a shell 12 kilometres

Technology and war: aircraft

Like many military innovations, the airplane was not immediately recognized by commanders as having any military potential beyond reconnaissance. This was perhaps understandable given that early model airplanes were little more than lacquered canvas stretched across a wooden frame with a seat, engine and fuel tank. But as with all completely new technology, advancements came quickly, with new models being churned out in a matter of weeks in some instances. Very soon airplanes were armed and fighting for domination of the sky, which meant impeding the reconnaissance of your enemy, sighting for more accurate artillery fire and eventually supporting the movement of ground troops with aerial fire.

Fighters: Designed for air-to-air combat, manoeuvrability and firepower were the key factors in a successful fighter. Innovations included the interrupter gear, which allowed machine guns to be fired forward through the propeller and triplanes such as the Fokker, which, though more difficult to fly, were far more manoeuvrable than two-winged planes. Fighters were used to harass enemy reconnaissance airplanes and balloons and later provide fire support for the infantry while protecting their own bombing aircraft.

Bombers: Fewer models of bomber aircraft were produced, but these were constantly improved upon, namely their range and the weight of bombs they could carry. Strategic bombing, whether by airplane or Zeppelins, targeted railroads and eventually factories in the enemy's rear from 1915.

Airships: Germany's Zeppelins flew too high for most fighter planes and as such could attack British cities at will early in the war. By 1916 better airplanes armed with incendiary ammunition curtailed the effectiveness of Germany's Zeppelin fleet.

▲ A British Sopwith Camel. How did the role of the airplane change over the course of the war?

The Battle of the Frontiers

As Schlieffen's Plan unfolded in the north, it was time for Plan XVII to be put into action. The Battle of the Frontiers was actually a series of offensives mounted by the French as part of Plan XVII and counteroffensives by the German Sixth and Seventh armies. As early as

7 August the French had started operations to recapture the Alsatian city of Mulhouse. On 14 August the French army launched itself into Lorraine to liberate the territories taken after the humiliation of the Franco-Prussian War. At first Plan XVII, relying on the doctrine of the offensive and its combination of boldness and *élan*, seemed to be working well. The Germans fell back and the French retook cities such as Mulhouse. The French advance, however, was not uniform and this fact opened up gaps between the advancing French units – gaps that the Germans would exploit in their counteroffensive launched on 20 August. Other engagements happened at places like Sambre and in the Ardennes, the net result of which was defeat for the French. By 24 August the French advance was halted and with it the hopes of Plan XVII.

Class discussion

Why did Plan XVII fail? What are the inherent problems with war plans?

The Battle of the Marne (5–12 September 1914)

Plan XVII had been a massive failure for the French army resulting in some 200 000 casualties including 75 000 dead, 25 000 of them killed in a single day (22 August). This staggering defeat seemed to indicate that the Schlieffen Plan, unlike its French counterpart, was working as had been intended.

The German armies resumed their great sweep through Belgium after subduing unexpectedly stiff Belgian resistance. The BEF delayed the German offensive briefly at Mons, but then pulled back in what would become known as the Great Retreat. Again, all seemed to be going according to plan for the Germans, but it remained to be seen if Paris would fall within the required 41 days from mobilization.

▲ German troops dig in at the Marne

Ironically, as the Germans pushed forward and the Anglo-French forces pulled back toward Paris, a number of factors began to emerge that would prove beneficial to the defenders.

- As they retreated, the Anglo-French shortened their supply and communication lines while the Germans extended theirs.

- A principle known as the "diminishing power of the offensive" was beginning to tell on the Germans. As they advanced, casualties, the need to garrison captured territory, physical exhaustion and

Thinking and communication skills

A vital component of the Battle of the Marne was the decision of Field Marshal Sir John French and the British to commit troops to General Joffre's plan for the Marne. French took some persuading. Choose to represent either Joffre or French and develop arguments as to why the BEF should risk annihilation to help the French and why they should not. How might emotion have contributed to the final decision? How does this link with TOK?

lengthening supply lines requiring more men to maintain them weakened the German attackers. The further the Germans advanced, the weaker their force became.

- The Belgian resistance had afforded the military governor of Paris, General Gallieni, time to cobble together a new army to defend the capital.

When a French aviator spotted the German First Army wheeling in front of Paris – and not around Paris as Schlieffen had intended – thus exposing its right flank to the French Sixth Army guarding Paris, the French commander, Joffre, saw his opportunity for a counteroffensive. He ordered the French Sixth Army defending Paris to slam into the right flank of the Germans. When the German First Army commander, General von Kluck, turned to meet this threat it opened up a 50-kilometre gap between the German First and Second Armies. Joffre pleaded with the BEF to join the fight and drive into the gap along with the French Fifth Army. These actions stopped the German advance and thus spelled the end of the Schlieffen Plan. The German Chief of Staff, von Moltke, far away in his Luxembourg headquarters, had an imperfect and delayed picture of events as they unfolded at the Marne owing to a tortured communications system. His cautious nature revealed itself in this stressful situation and on 9 September he ordered his army to withdraw and prepare defences 65 kilometres to the rear. The Schlieffen Plan had failed. Now what?

The Race to the Sea

The retreat and subsequent entrenchment of the German First and Second Armies set in motion a series of events that would determine the topography of the Western Front for the rest of the war and is sometimes referred to as "The Race to the Sea".

An enduring military manoeuvre is to outflank one's enemy. It threatens them with encirclement and requires that they defend in two directions. It was just such a manoeuvre to which the three major armies operating in France now turned their attention. The French and British armies probed north and west for a way around the German flank. The Germans did likewise. This series of movements and counter movements, accompanied by the entrenching of ground that was held, extended the front to the English Channel. Similar operations on the south-east end of the front resulted in a more or less continuous front stretching 700 kilometres from the Alps to the Channel. All along this front both sides were digging furiously.

Trench warfare

The stalemate that developed on the Western Front, a massively complex system of entrenchments, can be seen as an uneven clash of technologies in which, for the majority of the war, those that were defensive in nature were stronger than those that were offensive in nature. This imbalance favoured the Germans, as they were the defenders in this context, fighting to hold on to the territory gained in August and September of 1914. Paradoxically, the defensive technology that dominated the Western Front seems primitive in comparison to some of the technologies designed to overcome them. Defences were based on the shovel and barbed wire, later augmented with concrete. The machine gun, of more use as a defensive weapon early in the war, is an exception. Of flamethrowers, trench mortars, gas, **mines** and tanks only the latter seemed to hold any hope of breaching the ever-strengthening defenses.

Nor was strategy up to the task of overcoming the geography of the Western Front. Short of siege warfare, military strategy had always been predicated on some form of movement. Feints, outflanking, encirclement, all required a degree of mobility that the trenches denied both sides. Because the front was basically continuous from the Alps to the Channel, getting around the flank of the enemy was out of the question. Technology, such as aircraft, did not yet allow for troops to be moved over the front lines. Amphibious landings were incredibly dangerous and logistically taxing. In the absence of these strategic options, breaking through became the only feasible alternative. It is to this alternative that the Allies, and to a degree the Germans, resorted for the rest of the war on the Western Front.

The Second Battle of Ypres erupted five months after the Germans had abandoned the first, with the introduction in the west of a new weapon – poison gas.

The German army in the Ypres sector released 170 tonnes of chlorine gas on 22 April 1915, advancing behind the deadly cloud as it drifted toward the Allied lines held by French colonial troops. In a matter of minutes the gas had caused 10 000 Allied casualties and opened a huge gap in the Allied lines. The success of the attack shocked the attackers as much as the defenders and the gap was only exploited to a depth of three kilometres. A second gas attack two days later targeted newly arrived Canadian troops who, though giving some ground, blunted the German attack using improvised gas masks losing close to 6,000 casualties, including 1,000 dead. The entire peacetime Canadian army had numbered only 6,000 men. By the time the Germans called a halt to their offensive on 24 May they had significantly shrunk the size of the Ypres salient by taking important high ground to the north and east. But the city and a pocket measuring 5 kilometres by 8 kilometres around it remained in Allied hands. The Allies had suffered close to 70 000 casualties at the Second Battle of Ypres. The Germans suffered half as many.

---

mines

Explosive charges concealed underground. Mines can be massive with tonnes of explosives dug into deep subterranean shafts or small anti-personnel devices designed to maim a single individual.

ATL **Research skills**

The scale of the casualties in the first months of the war staggered even the most hardened generals. How did the casualties for August–September 1914 compare to the casualties in previous wars (Franco-Prussian, Anglo-Boer, and Crimean)? What are possible explanations for these differences?

TOK discussion

Fritz Haber was the German chemist who developed chlorine as a chemical weapon. He later won the Nobel Prize in chemistry for the Haber–Bosch Process.

"We should misjudge this scientist [Fritz Haber] seriously if we were to judge him only by his harvest. The stimulation of research and the advancement of younger scholars become ever more important to him than his own achievements."

Richard Willstätter

To what extent do you agree with Willstätter in terms of Haber's work with chemical weapons?

Technology and war: gas

Gas used in the First World War was generally of three types:

- tearing agents
- asphyxiants
- blistering agents.

The first gas to be used was deployed by the German army on the Eastern Front. It was a tearing agent and although it briefly incapacitated the Russians, it was generally ineffective.

Chlorine was the first common gas used by both sides. It was greenish in colour and caused irritation to the eyes and corruption of the lungs. Death came by asphyxiation.

Phosgene was a deadlier variant of chlorine that was hard to detect. It was often mixed with chlorine, combining the controllability of chlorine with the lethality of phosgene.

Mustard gas was the most common blistering agent. On contact with the skin, especially moist areas such as the armpits and groin, it would cause severe burns. If inhaled it would burn away the lining of the lungs. Death would often come some days or even weeks after inhalation. Mustard gas was heavier than air and would rest in the low areas of shell holes for days, impeding an enemy's movements on the battlefield.

More than one million casualties were caused by gas during the war.

▲ French soldiers and their mounts prepare for a gas attack

Source skills

Chemical warfare

Read the following two accounts of the use of gas in warfare and answer the questions that follow.

Kurds recall gas attack horror at Saddam Trial

BAGHDAD, Iraq — A survivor testified Wednesday at the genocide trial of Saddam Hussein that Iraqi warplanes bombarded a Kurdish village with chemical weapons in 1987 and helicopters pursued those who fled into the hills and bombed them.

For a second day, survivors took the stand in the trial, in which Saddam and six co-defendants are charged over the 1987–1988 Anfal campaign, a military sweep against the Kurds of northern Iraq in which tens of thousands of people were killed.

After hearing from four survivors, chief judge Abdullah al-Amiri adjourned the trial until Sept. 11, to give time to consider an appeal from defense lawyers about the court's legitimacy.

Earlier, Adiba Oula Bayez described the Aug. 16, 1987 bombardment of her village of Balisan, saying warplanes dropped bombs that spread a smoke that smelled "like rotten apples."

"Then my daughter Narjis came to me, complaining about pain in her eyes, chest and stomach. When I got close to see what's wrong with her, she threw up all over me," Bayez, a mother of five, said. "When I took her in to wash her face ... all my other children were throwing up."

"Then my condition got bad, too. And that's when we realized that the weapon was poisonous and chemical," she said.

Bayez said the villagers fled to nearby caves on mules, "but the helicopters came and bombed the mountains to prevent the villagers from taking refuge anywhere."

Like many villagers, she was blinded by the gas, she said. In the caves, people were vomiting blood, many had burns. "All I knew was that I was holding tight my five children," she said. "I couldn't see, I couldn't do anything, the only thing I did was scream, 'Don't take my kids away from me.'"

The villagers were taken by the military to a prison camp, and Bayez said four people kept in the same room with her died. On the fifth day in jail, she pried open her swollen eyes with her fingers to see, and "I saw my children's' eyes swollen, their skin blackened," she said.

Another Balisan resident, Badriya Said Khider, said nine of her relatives were killed in the bombing and the military sweep afterwards, including her parents, two brothers, husband and son.

A man claiming to be a former Kurdish guerrilla, or peshmerga, also took the stand, accounting several attacks he witnessed in 1987 and 1988, including an August 1988 chemical weapons attack on the village of Ikmala in which his brother's family was killed.

"On the ground outside their house, my brother Saleh and his son Shaaban were on the ground dead, hugging each other, and a few meters (yards) away was my brother's wife," said Moussa Abdullah Moussa. "I can't tell the feeling I had. Only the eye and heart that saw that can describe it."

The accounts resembled those of two other survivors of the attack on Balisan and the neighboring village of Sheik Wasan who testified Tuesday in the trial. Bayez's husband, Ali Mostafa Hama, testified on Tuesday.

The survivors are testifying as plaintiffs in the case. Asked by the judges whom she wished to file her complaint against, Bayez exclaimed, "I complain against Saddam Hussein, Ali Hassan al-Majid and everyone in the [defendants'] box. May God blind them all."

Source: www.msnbc.msn.com/id/14475531/ #storyContinued

Account of gas attack – 1916

Arthur Empey was an American living in New Jersey when war consumed Europe in 1914. Enraged by the sinking of the Lusitania and loss of the lives of American passengers, he expected to join an American army to combat the Germans. When America did not immediately declare war, Empey boarded a ship to England, enlisted in the British army and was soon manning a trench on the front lines.

We join his story as he sits in a trench peering towards German lines. Conditions are perfect for a gas attack – a slight breeze blowing from the enemy's direction. The warning has been passed along to be on the lookout:

We had a new man at the periscope, on this afternoon in question; I was sitting on the fire step, cleaning my rifle, when he called out to me: "There's a sort of greenish, yellow cloud rolling along the ground out in front, it's coming–" But I waited for no more, grabbing my bayonet, which was detached from the rifle, I gave the alarm by banging an empty shell case, which was hanging near the periscope. At the same instant, gongs started ringing down the trench, the signal for Tommy to don his respirator, or smoke helmet, as we call it. Gas travels quietly, so you must not lose any time; you generally have about eighteen or twenty seconds in which to adjust your gas helmet.

A gas helmet is made of cloth, treated with chemicals. There are two windows, or glass eyes, in it, through which you can see. Inside there is a rubber-covered tube, which goes in the mouth. You breathe through your nose; the gas, passing through the cloth helmet, is neutralized by the action of the chemicals. The foul air is exhaled through the tube in the mouth, this tube being so constructed that it prevents the inhaling of the outside air or gas. One helmet is good for five hours of the strongest gas. Each Tommy carries two of them slung around his shoulder in a waterproof canvas bag. He must wear this bag at all times, even while sleeping. To change a defective helmet, you take out the new one, hold your breath, pull the old one off, placing the new one over your head, tucking in the loose ends under the collar of your tunic.

For a minute, pandemonium reigned in our trench, Tommies adjusting their helmets, bombers running here and there, and men turning out of the dugouts with fixed bayonets, to man the fire step. Reinforcements were pouring out of the communication trenches. Our gun's crew was busy mounting the machine gun on the parapet and bringing up extra ammunition from the dugout.

German gas is heavier than air and soon fills the trenches and dugouts… We had to work quickly, as Fritz generally follows the gas with an infantry attack. A company man on our right was too slow in getting on his helmet; he sank to the ground, clutching at his throat, and after a few spasmodic twistings, went West [died]. It was horrible to see him die, but we were powerless to help him. In the corner of a traverse, a little, muddy cur dog, one of the company's pets, was lying dead, with his two paws over his nose. It's the animals that suffer the most, the horses, mules, cattle, dogs, cats, and rats, they having no helmets to save them.

A gas, or smoke helmet, as it is called, at the best is a vile-smelling thing, and it is not long before one gets a violent headache from wearing it.

Our eighteen-pounders were bursting in No Man's Land, in an effort, by the artillery, to disperse the gas clouds. The fire step was lined with crouching men, bayonets fixed, and bombs near at hand to repel the expected attack. Our artillery had put a barrage of curtain fire on the German lines, to try and break up their attack and keep back reinforcements.

I trained my machine gun on their trench and its bullets were raking the parapet. Then over they came, bayonets glistening. In their respirators, which have a large snout in front, they looked like some horrible nightmare. All along our trench, rifles and machine guns spoke, our shrapnel was bursting over their heads. They went down in heaps, but new ones took the place of the fallen. Nothing could stop that mad rush. The Germans reached our barbed wire…

Suddenly, my head seemed to burst from a loud "crack" in my ear. Then my head began to swim, throat got dry, and a heavy pressure on the lungs warned me that my helmet was leaking. Turning my gun over to No. 2, I changed helmets. The trench started to wind like a snake, and sandbags appeared to be floating in the air. The noise was horrible; I sank onto the fire step, needles seemed to be pricking my flesh, then blackness.

I was awakened by one of my mates removing my smoke helmet. How delicious that cool, fresh air felt in my lungs. A strong wind had arisen and dispersed the gas. They told me that I had been "out" for three hours; they thought I was dead.

I examined my first smoke helmet, a bullet had gone through it on the left side, just grazing my ear, the gas had penetrated through the hole made in the cloth.

Out of our crew of six, we lost two killed and two wounded. That night we buried all of the dead, excepting those in No Man's Land. In death there is not much distinction, friend and foe are treated alike.

Source: Eyewitness to History, www.eyewitnesshistory. com/gas.htm

Questions

1 Compare and contrast the two accounts of being attacked by gas. How might you account for the differences?

2 What can you surmise about the goals of the Iraqi forces? What were the goals of the German army?

3 Gas was not used extensively in 20th-century wars after 1918. Why might this be?

4 Construct a table comparing the advantages and disadvantages of gas as a weapon. Is gas any more or less "humane" than other weapons? Explain your answer.

The Battle of Verdun (February–October 1916)

The German attempt to break the stalemate on the Western Front centred on the French army entrenched around the city of Verdun. The operation was the brainchild of the German Chief of the General Staff Erich von Falkenhayn. Initially he wanted to attack the French with such ferocity that they could not surrender, that they would "bleed the French white" to use his chilling phrase. Like the British attack at the Somme later in the year, the German attack, code named Operation Judgment, would require the stockpiling of a massive amount of resources. Along 13 kilometres of front the Germans would deploy eight divisions plus reserves and 1,200 artillery pieces, including some of the enormous guns that had been so effective in Belgium during the first weeks of the war. To feed these guns the Germans had amassed 2.5 million shells.

▲ German artillery at Verdun. What role did artillery play in the German plan at Verdun?

The opening of the battle was postponed because of weather, allowing the French to bolster their defences. When it finally erupted on 21 February, the bombardment came close to smashing the French defenders – 100 000 shells an hour rained on the defenders hunkered down in their dugouts, trenches and forts. The German plan, however, called for cautious advance, as the intention was to kill as many French soldiers as possible rather than seize territory. The defence of the city and its environs was entrusted to General Pétain. He determined that the French would use the doctrine of active defence – contesting every bit of ground, giving way only to counter-attack later. The Germans, for their part, continued to hammer them with their artillery and then follow up with infantry. It became increasingly difficult for the Germans to move their heavy guns forward across the torn landscape. The city of Verdun was ringed by a series of forts and hills, which became the focus of the German attack. The doctrine of active defence meant that it was hard to keep track of which side held what ground. The village of Vaux changed hands 13 times in March alone. The key to French resistance was a single road supplying Verdun, which the Germans never managed to cut.

From April Falkenhayn ordered his army to attack along the whole front and so continued to press the French throughout the spring. The problem was that he was now being drawn into a battle of attrition, the exact thing into which he wanted to draw the French – the German army was beginning to bleed itself white. By the end of June the German casualties were on a par with the French, about 200 000. In the sporadic fighting around Verdun that would last until December, each side would lose approximately 350 000 casualties.

▲ Canadian infantry on the front lines in April 1916

Technology and war: communications

Directing the movement of groups of soldiers in as close to real time as possible has always been both the key to victory on the battlefield and a considerable challenge. When armies and formations were relatively small, runners or riders could carry commands verbally, the speed of communication limited only by the speed of the carrier and the distance travelled. As armies and battlefields grew in size and complexity, sound (bugles, drums, or pipes) or visuals (usually flags) were used. The amount of smoke and noise produced in a Napoleonic or American Civil War battle, however, made such advances impractical once a large engagement commenced. The telephone held some promise, but was dependent on stable wires.

The massive armies and immense battlefields of the First World War brought all these issues into sharp relief. Generals were often miles to the rear of fronts that themselves stretched for miles – the Germans attacked along 13 kilometres of front at Verdun. The Somme front on 1 July 1916 was twice as long. Timely information to a Brigadier General about the progress of his men could take hours and therefore the tactical situation could be, and often was, entirely different by the time new orders reached those who had to carry them out. Telephone wires were generally cut within the first minutes of a battle. Wireless sets were huge and unreliable, not to mention easily intercepted by the enemy. And so tactical communication in this modern war reverted to methods used for hundreds of years in some cases.

Trench runners: All armies employed soldiers whose sole responsibility was to convey messages through the labyrinthine trench system. This was very dangerous work and required a good knowledge of the trench system, a system that could change regularly.

Flags: Semaphore flags were used by all services. Competent signalers could send up to 12 words a minute if visibility was uninterrupted, which was a complication by the very nature of trench warfare.

Heliographs and lamps: Heliographs communicated Morse code by concentrating sunlight, making them useless at night. Paraffin and later battery operated lamps overcame this limitation, but were still limited by line of sight.

Carrier pigeons: Pigeons were a remarkably reliable communication method during the war. The British army had some 22 000 pigeons in service at any one time during the war and by the end had used some 100 000. Only about 2% of those released failed to return.

The Battle of the Somme (July–November 1916)

The epitome of offensive strategy to which the Allied generals on the Western Front aspired was to breach the enemy's lines with a combination of massive artillery pounding followed up with waves of infantry. Cavalry, held in reserve, would then exploit the breach in the lines, and pour into the open fields in the enemy's rear, restoring movement and a more familiar style of warfare to the front. Neither the sodden land on the north end of the front nor the broken, rocky land in the south was suited to this strategy. This left the centre from Verdun through Champagne and Picardy to Amiens as the logical place for such massive undertakings.

After the wasteful operations of 1915, both sides decided that the drive to end the war would be postponed until 1916. The interim would be spent amassing the enormous resources they thought would be required to break the stalemate. The process started with the British army itself. Tiny by pre-war standards – the Kaiser had famously referred to it as a "contemptible little army" – the British army had swelled to close to 2 million men. It was decided that this "New Army" would attack jointly with the French along the Somme River. The advance would require:

- the building of new rail lines with a total of 17 railheads
- 1,500 artillery pieces of various sizes
- 3 million shells for these guns
- 11 200 kilometres of buried telephone cable
- 69 000 kilometres of above ground cable
- thousands of carrier pigeons
- 100 000 horses
- lodging for 400 000 men
- 300 water trucks.

The plan seemed straightforward. A massive week-long artillery bombardment would target both the German barbed wire and the artillery (counter-battery targeting) with such devastating effect that there would be virtually nothing left to oppose the advance of the infantry. On 1 July 1916 this artillery assault would be supplemented by the detonation of massive underground "mines" which had been laboriously tunneled 18 metres under the German lines. As the attacking infantry rose from their trenches to advance across "no man's land" they would be preceded by a "creeping barrage" that would provide a theoretical shield delivering them unscathed to the destroyed enemy trench lines. In General Haig's mind, this breach would be filled by rushing British cavalry to a distance

▲ British wounded at the Battle of the Somme

of 11 kilometres on the first day. His subordinate General Rawlinson thought a more modest advance was more likely. None of this transpired.

The operation was to be launched at the beginning of August, but Joffre asked that it be moved up by a month in order to take pressure off the French army at Verdun. The bombardment, fierce though it was, did not destroy the barbed wire as much as it threw it around and jumbled it further. The creeping barrage on the whole "crept" too quickly, outstripping the advancing infantry and thus offering them little protection. The German dugouts were equal to the incredible pounding they took during this horrendous week and the German machine gunners clamoured out, dazed but operational, when the bombardment passed over them. What they saw amazed them: wave upon wave of British soldiers advancing toward them as though the Germans and their machine guns did not exist. While some elements of the attacking force did make it into the enemy trenches, the vast majority of the attacking troops were stopped in no man's land with horrific losses. Some units of the second wave were ordered to attack from the second (support) trench lines because the forward trenches were choked with the dead and wounded and were cut down before they reached their own front line. When the grim accounting was completed, 60 000 of an attacking force of 100 000 were casualties – 20 000 of these were dead.

Class discussion

What role did poor communication play in the disastrous first day at the Somme?

> ## Technology and war: machine guns
>
> The quintessential weapon of the industrial age, the machine gun was to mass killing as the assembly line was to mass production. Many had attempted to develop an automatically repeating weapon in the 19th century, but it was an American – Hiram Maxim – who designed a weapon that could fire up to 600 rounds a minute powered by the gas discharge from those same rounds.
>
> By the outbreak of hostilities in 1914 all modern armies had versions of Maxim's innovation. These were large weapons, which required a crew of four to six men to operate. Jamming and overheating were constant problems in the trying environment of trench warfare. Nevertheless, by the end of the war they could fire 1,200 rounds per minute and were mainstays of trench defences with ranges of up to 1,000 metres. Smaller, more portable machine guns were developed such as the Lewis gun or small Vickers machine guns. These could be mounted on aircraft and carried forward in infantry assaults.

Haig and the British would resume their attacks on the Somme front until November. The furthest advance was 12 kilometres. By November the British had suffered 420 000 casualties, the French 194 000 and the Germans 500 000.

Source skills

The Battle of the Somme

Source A

General Douglas Haig, dispatch summary of the battle, December 1916. (http://www.firstworldwar.com/source/haigsommedespatch.htm)

"Artillery bombardments were also carried out daily at different points on the rest of our front, and during the period from the 24th June to 1st July gas was discharged with good effect at more than forty places along our line, upon a frontage which in total amounted to over fifteen miles. Some 70 raids, too, were undertaken by our infantry between Gommecourt and our extreme left north of Ypres during the week preceding the attack, and these kept me well informed as to the enemy's dispositions, besides serving other useful purposes."

Source B

Private Tomlinson, 1/7th Sherwood Foresters. (Quoted in John Keegan, *The Face of Battle*.)

"When we got to the German wire, I was absolutely amazed to see it intact, after what we had been told. The Colonel and I took cover behind a small bank but after a bit the Colonel raised himself on his hands and knees to see better. Immediately he was hit in the forehead by a single bullet."

Source C

General de Lisle in a report to the Prime Minister of Newfoundland describing the efforts of the Newfoundland Regiment, which suffered 92% casualties on 1 July. (Quoted in Martin Gilbert, *The Battle of the Somme: The Heroism and Horror of War*.)

"It was a magnificent display of trained and disciplined valour, and its assault only failed of success because dead men can advance no further."

Source D

John Keegan, *The First World War*.

"If there was any exception to the unrelievedly disastrous results of 1 July 1916, it was that the German High Command ... had been gravely alarmed at the scale of the British attack, particularly because in one sector ... ground had been lost. ... Falkenhayn [Chief of the German General Staff] reacted to that loss in peremptory fashion, relieving the [commander] in whose sector it had occurred ..."

Questions

1 a   What does Keegan mean by "the scale of the British attack"? [Source D]

   b   What is General de Lisle implying in his statement? [Source C]

2   With reference to its origin, purpose and content, analyse the value and limitations of Source B for a historian studying the British attack on the Somme in 1916.

3   Compare and contrast what Sources A and B reveal about the bombardment that preceded the British attack on the Somme.

4   Using the sources and your own knowledge, evaluate the role that the bombardment played in the failure of the British attack on the Somme, 1 July 1916.

Passchendaele (July–November 1917)

After the great bloodletting of 1916, the Allies were near the point of exhaustion. The Russian army was near collapse as was the Russian Provisional Government that had taken control after the abdication of the Tsar in February of 1917. Fifty French divisions were in various states of mutiny, remaining in the trenches, but refusing to participate in any more of what they saw as fruitless assaults. The Italian army had bent but not broken in the face of an Austro-German assault at Caporetto, a route that had only barely been halted before Venice. That left the British.

In many ways the strategy for the British assault at the Battle of Passchendaele (also known as the Third Battle of Ypres) had not evolved much from the Battle of the Somme a year earlier. Expectations had though. The breakthrough was no longer the goal. Instead the British would advance after a longer and more intense artillery barrage than had preceded the Somme offensive and grab on to the German trenches, move the artillery forward and do it again. The barrage differed only in intensity – twice as long as before the Somme with twice as many guns firing four times as many shells across a narrower front. Needless to say, the attack was no surprise to the defenders. A new element of warfare – the tank – at first seemed to work well in the dry, though rough, surface of no man's land.

The progress was short-lived. A German counter-attack and the onset of torrential rain made any sort of advance impossible. The ground was so soft and the mud so oppressive that men were said to sink out of sight. Tanks became bogged down and the movement of artillery pieces became close to impossible.

Technology and war: tanks

A vehicle that could withstand withering machine gun fire and traverse the moonscape that was no man's land could theoretically lead to the breakthrough of which both sides dreamt. On paper the tank seemed to deliver exactly this. First developed by the British, the first tanks, so called to preserve secrecy and because of their resemblance to water tanks, posed as many problems as they solved. First introduced at the Somme front late in 1916, they were usually crewed by eight men, choked by the diesel and cordite fumes. These early tanks travelled 6 km/h and broke down frequently.

How to use these monstrosities? The Allies tended to divide the tanks up among infantry units and use them as armoured shelter for advancing soldiers. Following behind the tanks the British infantry was able to advance 3,500 metres with limited casualties at which time the unreliability of the new innovation began to tell. It was not until 1918 that the idea of massing tanks with coordinated artillery and air support was implemented. This approach worked very well and presaged the tank's use in the Second World War. In the end the Germans were the least enthused about the new technology, only producing about 20 tanks of their own, but using captured Allied tanks when they could. The French, on the other hand, produced over 4,000 of various models and the British about 2,600.

When the battle resumed the British won a series of smaller engagements in September that encouraged General Haig to attempt larger gains toward the village of Passchendaele. These assaults resulted in little more than a stalemate within a stalemate. British forces would bombard a section of the front and take the ground, only to have the German artillery pound the same ground and then have its infantry take it back. By the end of September the British units were exhausted. Haig called on Australian and New Zealand forces to resume the attack, which they did to little effect. The Canadian Corps resumed the assault on 26 October and on 6 November captured the now non-existent village of Passchendaele. Although casualty figures are disputed, the Allied Powers lost some 270 000 casualties taking the village and surrounding territory, the Germans around 200 000 defending it.

1918

The dawn of 1918 on the Western Front saw three exhausted armies staring at each other across a battered moonscape. Both sides, however, had some reason to hope. The Germans would soon being seeing new troops fresh from the now non-existent Russian front. For the Allies, hope stemmed from the thousands of American soldiers who were arriving in France each week – over 300 000 by March 1918 with another 1 million on the way by the summer. The German army knew, however, that despite the new soldiers, their economy and even their society could not outlast the economic juggernaut that was the United States. For the Germans 1918 would be a race – could they use their new forces and their submarines to knock Britain out of the war and thereby force the French to the negotiation table before they were crushed by the weight of US mobilization?

The German offensive that struck the British on 21 March was predicated on new tactics and these new tactics required speed. A debilitating three-hour artillery barrage was followed by "storm troopers" moving quickly, punching holes in the British lines and moving deep into the rear areas. Rather than contest strong points, the Storm Troopers bypassed them, leaving these for traditional infantry units to take. At the end of the day over 7,000 British soldiers had been killed. The speed of the offensive also resulted in the surrender of over 20 000 British soldiers. Although they had taken many of the British forward positions, the Germans had suffered over 39 000 casualties doing so, soldiers they could ill afford to lose if they were going to capitalize on the successes of the first day. The Allies were able to slow and, in some cases, reverse the German gains, but by the time the German offensive ground to a halt it was only 8 kilometres from Amiens. As impressive as the gains were, the overall goals of the operation were beyond the reach of the German armies. They had not "rolled up" the British line. They had not taken the channel ports and they had not separated the French and British armies. They had, however, exhausted themselves having lost 250 000 troops that they could not replace. The Allies jointly suffered a similar number of casualties, but with the steady influx of US troops the losses were less acutely felt. The Germans had lost the race.

By August it was the Allies' turn to try to end the war with a knockout blow. On 8 August they launched a massive attack in front of Amiens that coordinated tank forces, artillery, infantry and air support on a scale not previously attempted. German General Ludendorff called this "The black day of the German army". This set the tone for the rest of the war on the Western Front. In a series of actions collectively known as the Hundred Days, Allied forces progressively pushed the Germans back toward where they had started four years earlier. Once the German army, monarchy and government acknowledged this fact, the Germans asked for an armistice. By agreement, hostilities would cease at 11:00 am on 11 November 1918.

Key questions

→ How was the nature of combat on the Eastern Front different from that on the Western Front?

→ What role did naval forces play in the war?

→ In what ways did the Home Front contribute to the war effort?

Key concepts

→ Cause

→ Consequence

→ Perspective

The Eastern Front

In some ways the Schlieffen Plan did exactly the opposite to what its author envisioned. The entire plan had been based on the assumption of slow Russian mobilization. In fact the Russian First Army under General Rennenkampf invaded East Prussia well before many expected. Further, Schlieffen had envisioned a quick victory in the west and a long drawn out war in the east. The Germans in fact would have great success in the east at the end of August and early September 1914, at the same time that the Schlieffen Plan was unravelling at the Marne in France. In the words of John Keegan, it was "a plan pregnant with dangerous uncertainty". Those uncertainties became evident very early in the war.

The Russians invaded Germany with two armies that vastly outnumbered the German defenders. At the battle of Gumbinenn on 20 August 1914 the invaders bloodied the defenders. After a hasty reorganization of the German command in the east which saw Generals Ludendorff and Hindenburg, the two officers who would manage the German War effort from 1916 until the end of the war, rise to prominence, the Germans realized that the two Russian armies were not cooperating. In fact, there was deep personal animosity between the Russians commanding the two armies – Generals Samsonov and Rennenkampf. This allowed the Germans to transport their troops by train and defeat each army in turn without having to face their combined strength, which was considerably greater than their own. The result was the encirclement of the Russian Second Army at the Battle of Tannenberg. Rather than report to his Tsar that the Russian army had suffered 30 000 casualties and had 95 000 soldiers captured by the Germans, General Samsonov committed suicide.

One week later, Hindenburg wheeled his army to deal with the Russian First Army. At the subsequent Battle of the Masurian Lakes, Hindenburg's forces swept the invaders from Germany inflicting 95 000 casualties on the enemy. Rennenkampf withdrew to protect his army from encirclement and the Germans followed.

The topography and space of the east ensured that the war of movement would last longer on the Eastern Front than it had on the Western Front. After the twin defeats of Tannenberg and Masurian Lakes, the Russian army regrouped and returned to the offensive. The Austrian forces were not nearly as successful as their German allies and at one point in the autumn of 1914 the Russians threatened to sweep through Hungary. This came to nothing and the Eastern Front settled into a stalemate, though not as trench bound as the Western Front had become.

When Italy entered the war on the side of the Allies in 1915, the Austrians were obliged to move troops facing the Germans to the Italian front. The Russian General Brusilov judged this to be a good time to press the Germans on his front in the south. His offensive regained almost 100 miles of territory lost the previous year.

Gallipoli

With the stalemate in France becoming more intractable by the week, it seems, in hindsight, only obvious that the Allies would seek to open a new front in another theatre of war. By November 1914 both the French and the British were exploring such options. Over the objections of the commanders on the Western Front, a plan to attack the Ottoman Empire began to take shape.

> ## Class discussion
> What were the strategic benefits of attacking the Ottoman Empire at the Dardanelles?

The original plan was for a squadron of older model battleships, both French and British, to force their way up the narrow Dardanelle Straits with the help of mine sweepers, pounding at Turkish defenses as they went. While they were moderately successful at destroying the Turks' fixed guns, the defenders' mobile guns proved elusive. Within two hours of starting the operation the squadron was reduced by a third and had retired. The shore guns would have to be neutralized by land forces. On 25 April 1915 British forces landed on the southern tip of the Gallipoli Peninsula, followed four days later by soldiers of the Australia and New Zealand Army Corps (ANZAC). These two landings managed to carve out small patches of beach and surrounding hills, but nothing more. They were stopped by a combination of bad military intelligence, poor navigation, very rough terrain and the decisive action of the Turkish commander on the spot – Mustapha Kemal (later to be known as Kemal Ataturk when he became the president of post-war Turkey.) The British tried to break the stalemate with a third landing at Suvla Bay, which succeeded only in creating a third narrow enclave surrounded by Turkish forces.

> ## Class discussion
> Why are amphibious landings so dangerous for the attacking forces?

By the end of 1915 the Allied leadership acknowledged the fiasco for what it was and made plans to withdraw all their forces from the Gallipoli Peninsula. Between 28 December 1915 and 6 January 1916, the British and ANZAC forces abandoned their positions. The evacuation was perhaps the most successful military operation of the campaign, a campaign that cost the Allies 300 000 casualties and the Turks 250 000 casualties.

The war would drag on in the east as in the west. The war would bring with it economic and social pressures that would prove too great for the Russian Empire, which descended into revolution in 1917, eventually signing a separate peace, the Treaty of Brest-Litovsk, abandoning the conflict.

The War at Sea

It is one of the great ironies of the war that while the naval arms race between Britain and the German Empire was a major long-term cause of the war, the massive fleets created by this same race clashed only once during the war.

There were two critical problems that faced the German High Seas Fleet and therefore her naval strategy. The first was that, despite her frenzied pre-war shipbuilding, Germany still fell short of the numerical advantage of the Royal Navy. By the time the only major fleet engagement happened at Jutland in 1916 the Royal Navy had 31 Dreadnought battleships and Germany 18. It had a 2:1 advantage in battle cruisers and in all other ships the Royal Navy enjoyed a 1.6:1 numerical advantage.

The second disadvantage that weighed on German naval ambitions was geographical. The end goal of a surface fleet was to wage economic warfare on the enemy. One way to accomplish this was to bombard ports, something the Royal Navy's numerical advantage precluded. The other was to sink merchant ships in the shipping lanes of the open ocean. For the Germans the only access to these shipping lanes was through the English Channel, 34 kilometres wide at its narrowest, and the North Sea between Norway and Scotland, both bottlenecks controlled by the Royal Navy.

Throughout 1914 and 1915 the German High Seas Fleet adopted a hit and run approach. The fleet would emerge from its ports in less than full force, engage the Royal Navy advance force and retire before the bulk of the Grand Fleet could arrive. This strategy had resulted in the defeats at Heligoland Blight in 1914 and Dogger Bank in 1915, but not before inflicting some damage on their enemy. In 1916, however, a new commander brought a new attitude. Admiral Rheinhard Scheer began taking the fleet to sea looking for action. In May 1916 the Royal Navy decrypted German ciphers giving them advanced notice of a large sortie into the North Sea. The subsequent clash was the largest naval battle in history with both sides claiming victory. More efficient battle communications and safer ammunition and propellant storage meant that the Germans were able to inflict more damage than the Royal Navy. Unwilling to risk the rest of their fleet, however, the Germans returned to their bases, leaving the Royal Navy in command of the North Sea once again. The German High Seas Fleet would not emerge for the remainder of the war.

ATL Research skills

1 With the signing of Brest-Litovsk the German army was free to transfer all its units from the Eastern Front to the Western Front. How many soldiers were transferred?

2 How did this affect the balance of forces on the Western Front?

3 How long did it take the flow of American soldiers to nullify this increase?

Technology and war: submarines

The submarine, or U-boat, seemed to hold out the promise of blockading an enemy without the expense of a massive surface fleet. This was especially attractive to Germany whose surface fleet could not match the British Royal Navy and was in fact holed up in its North Sea ports for the vast majority of the war.

The German Imperial Navy began the war with about 30 functional U-boats. These were deployed both against the Royal Navy and the British merchant fleet plying the waters between North America and Britain. Early models were equipped with one torpedo tube, but later models could discharge multiple self-propelled torpedoes. The U-boat

brought new ethical dilemmas to naval warfare. They were unable to take on survivors of their attacks and lost all their advantage if they surfaced and warned their targets, as maritime law demanded they do. If the U-boats practised so-called "unrestricted" submarine warfare and attacked any ship deemed to be headed to an enemy port, however, they proved deadly. Unrestricted submarine warfare also solved the perpetual problem of having to accurately identify targets and from which country they sailed.

While the U-boat menace was very real, countermeasures such as convoys, depth charges and rudimentary sonar turned the tide in favour of the Allies.

The Home Front

By the time the terrible machine of the First World War ground to a halt in November 1918, tens of millions of men had been mobilized by the belligerent nations. It would be understatement to say the process of feeding, clothing and arming these vast armies was a massive undertaking – an undertaking that proved too much for a number of countries.

As we have discussed a total war is one in which a nation mobilizes all resources in the war effort. This includes industrial resources, financial resources, educational resources, agricultural resources, cultural resources and human resources. In the First World War this mobilization became known as the Home Front. The deadly logic of total war, however, is that if all of these resources are being used in the war effort, they will also become military targets.

The Home Front looked different in all countries, but we can identify certain aspects common to each. The major powers shared a belief that such vital economic activity could not be left to the whims of the free market and so they all created various government agencies to manage and coordinate the Home Front. Many countries passed sweeping legislation such as the War Measures Act in Canada and the Defence of the Realm Act in Britain that allowed governments to more directly control the economy and the lives of its citizens. Government agencies were established to directly manage wartime production. In the United States the War Industries Board coordinated production and procurement. In Canada the Munitions Resources Commission ensured a steady supply of raw materials for war production. Sometimes these agencies acted across national borders such as in the case of the Imperial Munitions Board.

The net result of these activities was a drastic increase in war production. What could not be produced domestically had to be imported. While Germany was able to maintain a fairly high level of steel and coal production and feed its army, partly as a result of the foreign territories it occupied, it was at the expense of consumer goods and food for civilians. Britain and France, on the other hand, had to import vast amounts of food and munitions from the United States, Australia, Canada and other countries not physically affected by the war.

UK Munitions Production, 1914–1918					
	1914	**1915**	**1916**	**1917**	**1918**
Artillery pieces	91	3390	4314	5137	8039
Tanks	–	–	150	1110	1359
Aircraft	200	1900	6100	14 700	32 000
Machine guns	300	6100	33 500	79 700	120 900

Source: Kennedy, Paul. 1988. *Rise and Fall of the Great Powers: Economic and Military Conflict from 1500 to 2000*. London, UK. Fontana Press.

This increase meant that resources had to be reallocated to the war effort and this meant consumer goods and even food had to be rationed. This reallocation of resources applied to the workforce as well. As men filled the ranks of the massive armies – 20% of France's population and 18% of Germany's population joined the military – their places in civilian walks of life were filled by women. In Britain over 1.5 million women took "non-traditional" jobs during the war.

The cruel logic of war is that if something is important to your enemy it must become a target. Both the Allies and the Central Powers took economic warfare to a new level during the war. The naval blockade had been the cornerstone of Britain's national defence for 300 years. While there had been an effort in 1909 to differentiate between war materials – contraband – and goods destined for non-military use, the issue was still disputed. International law permitted blockading contraband only. This designation, however, was meaningless once the war started. Britain used its massive surface fleet to turn back all ships bound for Germany. Eventually this blockade began to take its toll on both the German army and its civilian population. In the last two years of the war an estimated 800 000 German civilians died of undernourishment and related disorders.

For their part, the Germans used new military technology to conduct economic warfare. The German submarine fleet attempted to cut the vital flow of supplies to Britain, sinking over 15 million tonnes of shipping throughout the war and at one point in 1917 reducing her to only six weeks' reserve of food for the whole country. Her fleets of Zeppelin airships and later bomber aircraft, such as the Gotha, dropped bombs on British cities inflicting close to 5,000 casualties but causing no meaningful disruption in production.

5.5 Effects of the First World War

Political

By the time the leaders, diplomats, economists and various other functionaries gathered in Paris to grope their way to a peace settlement, the war had already imposed a number of significant political changes on Europe. The new Bolshevik state was beginning its rule in Russia. Germany had become a republic and was itself rocked by revolution. The Dual Monarchy of Austria had collapsed and had split into its constituent components. For its part Hungary would experiment with a communist state for a few weeks in 1919. In a flurry of competing interests, incomplete information, confused goals, and imperfect communication the leaders at Paris would try to redesign the map and power structure of Europe.

ATL Research and communication skills

Choose one of the following:

- Germany
- Austria-Hungary
- United States
- Great Britain
- France
- Reporters

For those representing a country, research your country and the Paris peace settlement according to the following categories:

- Economic, social, military condition in November 1918
- Military provisions of the treaties
- Territorial provisions of the treaties

For the reporters, research the terms of the treaties and generate a series of questions that attempt to elicit the motivations of the countries and what they think the strengths and weaknesses of the treaties are for their country.

Conduct a press conference in which:

- each country makes a presentation to outline its research findings
- the reporters ask each country representative questions and follow up questions
- the country representatives answer the questions.

Discuss and analyse the treaties and evaluate the Paris peace settlement.

Economic

The First World War was economically disastrous for all countries involved with the possible exception of the United States. The British Empire spent $23 billion on the war, France spent $9.3 billion and Germany $19.9 billion. Because these countries did not have this money, each incurred staggering amounts of debt. In the short time that the United States was in the war it managed to spend $17 billion. When belligerent countries went off the gold standard it expanded the money supply. Coupled with skyrocketing demand, this expansion created disastrous inflation. Demobilization brought the blight of high unemployment. Huge areas of northern France and eastern Europe were physically ravaged by the war and would not return to significant productivity until the mid-1920s. The terms of the peace treaties brought with them their own contribution to the economic devastation of the war. Although many historians believe that the amount of the reparations imposed was within Germany's ability to pay, the wisdom of requiring it to do so is doubtful. Likewise the schedule of reparation payments was unrealistic.

Social

As a watershed, the First World War had wide-ranging effects on society. Women flooded into the workplace like never before. While women had always composed an important part of each country's workforce, the war required they take up occupations traditionally monopolized by men. Middle-class women entered the workforce in greater numbers than ever before. With this independent income also came a degree of social independence. When demobilization dumped millions of male workers back into the economy and industrial demand shrank to peacetime levels, many of these women found themselves out of work. Nevertheless the wartime contributions of women and political necessities combined to expand the franchise to women in many countries.

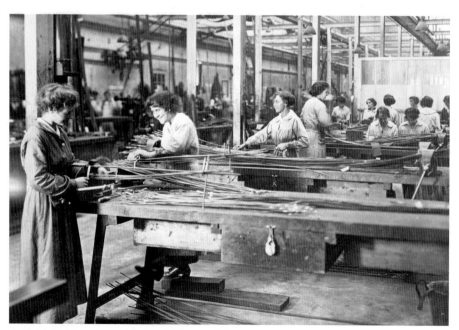

▲ British women at work in a steel factory. Why was it that many of the gains that woman had made during the war were short-lived?

As reflections of the wider world it is not surprising that the arts were affected by the war. The horrors of the trenches spawned new artistic movements such as Dada and Surrealism. The German artist Otto Dix and the works of the British war poets such as Wilfred Owen and Siegfried Sassoon brought the emotional power to bear on their wartime experiences. In the post-war years personal memoirs by the likes of Robert Graves and Erich Maria Remarque were very popular and remain an intriguing source of information on the war. The entry of the United States brought jazz music, that uniquely American music form, to Europe, with it becoming wildly popular in the cafés of France and Germany in the 1920s and 1930s.

ATL Thinking skills

On an outline map of Europe in 1914 draw the borders of the following successor states:

- Latvia
- Lithuania
- Estonia
- Czechoslovakia
- Yugoslavia
- Hungary
- Poland
- Finland

1 On what basis did the diplomats and leaders at Versailles draw these borders? Did the same principles apply to territories outside of Europe? Why or why not? Give an example.

2 Which 1914 countries would have objected to these boundaries? Why?

3 Identify points of potential conflict based in the 1919 map.

Exam-style questions and further reading

Exam-style questions

1 Examine the role of domestic concerns in causing the First World War.

2 Evaluate the role technology played in the outcome of the First World War.

3 To what extent did strategy determine the outcome of the First World War?

4 Discuss the economic causes of the First World War.

5 Evaluate the importance of sea power in the outcome of the First World War.

6 Evaluate the strengths and weaknesses of the Schlieffen Plan.

7 To what extent was the First World War a total war?

8 Discuss the role of the United States in the First World War.

9 Compare and contrast military operations on the Eastern Front and the Western Front.

10 Examine the failure of both German and Allied offensives in 1916.

Further reading

Ferguson, Niall. 1999. *The Pity of War: Explaining World War I.* Basic Books. New York, USA.

Fromkin, David. 2004. *Europe's Last Summer: Who Started the Great War in 1914?* Alfred Knopf. New York, USA

Fussell, Paul. 1975. *The Great War and Modern Memory.* Oxford University Press. Oxford, UK.

Gilbert, Martin. 2006. *The Battle of the Somme: The Heroism and Horror of War.* McClelland and Stewart. Toronto, Canada.

Herwig, Holger H. 2011. *The Marne, 1914: The Opening of World War I and the Battle that Changed the World.* Random House. New York, USA.

Keegan, John. *The First World War.* A. Knopf (distributed by Random House). New York, USA.

Kennedy, Paul. 1988. *Rise and Fall of the Great Powers: Economic and Military Conflict from 1500 to 2000.* London, UK. Fontana Press.

MacMillan, Margaret. 2013. *The War That Ended Peace: The Road to 1914.* Allen Lane. Toronto, Canada.

MacMillan, Margaret. 2002. *Paris 1919: Six Months That Changed the World.* Random House. New York, USA.

Sondhaus, Lawrence. 2014. *The Great War at Sea: A Naval History of the First World War.* Cambridge University Press. Cambridge, UK.

Strachan, Hew. 2003. *The First World War.* Oxford University Press. Oxford, UK.

Writing introductions and conclusions

Introductions and conclusions are key elements in any essay and yet they generally receive little attention. This is especially true in timed, high-stress situations such as IB exams. When time is a factor you need to make sure that everything you write contributes to the completion of the task. There should be no "throwaway" sentences or paragraphs. Introductions and conclusions count.

Introductions

The introduction contains the most important element of the essay – your thesis. The thesis is essentially your answer to the question and must be the focus of the rest of the essay.

Generally speaking, you should structure the sentences in your introduction from general to specific, with the thesis as your last sentence being the most specific. While these sentences are general in nature, they should still address the question. While context is important, the introduction should not be used to go into elaborate detail on the context of the question.

Balance relative to the rest of the essay is also important when constructing your introduction. It should be slightly less than your average paragraph. Too often, students get carried away writing their introductions, not leaving enough time for the rest of the essay. If this is a concern for you, try writing just your thesis and then proceed with the rest of the essay, leaving room for the rest of the introduction. You can go back once you have finished the body of the essay and fill in the beginning of the introduction.

Conclusions

If students tend to spend too much time on their introductions, the opposite is true of conclusions. This is partially a function of time management and partially a function of using the conclusion simply to repeat what has been said in the rest of the essay. A good conclusion should do a number of things:

- Refocus on the thesis
- Summarize the arguments – not the evidence – and how they relate to the thesis
- Include any overarching task required by the command term
- Indicate the significance of the topic to other events.

In the same way that you should structure your introduction from general statements to more specific statements, the conclusion should start with a specific statement, usually some form of the thesis, followed by more general statements.

6 THE SECOND WORLD WAR IN EUROPE AND NORTH AFRICA: A RETURN TO TOTAL WAR

Global context

It is to some extent a cliché to say that the Second World War erupted out of the ashes of the First World War. Nevertheless, the First World War left a deep impression on the political, economic and social climate of the 1920s and 1930s in Europe. No country had been untouched by it. It was out of this context of poverty, humiliation and dependence on other countries that the totalitarian ideologies which dominated central and eastern Europe during this period grew. The three dominant ideologies in Europe during this period – liberal democracy, fascism and communism – were in many ways mutually incompatible. When this incompatibility was coupled with the uncompromising and expansionist nature of one of these ideologies, namely fascism, conflict became far more likely. This dangerous mix was made more volatile by the isolationist policies of the US and the introverted stance of France and Britain.

Timeline

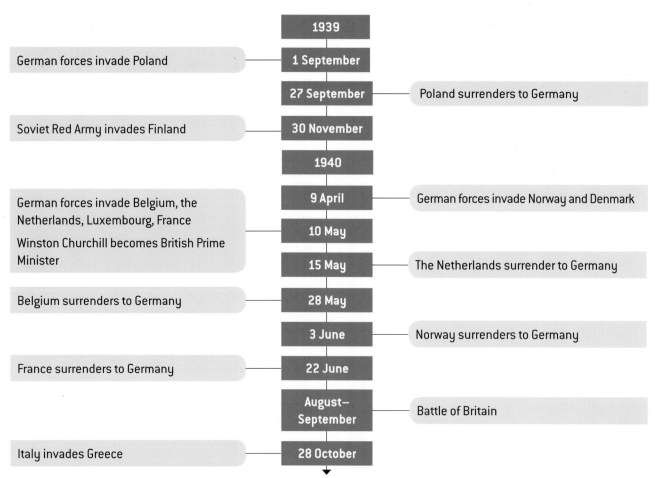

	1939	
German forces invade Poland	1 September	
	27 September	Poland surrenders to Germany
Soviet Red Army invades Finland	30 November	
	1940	
German forces invade Belgium, the Netherlands, Luxembourg, France	9 April	German forces invade Norway and Denmark
	10 May	
Winston Churchill becomes British Prime Minister	15 May	The Netherlands surrender to Germany
Belgium surrenders to Germany	28 May	
	3 June	Norway surrenders to Germany
France surrenders to Germany	22 June	
	August–September	Battle of Britain
Italy invades Greece	28 October	

1941

11 March — Roosevelt signs Lend-Lease Act

German forces invade Yugoslavia and Greece — 6 April

22 June — German forces invade USSR

Soviet counter-attack halts German advance — 5 December

11 December — Italy and Germany declare war on the US

1942

Stalin and Churchill meet in Moscow — 12 August

September — Battle of Stalingrad begins

Battle of El Alamein begins — 23 October

8 November — US troops land in North Africa

1943

Casablanca Conference — January

5 July — Battle of Kursk begins

Italian fascist regime falls — 25 July

1944

January — Soviet Red Army enters Poland

Allies land at Normandy in France — 6 June

25 August — Paris is liberated

Allied airborne attack on the Netherlands — 17 September

16–27 December — Battle of the Bulge

1945

Soviet Red Army captures Warsaw — 17 January

16 April — Soviet Red Army begin final assault on Berlin

Adolf Hitler commits suicide — 30 April

7 May — All German forces surrender to Allies

6.1 Causes of the Second World War

Long-term causes

The legacy of the First World War

It has become popular to see the roots of the Second World War in the unsatisfactory conclusion to the First World War and there is certainly evidence to support this view. With the exception of the US, the victors were themselves near ruin. Germany and the other Central Powers were sliding into chaos and denied a seat at Versailles and with it any meaningful say in the future of their countries. The Nazi Party came to power partially on a promise of reversing the verdict of Versailles and Germany's subsequent military programme had this as one of its key aims. The Bolshevik government in Russia extracted itself from the war only to face three more years of devastating civil war during which she was ostracized from European politics. The commander of the French army, Marshal Ferdinand Foch, recognized that the end of the war brought little stability to Europe when he said at the signing of the treaty of Versailles, "This is not a peace. It is an armistice for 20 years".

Insofar as wars are often fought to address issues in international relations, the unsatisfactory outcome of the First World War seems to suggest that at least some of these issues were outstanding for some if not all the combatants. Indeed the victors sought to recreate the conditions of the 19th century that had brought them to the commanding positions they had enjoyed in international politics and economics.

Britain eschewed the politics of the continent after Versailles and instead looked to its empire to return it to its former position. It would take part in the League of Nations insofar as it helped to confirm its worldview – that it was the natural leader of its empire and this empire should serve first the mother country. For Britain this desire to return to the balance

of the 19th century also meant a return to the belief that international disputes could be sorted out by discussion and compromise. War as a tool of diplomacy was to be used as a last resort.

Such an approach, however, could no more be expected to resolve issues in the 1930s than it could in 1914. And many of the same issues remained, if in somewhat altered forms. Germany was dissatisfied with its place in European and world politics. Versailles had stripped it of its colonies and these sources of income needed to be replaced, especially in light of the massive public spending that Germany undertook once the Nazis came to power. Nationalism in the Balkans riled Mussolini and the Italians. Nationalism also posed a threat to more established empires such as the British and French. The Soviet Union can be seen as an exception. Russia's position and interests were more of an enigma to the West than it had been in 1914 and she was certainly not the continental power she had been in 1914, although her industrial and thus her military potential was still massive.

Between them Britain and France controlled a third of the world by the 1930s and each country saw its empire as vital to its economic health. This was especially true in the years after the stock market crash of 1929. Of course, it was an advantage denied to Germany, Italy and Japan in 1919. While colonies may have been an economic asset, strategically they could also be a liability, as they had in the years leading up to 1914. While countries may have little to bring them into conflict in Europe – say Britain and France – colonial issues could collide in Africa or Asia thus destabilizing Europe. Protecting such large empires was expensive and in the 1930s neither country could afford to do so adequately. Britain and France were faced with using their limited military to police and defend their empires, thus leaving them only diplomacy to maintain their international interests.

If continuity marked western governments' approach to the international situation after the First World War, change was the key word for the attitude of the general population. In contrast to the bellicose attitude of many Europeans in 1914, western Europeans looked on the international situation of the inter-war period with a sense of unease and pacifism. This took many forms, from popular support for official neutrality in the US to student-led peace movements throughout Europe.

The legacy of the First World War in western Europe was one of military and diplomatic weakness. This weakness was obscured by the absence of any power to challenge it. The rise of fascism in the 1920s and 1930s would provide such a power and expose that weakness.

Fascism

The catastrophe of the First World War convinced many, and confirmed the conviction of others, that political systems based on liberal democracy were incapable of organizing and governing modern states to the benefit of the many. Two ideologies that rejected liberal principles, one from a class perspective and the other from an ultra-nationalist perspective, rose to the fore in the dislocation of the First World War.

TOK discussion

To what extent can the citizens of a country be held accountable for the actions of its government? To what extent can they be held accountable for the actions of governments in the past?

Fascism, based as it was on ultra-nationalism, had expansionism built into its central tenets.

In Italy, Mussolini used theatre and violence to ride socio-economic unrest and parliamentary weakness to power. Part of Mussolini's political theatre was to invoke the grandeur of the Roman Empire with rhetoric and symbols, but with the Great Depression and Mussolini's policy of autarky this rhetoric would take on more substance. The Italian military was expanded as an expression of national strength and virility. Initial forays into the Balkans proved insufficient and in 1935 Italy invaded Abyssinia in a quest for an empire of its own, in the process destabilizing the diplomatic situation in Europe even further.

The form that fascism took in Germany was of a kind, but more lethal in its execution. Taking as its premise the racial superiority of Germans and certain social Darwinian concepts, Nazism preached the need for Germany to expand in response to economic and demographic pressures. A belief that Jews and Slavs were inferior provided a racist justification for expansion to the east. The tool of this expansion, or *Lebensraum*, was to be a massive and modern national military seen, as it was in Italy, as an expression of national strength. Restoration of terrritory also fuelled Nazi ideology. The fact that German-speaking people in Austria, parts of Czechoslovakia and Poland were not part of Germany was anathema to the Nazis' ultra-nationalism. The means and justification for war was built into Nazism.

Short-term causes

The Great Depression

After the First World War it became clear that the only national economy that could in any way claim to be healthy was that of the United States. Any kind of recovery in the post-war years, therefore, would in some way, shape or form be dependent on the US economy. This proved true with the adoption of the **Dawes Plan** as a solution to the Ruhr Crisis and attendant economic turmoil. Money in the form of loans and capital flowed from the US to Germany. Reparations in turn flowed from Germany to France and Britain, which then paid back wartime loans to the US. This triangular flow seemed to work at first. The German economy, with its new currency, began to recover in the years 1924–1929, the so-called Golden Age of the Weimar Republic.

After the Wall Street Crash of 1929, cash-strapped US banks recalled German loans and investors sold German securities, plunging Germany into depression. Eight million Germans were unemployed by 1932 and Hitler and the Nazis rode this wave of economic hardship into office. In this sense the Great Depression can be seen as a long-term cause of the war in that it brought an expansionist ideology to power. The depression also prompted countries into adopting protectionist economic policies that isolated countries such as Germany and Japan, who had to look elsewhere for markets. This increased economic rivalry between European powers in South America, China and the Balkans. Economic isolation helped fuel diplomatic isolation, especially in the

Dawes Plan
A financial aid package from the US to Germany. The package was in response to the French invasion of the Ruhr and subsequent German hyperinflation. The plan provided US dollars to refinance the German currency as well as capital to German banks and businesses.

case of the United States, which emboldened expansionist powers. Economic hardship also hampered the rearmament of the western allies at exactly the time the expansionist powers were rapidly increasing the size of their militaries.

German expansion

With the ideological justification of National Socialism and a mandate, manipulated though it was, from the German people, Hitler set about undoing the hated Treaty of Versailles. In 1935 he tore up the disarmament clauses of the treaty and announced conscription and rearmament, responding, he said, to the lengthening of French conscription terms. This was to be the first example of Hitler's approach to the West. He would push the envelope and wait for the Allies' reaction and judge his next step accordingly. When Britain and France did not react to his rearmament programme he accelerated it. The Anglo-German Naval Agreement of 1935, although seeming to limit German naval building, signified for Hitler a tacit approval of German rearmament.

In 1936 he again tested the West's commitment to Versailles. Hitler ordered the German army to re-occupy the Rhineland, German territory demilitarized by Versailles, and waited for the Allies' response. German commanders had orders to pull back across the Rhine should France show the slightest inclination to intervene. Hitler did not want to risk his fledgling army. When France did nothing, Hitler was again emboldened. The next year, Germany intervened in the Spanish Civil War on the side of Franco and the rebels while France and Britain rigorously upheld their non-interventionist stance. If France and her British ally did not respond to threats on its border, why would they object to German expansion in the east?

The territorial ambitions of Nazism pushed Germany to annex Austria, the *Anschluss*, in 1938, an act forbidden by Versailles. Again the British and French raised no objections. Versailles was clearly dead. Perhaps more disturbingly for the British was Hitler's preference for unilateral action, without recourse to diplomacy or negotiation. If Germany no longer played by the rules that Britain assumed underpinned international relations, rules like the sanctity of treaties and agreements and the use of war as a last resort rather than a preferred response, then her whole approach to European relations was built on sand. Hitler's ephemeral promises were illustrated when he ignored the Munich Agreement within six months of signing it and occupied what remained of Czechoslovakia. When France and Britain guaranteed Poland's borders in response Hitler had no reason to believe that this commitment was any more solid than the Allies' commitment to Munich.

Appeasement

Very simply, appeasement is to give in to demands in order to avoid conflict. This, however, obscures the great complexity with which appeasement was used in the 1930s. With the benefit of hindsight, many post-war commentators used the word with disdain to denote what they saw as British Prime Minister Neville Chamberlain's naive and weak approach to German foreign policy in the late 1930s. Superficially this assessment seems to hold, however, more recent scholarship interprets appeasement differently.

Appeasement can be seen as a continuation of traditional British diplomacy:

- based on discussion and negotiation
- based on Britain's economic and military strength
- considering the global scope of Britain's interests
- treating each issue on its own merits
- avoiding war when possible
- resorting to war if it were in Britain's interest to do so.

These principles were applied by the British to each of Hitler's foreign policy adventures. When he re-occupied the Rhineland, it was clearly no direct threat to British interests and could be seen as a return to a more normalized situation of German autonomy. Likewise it was not clear how the *Anschluss* threatened British interests. Certainly the Sino-Japanese war was more of a concern for Britain globally. At Munich, Chamberlain judged the Czechs' sovereignty to be less of a concern than the costs of any kind of British intervention, if such an intervention was even feasible, and negotiated an end to the crisis. Germany's actions did not threaten her shores as any movement toward France or Belgium would. It did not threaten their sea routes and communications through the Mediterranean. It in no way impeded the operation of the British Empire. Rearmament, started in 1938, nevertheless continued in Britain.

There were two underlying assumptions when it came to applying this policy to German actions in central Europe. This first assumption was that German leadership held the same values as did Britain and France in terms of international agreements. The second assumption was that German ambitions could be satisfied. Both assumptions in the end proved to be false. Once it became obvious that they were false, and the British rearmament programme was close to putting Britain on par with German military output, war became a more feasible solution to future situations.

This interpretation suggests that the key question is not why did the Allies not fight for Czechoslovakia, but rather why did they fight for Poland? As mentioned, British rearmament had reached peak production by mid-1939 and French rearmament was progressing. Globally, the Sino-Japanese war seemed to be sapping Japanese ability to menace British holdings. The Nazi-Soviet Non-aggression Pact removed the USSR as a deterrent to German expansion. In the end, the British abandoned their assumption that Hitler could be sated and thus their ability to affect the course of world affairs and by so doing protect their interests through diplomacy was no longer feasible. Appeasement had worked until it did not.

Class discussion

Is there a moral or ethical element to appeasement?

Research and thinking skills

For each of the following positions, research the views of the historians listed. Each historian may either support or reject the perspective. What are the strengths and weaknesses of each historian's position?

The policy of appeasement caused the war

- RAC Parker
- AJP Taylor

Nazi ideology caused the war

- Eric Hobsbawm
- AJP Taylor
- Hugh Trevor Roper

Source skills

Chamberlain and appeasement

The following is an extract from the memoirs of Lord Halifax, Chamberlain's Foreign Secretary.

Source A

The other element that gave fuel to the fires of criticism was the unhappy phrases which Neville Chamberlain under the stress of great emotion allowed himself to use. 'Peace with Honour'; 'Peace for our time' – such sentences grated harshly on the ear and thought of even those closest to him. But when all has been said, one fact remains dominant and unchallengeable. When war did come a year later it found a country and Commonwealth wholly united within itself, convinced to the foundations of soul and conscience that every conceivable effort had been made to find the way of sparing Europe the ordeal of war, and that no alternative remained. And that was the best thing that Chamberlain did.

Source: Halifax, Edward. 1956. *Fullness of Days*. Dodd, Mead and Co. London, UK.

http://spartacus-educational.com/PRchamberlain.htm

Source B

Winston Churchill's speech to the House of Commons on Neville Chamberlain's death, 12 November 1940.

It fell to Neville Chamberlain in one of the supreme crises of the world to be contradicted by events, to be disappointed in his hopes, and to be deceived and cheated by a wicked man. But what were these hopes in which he was disappointed? What were these wishes in which he was frustrated? What was that faith that was abused? They were surely among the most noble and benevolent instincts of the human heart – the love of peace, the toil for peace, the strife for peace, the pursuit of peace, even at great peril, and certainly to the utter disdain of popularity or clamour.

Source: *http://www.winstonchurchill.org/resources/ speeches/1940-the-finest-hour/neville-chamberlain*

Source C

Duff Cooper, First Lord of the Admiralty, Diary entry 17 September 1938 describing a cabinet meeting with Chamberlain.

Power from obtaining undue predominance in Europe; but we were now faced with probably the most formidable Power that had ever dominated Europe, and resistance to that Power was quite obviously a British interest. If I thought surrender would bring lasting peace I should be in favour of surrender, but I did not believe there would ever be peace in Europe so long as Nazism ruled in Germany. The next act of aggression might be one that it would be far harder for us to resist.

Source D

The following is an extract from *The Origins of the Second World War*, written by British historian AJP Taylor.

The settlement at Munich was a triumph for British policy, which had worked precisely to this end; not a triumph for Hitler, who had started with far less clear intentions. Nor was it merely a triumph for selfish or cynical British statesmen, indifferent to the fate of far-off peoples or calculating that Hitler might be launched against Soviet Russia. It was a triumph for all that was best and most enlightened in British life; a triumph for those who had preached equal justice between peoples; a triumph for those who had denounced the harshness and short-sightedness of Versailles.

Source: Taylor, AJP. 1961. *The Origins of the Second World War*. Hamish Hamilton. London, UK

Questions

1 **a** What does Churchill mean when he says Chamberlain was "contradicted by events"? (Source B)

   b What are the implications of Source D?

2 With reference to its origin, purpose and content discuss the strengths and weaknesses of Source B for historians studying Chamberlain's role in the war.

3 Compare and contrast the perspectives of Source A and Source B on Chamberlain's policy of appeasement.

4 Using your own knowledge and these sources evaluate appeasement as an effective foreign policy.

6.2 Combatants

Conceptual understanding

Key questions

→ At what point could the western powers challenge the Axis Powers in terms of military strength?

→ What was the relationship of industrial power to military strength in 1939?

Key concepts

→ Continuity

→ Change

→ Significance

Axis Powers

The Treaty of Versailles had placed severe restrictions on the size of the German army. This did not mean, however, that the German High Command was idle during the 1920s. The small officer corps undertook a thorough analysis of both the lessons of the First World War and what this meant for Germany in the context of Versailles restrictions. It was this analysis and subsequent doctrine that would structure the German military when it began to expand in the mid-1930s. The lessons that the German general staff took from the battles of 1918 were that flexibility, initiative and active combat leadership were the key to mobile warfare. Even before Hitler came to power, the German army had a plan for expansion beyond its Versailles restrictions.

In 1935 conscription raised the strength of the German army from its 100 000 men to 21 divisions. By the eve of war in 1939 it was 103 divisions – some three million men. These six divisions included armoured divisions boasting close to 2,400 tanks. The German air force, banned by Versailles, boasted over 4,000 aircraft in 1939. Likewise the navy also expanded both its surface and submarine fleets. Nevertheless, it is one thing to build and maintain a peacetime army and quite another to keep it supplied with men and material while fighting a modern war, and in 1939 many within the German command believed the German economy was incapable of sustaining a fight over the long term without the conquest of significant productive land. Over half of its government expenditure went to rearmament consuming over 15% of its GNP.

Throughout the war the Germans were famously handicapped by their Italian allies. Italy had suffered in the First World War without the compensation she deemed owed to her. The economic crisis that accompanied the peace brought Mussolini to power, with his chaotically dangerous blend of ultra-nationalism, economic planning, militarism, terror and incompetence, and with him a vague notion of regaining the glories of ancient Rome. He expanded the Italian navy in both surface vessels and submarines. Counter-intuitively, though, because Italy rearmed before all the other European powers, her material was obsolete first as well and she lacked the economic resources to modernize before she entered the war. The Italian military/industrial complex had some of the same economic weaknesses that the German military did, without the real ability to conquer new territories to compensate for them. These weaknesses were exacerbated by poor leadership in all branches of the military and indeed up to *Il Duce* himself.

Axis ground forces (Europe, Asia, Africa and the Pacific)	
Country	Maximum strength
Germany	Army: 6 500 000
	Waffen SS : 800 000
Italy	3 700 000
Japan	5 500 000
Romania	600 000

Class discussion

Hitler stood by Mussolini to the end, even having him rescued from a mountain prison. How can we account for this loyalty in light of Italy's military shortcomings?

Allied Powers

As with the Axis Powers, the legacy of the First World War deeply affected military expenditure in the inter-war period. In the 1930s, France spent nearly 50% of its budget on debt and pensions accumulated between 1914 and 1918. This meant there was less money available to rearm in the face of German rearmament. The economic and social malaise that settled on France in the 1930s fed the deeply conservative army. Tanks theory was still based on 1918 experiences. Aircraft production fell far below other European powers. Although her navy was a reasonably modern force, it was of little use against France's key rival. As much as French command had been besotted with the idea of the offensive fueled by dangerously vague notions of *élan* in 1914, it was defensive and statically minded in the 1930s. The most complete expression of this was the reliance on the massively expensive Maginot Line. France could muster 90 divisions of infantry. Five million were theoretically available for call up in case of war. At the outbreak of the war she had not organized her tanks into divisions, preferring instead to distribute tanks among infantry divisions as she had in 1918.

In the inter-war period, British policy turned inward, as, indeed, her voting public demanded. It was poverty and standard of living, not European stability, to which the British governments turned their attention. If she was to look abroad, it was to bolster her empire in the face of dominion independence and nationalism in the colonies. In the 1920s and 1930s she had returned to a policy of maintaining a small army. The economic crisis of the 1930s precluded anything else, even if there had been public support for rearmament. Nevertheless when

Relative war potential of the powers in 1937	
United States	41.7%
Germany	14.4%
USSR	14%
Great Britain	10.2%
France	4.2%
Japan	3.5%
Italy	2.5%

Source: Kennedy, Paul. 1988. *Rise and Fall of the Great Powers: Economic Change and Military Conflict From 1500 to 2000*. Fontana Press. London, UK.

Research skills

To what extent was Britain ready for war in:

- September 1938
- March 1939
- September 1939

Rate each date between 1–10, with 10 being very prepared and 1 being completely unprepared. Do the same for France and the USSR.

1 How did the preparedness of each country compare? What might be some reasons for the differences?

2 How did each country's level of readiness affect its foreign policy at these three points in time?

the war broke out the British army mustered four divisions to send to France. By May 1940 conscription had raised this number to 50 divisions. By the time the smoke of the Battle of France had settled, the British army numbered some 1.6 million men. The Royal Air Force (RAF) had 900 bombers and 600 fighters with which to defend the island. The Royal Navy was the largest in the world, although still stretched thin having to defend outposts as far away as Hong Kong and Singapore, the Mediterranean and the home islands.

Allied ground forces (Europe, Asia, Africa and the Pacific)	
Country	**Maximum strength**
Great Britain	3 100 000
USA	8 200 000
USSR	6 900 000
France	5 900 000 (with reserves)
Canada	730 000
India	2 500 00
Australia	727 000
New Zealand	157 000
South Africa	255 000

Wartime production

John Keegan has argued that Germany's economic strategy mirrored its military strategy, that is to say, like the German army it was designed for quick victory. The same can be said for the Japanese economy. In fact none of the Axis economies could withstand a long war of attrition with the likes of the United States and the Soviet Union. This weakness was exacerbated by the fact that the Allied production facilities were well out of reach of Axis forces. Even the Soviet factories that lay in the path of the German onslaught were for the most part spared when they were torn down and transported out of harm's way into the Ural mountain region. This evacuation had the added benefit of moving Soviet production closer to its supply of raw materials. Germany and Japan did not enjoy any such luxury. From 1943 Germany's industrial complex was subject to day and night bombing.

Both Germany and Japan managed to maintain war production for some time in the face of these offensives. Japan moved production out of large centres and decentralized it, making targeting and concentration of firepower more difficult and ineffectual. Until 1942, the German economy had not fully committed to war production. Consumer goods were still being produced in an attempt to maintain the standard of living and women were not used to augment the industrial workforce. When Albert Speer became Minister of Armaments and War Production early in 1942, he rationalized production and centralized control of the economic system. Production began to rise, even in the face of Allied bombing. Initially its occupied territories were used to help meet the economic demands of the war, but as time went on this was far from sufficient, especially after 1944 when the size of Germany's occupied territory shrank. Thereafter war production plummeted.

Unlike their enemies, the Allies, specifically Britain, understood it would have to sacrifice consumer production for war production. About half of British production went to the war effort during the war. Despite their impressive production figures, both Britain and the USSR depended on aid from North America. The US economy produced a staggering amount of material. This included 36 billion yards of cotton cloth and 41 billion rounds of ammunition. By 1943 a liberty ship was being completed every three days.

Armaments production of the powers, 1940–1943 (billions of 1944 dollars)			
	1940	**1941**	**1943**
Great Britain	3.5	6.5	11.1
USSR	(5)	8.5	13.9
United States	(1.5)	4.5	37.5
Total of Allied combatants	3.5	19.5	62.5
Germany	6	6	13.8
Japan	(1)	2	4.5
Italy	0.75	1	–
Total of Axis combatants	6.75	9	18.3

ATL Research and communication skills

Research the production quantities for one of the following items for each of the six major combatants in the years 1939–1945 (Germany, USSR, US, Britain, Japan and Italy):

- Aircraft
- Tanks
- Naval vessels
- Merchant vessels
- Trucks

Plot a graph depicting production quantities by year using a different colour for each country. Compare your graph with others of different items.

1   What patterns emerge from the graphs?

2   How do these patterns help explain the course of the war?

▲ A tank is produced at a General Motors assembly line in the US

6.3 Strategy

Axis Powers

As vaguely sketched out in *Mein Kampf*, Hitler sought *Lebensraum* – space in the east into which the German population could expand. This was Poland. He then turned his sights on readjusting the hated Versailles settlement in the west – again alluded to although not detailed in his autobiography. His calculation had been that the Allies would not intervene in Poland and that it could be taken quickly, leaving German forces to deal with western Europe with no enemy at her back. In other words to accomplish what the Schlieffen Plan was designed, but failed, to do in 1914 – capture France while avoiding the effects of a two-front war.

In Hitler's worldview there was to be a cataclysmic struggle between fascism and communism at some point in history and this belief formed the core of his strategic thinking, even before the fall of France. When, in the wake of France's defeat, Churchill and the British did not accept what Hitler believed to be the reality of their defeat, the German Führer had to re-evaluate. Should he postpone the conflict with the USSR and invade the British Isles? Or should he risk Napoleon's fate and turn east to settle ideological accounts with Bolshevism and secure the productive fields of western Russia and the oil of southern Russia? Regardless of ideology and supply, strengthening the German army in the east can be seen as a response to aggressive Soviet actions in the Baltic States and in Romania. True to his leadership style, Hitler did not choose, but rather let circumstances help dictate the course of events. While he had his military chiefs drafting plans for the invasion of the Soviet Union, he had his air force wage a desperate struggle to destroy the RAF in preparation for the invasion of Britain. Once they had been defeated in the skies

over Britain, the Germans devoted all their energy to the invasion of the Soviet Union.

From 1942 on, German strategy was dominated by the search for resources, particularly oil, and securing her previous conquests. Thus, Rommel's exploits in North Africa can be understood as a quest for the oil of the Middle East. When the German army swung south in Russia, it was with a view to securing the oil of the Caucasus Mountains. For the Germans 1943–1945 can be seen as a series of rearguard actions with occasional offensive thrusts, as in the case of the Battle of the Bulge in December 1944. The defensive posture that Germany had to adopt was in some ways a function of her early success or we might say overreach. German forces were forced to defend a massive front in Russia, her conquests in Greece and the Balkans. The Italian collapse added the Italian peninsula to German responsibilities. When the British, Canadian and United States armies secured their beachheads at Normandy on 6 June 1944 it added immeasurably to the defensive burden of the German forces.

German tactics, especially early in the war, were dominated by *Blitzkrieg*, so-called "Lightning War". This operational doctrine integrated precision dive-bombing – "flying artillery" – and other air support with very mobile massed armour. Offensive thrusts were to bypass enemy strong points, isolating them for later reduction. Traditional infantry would follow to secure and "mop up" any remaining resistance. *Blitzkrieg* required open spaces and a definitive and attainable end point. Both of these conditions existed in France and Poland. Both had relatively open territory through which the German tanks known as panzers could dash. The panzers pressed the Anglo-French forces against the channel. In the east the retreating Polish forces ran headlong into the Red Army. In the Soviet Union, however, only one of these conditions existed. It may have had wide, open spaces in abundance, but these spaces went on forever and would swallow the German army as it had Napoleon's.

The Allied Powers

Between January and March 1941, British, US and Canadian military planners secretly met in Washington to discuss a common strategic approach to the war. Secrecy was paramount given that the US was still neutral. US planners had already developed a contingency should they find themselves in a war with both Germany and Japan, and the ABC 1 plan followed from these strategic schemes. According to the plan:

- Italy was to be eliminated as quickly as possible

- Allied Powers would concentrate on the defeat of Germany before the defeat of Japan

- strategic bombing would become a key component of the overall strategy

- British and US holdings in the Pacific would be defended.

For the most part the broad-brush strokes of ABC 1 were realized throughout the war. The Allies did prioritize victory in Europe, which seemed all the more justified with the suspicion that the Germans were working on an atomic weapon. The North African landings and the subsequent Sicily and Italian campaigns knocked Italian forces out of the war although they did not eliminate Italy as a theatre of war. The Allies may have differed on how strategic bombing was to be implemented, but they persevered through heavy losses and questionable efficacy throughout the war. The US did go on the offensive in the Pacific, but really only after their economy had been fully mobilized for war production and they had won the essentially defensive Battle of Midway.

Even before the entry of the United States in the war in December of 1941, it was clear that a key component of the Allied strategy would be to outproduce their enemy. The **Lend-Lease policy** was a part of this strategy as was the Soviet decision to dismantle over 1,500 industrial factories ahead of the German onslaught and reassemble them in the relative safety of the Ural Mountains. This strategy played a vital role in all the Allied victories, especially once the United States entered the war in December 1941. Liberty ships were produced at a rate far in excess of the German U-boats' ability to sink them. The exchange ratio during the Battle of Britain favoured the RAF. The Red Army may have lost more tanks than the Germans in the Battle of Kursk, but they could afford to do so. The Soviet Union would produce more than 54 000 tanks to Germany's 20 000. This gap was made even wider given that for much of the war Germany had to distribute this tank production over multiple fronts, while the Soviets could concentrate all their production on one front.

Lend-Lease policy

The Lend-Lease Act set up a scheme through which the US sent aid to the Allies during the Second World War. Immediate payment was not required as the US was "lending" the materials to the Allies. The programme also provided US warships (destroyers) to Britain in exchange for the lease of a number of military bases in the Caribbean. The US had Lend-Lease agreements with a number of Allied countries.

Tank production		
Tank	Country	Number Produced
Sherman	USA	49 300
T-34	USSR	57 000
Panzer IV	Germany	8500
Crusader	Great Britain	5400
Tiger I and Tiger II	Germany	1850
Churchill	Great Britain	7300
Pershing	USA	2200

6.4 Operations

Conceptual understanding

Key questions

→ What factors led to the early success of the Axis forces?

→ To what extent did each side integrate land, air and sea power?

→ To what extent did the Allies outproduce the Axis Powers?

→ Why did the Allies win the war?

Key concepts

→ Cause

→ Consequence

→ Significance

Poland

Poland would be the first trial of *Blitzkrieg*. On the surface, Poland seemed the ideal terrain for the innovative tactics. Large, open plains allowed for unrestricted movement of large tank formations. The relative lack of cover would give the screaming Stuka dive bombers unobstructed sightlines to their targets, allowing Germany's air power to be fully integrated with its ground operations, an essential element of *Blitzkrieg*. While the topography of Poland theoretically would allow the Polish army a fairly easy path of withdrawal, after which it might regroup in the east, the secret codicils of the Molotov-Ribbentrop Pact made that prospect an illusion. The Polish army would instead be driven mercilessly east only to come up hard against the anvil of the Soviet Red Army, claiming its portion of the spoils.

Just before 5 am on 1 September 1939, the Luftwaffe launched massive air raids against Polish air force facilities, eradicating it by the end of the day. Those Polish planes which managed to get off the ground were destroyed. The air raids also targeted those infrastructure elements essential for a modern army to function: roads, rail lines and communication centres. Terror was a deliberate aspect of the air raids and as such these raids also targeted Polish cities and towns. The resulting civilian panic would clog the roads with fleeing refugees and thus hamper the operation of both civilian authorities and the Polish military.

The 1.5 million German soldiers that crossed the frontier into Poland on 1 September were divided into two army groups. One went north and then quickly east, driving behind Polish lines. The main attack would drive toward Warsaw, avoiding large Polish formations, preferring instead to get to the capital while at the same time encircling and isolating those same formations. This is, in fact what transpired. Some of the Polish forces managed to disengage and withdraw to Warsaw where they would set up a defensive perimeter around their capital.

▲ German soldiers break down a barrier on the German–Polish border, 1 September 1939

Schutzstaffel (SS)
Originally Hitler's personal bodyguard, the SS grew into a massive organization within the Nazi Party. Broadly tasked with party and state security, the SS managed domestic and foreign intelligence gathering, the Gestapo, policing and racial policies including the concentration camp system. The *Waffen* SS was the military branch of the SS, which fought throughout Europe alongside and in coordination with the German army, the *Wehrmacht*.

Class discussion

Frederick the Great of Prussia once said "he who defends everything, defends nothing". To what extent does this apply to the Polish army in September of 1939?

Following the main force were units of the *Schutzstaffel* **(SS)**, the Death's Head Regiments. Hitler's orders to these units were to rid Poland of the "enemies of Nazism"– a long list. These regiments rounded up Jews, communists, socialists and any local leaders deemed to be a threat. Whole villages and towns were burned to the ground. Civilians were a deliberate target in this war from the very beginning.

The siege of Warsaw began on 17 September. The Luftwaffe pounded the city for ten days. Although the city was defended by 140 000 Polish soldiers the suffering that the terror bombing created persuaded the Polish authorities to surrender the city on the 27 September.

True to their pledge, the British and French declared war on Germany on 3 September. By 10 September, Canada, Australia, New Zealand and South Africa had followed suit. But this meant very little in terms of practical aid to the beleaguered Poles. On 4 September British bombers attacked German ships at their births in Wilhelmshaven resulting in limited damage. French army units made tentative advances across the frontier with Germany.

ATL Thinking skills

- What lessons might the French and British allies have taken from the brief Polish campaigns that may have better prepared them to face the German army?
- What challenges would a campaign in western Europe pose for the German army that it had not encountered in Poland?

Casualties: Polish campaign			
	Dead/missing	Wounded	Captured
Poland	70 000	133 000	700 000 in German hands
			217 000 in Russian hands
Germany	13 900	30 000	
Civilians	25 000		

Battle for western Europe

Hitler had hoped that his army could be quickly turned west to conquer what he believed to be a hesitant and weak France. His generals were far more cautious. They argued for more time to better prepare for what they believed to be a more formidable enemy, one bolstered by a growing British army. It became evident, however, that the German advance in the west would have to wait until the spring of 1940. The interim, known as the Phoney War or to some of the British and Canadian soldiers waiting in Britain "the *Sitskrieg*", provided an opportunity for the British to raise 15–20 divisions, the French to mobilize reserves and reinforce the Maginot Line and the Germans to correct the deficiencies that became apparent in the Polish campaign and transfer their forces to the western front.

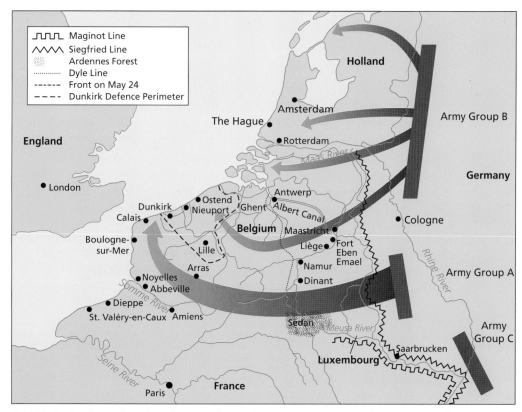

▲ Hitler's plan for the invasion of western Europe. Compare and contrast this plan with the Schlieffen Plan of 1914.

The war in the west did not open with a German drive into western Europe, but rather with an attack on Norway. Although officially neutral, Norway would provide the German navy with an important base of operation. Its occupation would also help secure the resources Germany obtained from Sweden. In March 1940 German mountain troops landed at Narvik in the north supported by German paratroopers. Stiff resistance from the Norwegians, reinforced by French and British troops and strong support from the Royal Navy, slowed the German advance. By the end of April, however, the British and French high command had decided that the prospects of success were slim and in any event, the expected thrust into France could not be far off.

That thrust was an object of some debate among German generals and their Führer. In the end, Hitler opted for the bolder plan that would send a smaller force to attack Belgium and the Netherlands – in a seeming repeat of 1914 – in hope of pulling French and British forces north. The vast majority of the German armour would then push through the forests of the Ardennes thought to be impenetrable by large forces, especially with tanks, separating the bulk of the Allied forces from the bulk of France. A third force would attack the Maginot Line. The plan, devised by the ambitious General Eric von Manstein, was daring and fraught with danger. What if the Ardennes proved to be as impenetrable as the French hoped? What if the garrison manning the Maginot Line emerged from its fortress and attacked the exposed flank of the main force as it plodded through the Ardennes? In any event, Hitler always gravitated to the bold over the cautious and therefore, this was his kind of plan. The plan was codenamed "Sickle Stroke".

The French plan was to rely on the Maginot Line and deploy their mobile troops, including their reserves in the north. Once again, as in 1914, the French strategy played right into the hands of the Germans. To call the French troops mobile is not to say they were the equivalent of the panzer divisions that would smash through the Ardennes. The French army, like its German counterpart with the exception of the panzer divisions, was road-bound and on foot, relying on horses to pull much of its artillery. On a forced march an infantry soldier could move about 31 kilometres on a road in a day. In Poland, the Wehrmacht's panzers covered 35 kilometres a day off road.

On 10 May Germany launched Operation Sickle Stroke. Paratroopers seized bridges, canals and forts in the Netherlands and Belgium. The Luftwaffe began to do to Rotterdam what it had done to Warsaw some months earlier. The Dutch surrendered on 19 May. This swing into the Low Countries prompted the Allies to rush troops to the north. They did not want to repeat the mistakes of 1914.

The nine panzer divisions of the main German force took only three days to push through the Ardennes and one to cross the Meuse River. As they prepared to begin the race to the English Channel, the Anglo-French forces still believed that the main attack would come down from the north. As the folly of this view became evident, the Allies began to panic. Some units of the British Expeditionary Force (BEF) dug in around their positions and prepared for a prolonged fight. Those French units that managed counter-attacks did so with little coordination and even these fell off as the German advance gained momentum.

Class discussion

How did operation Sickle Stroke differ from the Schlieffen Plan?

This momentum actually concerned Hitler and some of his commanders. The panzer divisions were outstripping their infantry support and Hitler worried about his tanks getting mired in the wet lowland areas of coastal Belgium and France. With the British army trapped against the coast and the French forces in disarray, Hitler ordered his panzers to stop – a controversial decision. The best German intelligence report put the number of British soldiers trapped within the Dunkirk perimeter at 100 000. The prospects of a sea evacuation, by German estimates, were negligible. The head of the Luftwaffe, Hermann Goering himself, assured Hitler that his aircrew could prevent any such rescue.

Close to 400 000 British, French and Belgian troops were trapped in the Dunkirk pocket. The plan to get them home was code named Operation Dynamo and consisted of some 222 Royal Navy vessels as well as 665 civilian boats – British, Belgian and Dutch – of all shapes and sizes, from commercial fishing trawlers to luxurious private sailing yachts. The key to the success of Dynamo is twofold. First the halt of the panzers bought the British time. Second, the RAF was able to keep the skies over the exposed beaches of Dunkirk and its approaches relatively clear of German aircraft.

By 4 June, over 337 000 Allied soldiers had been taken off the beaches. Of these 110 000 were French soldiers who quickly returned to France through secure ports. Although the "Miracle of Dunkirk" was proclaimed by the British media and preserved the fighting ability of the British army, it had come at a cost.

The Battle of Dunkirk: British losses	
Dead/missing	11 000
Captured	40 000
Tanks	475
Vehicles	38 000
Motorcycles	12 000
Anti-tank guns	4 000
Heavy artillery	1 000
Bren guns	8 000
Rifles	90 000

Now on their own, the remnants of the French military attempted to fortify a line of encampments running east to west perpendicular to the Maginot Line – so-called hedgehogs that could form pockets of resistance and attack the extended flank of the German "sickle stroke". It was too little, too late. Morale was nearly broken and the infrastructure required for a concerted military effort was close to non-existent. Although there was continued resistance in the Alps and along the Maginot Line, the French government, under Marshal Pétain from 17 June, signed the terms of surrender. The terms included:

- 60% of France, including Paris, the Atlantic coast and the industrial north, would be a zone of German occupation

- 40% of France and her colonies would be controlled by Pétain's puppet government with its capital at Vichy
- the French army would be reduced to 100 000 men
- French prisoners of war, over 1.5 million men, would be kept in captivity with no guarantee of their release
- the French would have to pay "occupation costs"
- the French navy was to be turned over to Germany.

Technology and war: Enigma and codebreaking

Enigma was an encoding machine used by the German military throughout the war. Enigma had a keyboard attached to three rotors. Each keystroke turned the rotors encrypting the message. An associated code key was required to decipher the message at the receiving end. By 1939 with the help of Polish mathematicians, the Allies were beginning to decipher German military code keys. The British mathematician Alan Turing developed a mechanized deciphering machine, which accelerated the process considerably. When the Germans created a four-rotor Enigma machine, the British modified their machine to decipher these codes as well. There were, however, hundreds of Axis code systems that were used and changed with varying degrees of regularity, making the task of the codebreakers vastly more complicated.

The program which deciphered and analysed the intelligence derived from Turing's machines was known as Ultra and at its height was deciphering over 2,000 messages a day. In a way the success of the program posed its own problems. Ensuring that the 2,000 decoded messages were analysed for their military importance and sent to the units to which the information was the most use in a timely fashion was an enormously complex undertaking. Allied leaders had to be careful which intelligence they acted on and how they did so for fear of tipping off the enemy who could then change the encryption system. The Allied militaries

▲ The Enigma machine. What were the challenges presented by this technology for both sides?

each had their own cryptographic systems and shared intelligence regularly. It was Ultra intelligence on Japanese intentions in northern China, released to the Soviets on Churchill's orders, which persuaded Stalin to allow his Siberian divisions to be transferred to the west. These divisions played a major role in the counteroffensive of December 1941 that threw the Germans back from the outskirts of Moscow.

Barbarossa to Stalingrad

While the autumn of 1940 was seemingly consumed with the vicious fighting in the skies, Hitler's attention was increasingly focused on the east – Germany's invasion of the Soviet Union. To an extent unknown in modern history, this was to be an ideological war, not simply a war of territorial conquest. Hitler had long envisioned the destruction of the communist edifice and the enslavement of the people who lived under it. It was to be a massive undertaking even by the standards of the Second World War. Three million men were to attack in three army groups along a 3,200-kilometre front supported by close to 1 million men from her allies. This force which included 3,350 tanks would be supported by

7,000 artillery pieces and 2,000 aircraft. To outfit such a formidable invasion the Germans were forced to use tanks and equipment from all over Europe including tanks from Czechoslovakia, artillery from Norway and trucks from France.

Opposing the Germans was a Red Army still reeling from the comprehensive purge of its officers in 1937–1938 and its humiliating performance against the Finns in 1940. Nevertheless, the Red Army numbered some 3.2 million infantry, 50 tank divisions (about 24 000 tanks in total) and 25 mechanized divisions.

Stalin's purge of the Red Army	
Rank	Executed or imprisoned
Marshall	60%
Army Commander	87%
Divisional Commander	56%
Brigadier	46%
Deputy Commissar of Defence	100%
Total officers purged	36 671

▲ German dispatch riders take a break during Operation Barbarossa. What role did communications play in *Blitzkrieg* tactics?

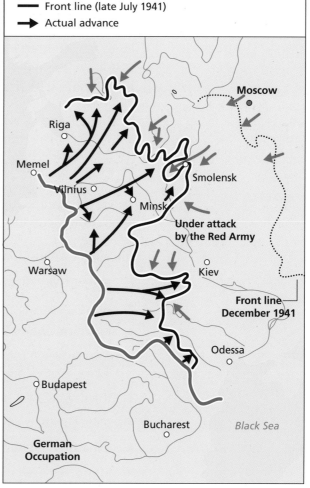

▲ Operation Barbarossa

More than Stalin's purge handicapped the Red Army. The Soviet leader's willful blindness to the coming invasion ensured that no proper military preparation had been made. Not wanting to offend Hitler or to violate the spirit of the Molotov-Ribbentrop Pact, Stalin forbade any "provocative" mobilization. Field commanders had no access to intelligence that very clearly showed that the Germany army was mobilizing along the frontier. As late as a few hours before the onslaught, Stalin refused to believe that anything was amiss, despite all telephone wires between Germany and Russia having been cut.

The German plan was to send its three army groups toward Leningrad, Moscow and Kiev. En route the Germans were to wash over Minsk, Smolensk, Riga and Tallin.

The *Blitzkrieg* blueprint was to be used again. Shortly after 3 am, the German artillery opened up along the entire front. The Luftwaffe began sorties against the Red Army air force almost immediately, destroying 3,000 aircraft in the first four days of the operation, many of these while they were still on the ground. Bridges and river crossings were secured quickly and the panzer divisions began to pour across the frontier. The opening weeks of the campaign were marked by massive battles of encirclement, "cauldrons". Within four days of the attack, **Army Group Centre** had encircled and captured 300 000 Soviet troops, destroying some 2,500 tanks. Such battles were to be repeated throughout the first months of the war.

By midsummer cracks had begun to show in the German army. As her panzers raced into Russia, they quickly outstripped their supply lines. Fuel shortages became more common as the advance moved east. Infantry on foot and guns being dragged by horses could not keep up. Perhaps most distressing for German military planners was that, although beaten badly, the Red Army showed no sign of complete collapse. In fact, it was finding its fight. Commanders who had been paralysed with the fear of making mistakes and the certain firing squad that would follow figured there was little difference between a German bullet or a Russian bullet, and began to take the initiative. German planners began to doubt their intelligence estimates. In June they had estimated that the Red Army could field about 200 divisions. By mid-August the Germans had encountered 360. German casualties, though small by Soviet standards, were still higher than anticipated – 400 000 by the end of August. The advance was slowing for a variety of reasons:

- higher than anticipated casualties

- the logistics of dealing with so many prisoners

- rapid use of fuel

- gaps between infantry and panzer units (infantry moving 32 kilometres per day; panzer units moving 80 kilometres per day)

- Russian railway tracks could not be used

- poor quality roads

- exhausted infantry and panzer troops

- efforts required to supply three full army groups.

Army Group Centre
The German army group tasked with advancing toward Moscow during Operation Barbarossa.

At this point Hitler interceded and changed the course of the campaign. Convinced that the capture of Leningrad would secure trade routes with Sweden, he diverted part of Army Group Centre to assist with the advance in the north. Equally concerned with the grain that the Ukraine could provide, he further weakened the centre by sending panzer units toward Kiev. By the time these units could return for Operation Typhoon, the advance on Moscow, valuable time had been lost – the mud of the autumn and snow of the winter approached.

While Typhoon went smoothly at first, after 6 October wet snow began to fall, turning all roads into quagmires. Meanwhile, the citizens of Moscow had been mobilized to its defence. Women dug tank traps while the men formed militia units. As November wore on and the weather deteriorated, the Red Army's defences stiffened. When winter arrived in force, German tank engines froze for lack of anti-freeze and German soldiers froze for lack of winter clothes.

What the Germans did not know was that the Red Army had assembled a massive force behind Moscow. This was partially composed of Siberian divisions trained in winter warfare that had been guarding against a Japanese attack in the east and were equipped with new aircraft and the T-34 tank. Zhukov, the Red Army Chief of Staff, unleashed this force as the temperature dipped to –25° C. The Soviet plan was to do to the Germans what had happened to the Red Army repeatedly in the summer – encirclement. After two weeks of vicious fighting, the Red Army had recaptured the territory lost since the beginning of Operation Typhoon. Both armies then dug in to endure the winter.

Stalingrad

The Russian spring brought the same mud and quagmire that the autumn had delivered. The German army was not on the move again until May 1942. Both armies had rebuilt during the winter. In the frantic days of Barbarossa the Soviets had dismantled factories in the west before they fell into German hands and reassembled them in the relative safety of the Ural Mountains. These factories were now producing tanks, aircraft and weapons. Despite replacing the losses of the winter, the German divisions were still short some 500 000 men. It was production that dominated German strategy in 1942. Hitler ordered his army to drive south to secure the Baku oilfields across the Caucasus Mountains as oil was becoming an urgent issue for the German army. Again the Red Army withered in front of the German onslaught. The German Sixth Army moved down the Don River, its goal being the city of Stalingrad on the Volga River where it would use the city to secure Army Group A's flank as it pushed toward and through the Caucasus Mountains. As the Germans drove south they used Romanian, Hungarian and Italian troops to guard the flank of their advance. By the last weeks of August the German Sixth Army was fighting on the outskirts of the sprawling city of Stalingrad on the west bank of the Volga River.

The assault on the city was heralded by a massive bombing raid on 23 August that left much of the city a pile of rubble. The rubble would pile ever higher in the ensuing months. This destruction had a curious effect on the nature of the battle. As the streets became ever more impassable, the Germans found it hard to use its great advantage in armour. It essentially turned the Battle of Stalingrad into a series of small unit actions in which the tenacity and growing expertise of the Red Army would tell, evening the odds somewhat. The Soviet strategy was to fight for every house, factory, sewer or ditch, all of which were filled with rubble. The Germans referred to it as *Rattenkrieg* – War of the Rats.

▲ A Red Army soldier fights in the ruins of Stalingrad. How did the German success in destroying the city work against them?

The Soviets mobilized every aspect of Stalingrad society in defence of the city that bore their leader's name. Two hundred thousand citizens of the city were organized to dig entrenchments and fortify defences. A potent mixture of patriotism, survival and fear motivated all who defended the city. Stalin had issued his famous "Not One Step Backward" order in August in which he ordered anyone who retreated without orders to be arrested. It also provided for the creation of units whose job it was to form a line behind advancing troops to gun down those who turned around to flee. The Red Army would cling to the west bank of the river while trying to resupply these forces from staging areas on the east bank of the river. Such resupply was treacherous under constant attack from the Luftwaffe and from 21 September with artillery fire.

Initially the Red Army defended the city itself with three divisions and less than 70 tanks. The perimeter steadily shrank from the repeated thrusts by the German infantry and tanks. The effort, however, was exhausting the Germans as well and the Sixth Army commander von Paulus called a halt to bring up fresh troops and supplies for another

push. This push came on 4 October and took them within 300 metres of the river. With over half its fighting strength gone, the Sixth Army tried one last time to dislodge the Russians, but this too failed.

The city of Stalingrad itself had only been a part of the Soviet strategy. Stalin's inclination had been to use absolutely all his available troops to defend the city. Zhukov, however, persuaded "The Boss" as he was known, to defend the city with the smallest force possible. Meanwhile they would gather a huge force north of Stalingrad where the German line bowed west and was defended by inferior Romanian and Italian troops. By September 1942 the Russians were producing 2,200 tanks a month, while the Germans were building 500 a month, which then had to be divided among the various theatres in which the Germans were fighting. This massive Red Army force would drive south and east, while a smaller force south of Stalingrad would drive north and west in a bid to encircle the German Sixth Army. Operation Uranus began on 19 November and within a few days the encirclement was complete.

Had Hitler allowed him, von Paulus and the Sixth Army could have fought their way out at that point, but the Führer had his own version of the "Not One Step Backwards Order". His scheme involved an outside force fighting its way to von Paulus's position, which would meanwhile be supplied by air with 300 tonnes of supplies a day landing at three airfields within the German perimeter. About 280 000 Germans were caught in the cauldron. As the weather deteriorated and the temperature fell, so too did the amount of supplies that reached the surrounded Germans, averaging only 70 tonnes per day. Unable to evacuate the wounded or maintain ammunition supplies, the perimeter gradually shrank and von Paulus surrendered on 30 January 1943. Ninety-one thousand Germans were captured. Between 1945 and 1955 the Russians released 5,000 prisoners. The final 2,000 were released in 1955 – the rest had perished in captivity. Since the beginning of the Stalingrad operation in August it is estimated that Germany and her allies suffered 500 000 casualties. The Red Army suffered 1.1 million casualties of which some 485 000 were dead. Stalingrad was the furthest point to the east the German army would reach during the war.

Class discussion

To what extent did tanks affect the nature of the Second World War compared to the First World War?

Technology and war: tanks

Tanks had originated in Britain during the First World War. Initially small numbers of tanks were assigned to infantry units. Later, the Germans and British pioneered the idea of massing tanks in their own divisions with supporting infantry. Coordination between large formations of tanks was made more practical with advances in wireless radio technology.

Tanks were generally classified according to size and armament – light, medium and heavy. Medium tanks such as the US Sherman with a 108 mm gun and the German Panzer Mark IV were excellent machines and the workhorse of their armies. The Soviet T-34 was perhaps the best all-round medium tank of the war. Sloped armour made it difficult to pierce with anti-tank shells. Its diesel engine could

power it to over 50 kmh. Wide treads made it more versatile in snow and its 76 mm gun, though not as big as some medium tanks, was more than sufficient. Perhaps one of the greatest attributes of the T-34 was that it could be readily produced in huge quantities. More T-34s were manufactured than any other model of tank in the war – over 57 000.

While the T-34 and Sherman were both relatively simple tanks to produce, the German heavy tanks were more complicated. The Tiger I and Tiger II were fearsome weapons designed to outmatch the T-34. The intricate mechanics, however, made for cumbersome manufacturing and difficult repair. By the end of the war the Germans had only produced about 1,350 Tiger Is and less than 500 Tiger IIs.

North Africa

The war in North Africa from 1940 to 1943 was a running battle between three combatants. As in Russia and the Pacific, geographic location, topography, climate and vegetation – or lack thereof – in North Africa determined much of the nature of combat there. The absence of obstacles, except for impassable features such as the Qattara Depression, on the surface seems a perfect environment for the mechanization of the Second World War. The lack of roads, harsh climate and interminable sand and dust, however, made waging war here its own particular hell. What obstacles there were – the sea, highland or depression – would limit mobility to a narrow strip along the coast. Despite this, the war in North Africa would prove to be one of extreme mobility, albeit a confined mobility. As a theatre it also would depend on control of the Mediterranean Sea as the only feasible supply route.

Initially the North African war would see some 200 000 Italian troops in Libya facing 63 000 British soldiers in western Egypt. In September 1940 Italy launched an attack on Egypt after which it tried to consolidate its gains. The expedition into Egypt was short-lived and a British counter-attack in December 1940 sent the Italians retreating 650 kilometres along the coast roads. When the advancing British managed to get ahead of the retreating Italian army the victory seemed complete. It could not, however, get as far as Tripoli for reasons that would become commonplace. The advancing force could not maintain supplies and manpower to sustain such a rapid advance and the German army was coming to the aid of its beleaguered Italian ally. In this case the Germans sent a panzer division and infantry division that would become an elite fighting force known as the Afrika Corps under a confident and supremely competent general, Erwin Rommel.

Rommel wasted no time in throwing the British back to where they had started, which he had done by 3 April, where he too outstripped his food, fuel and water and came to a halt, where his troops dug in. A British effort to dislodge them came to nothing. Another attempt, Operation Crusader, eventually succeeded in pushing the German-Italian force back to where they had started, relieving the siege of Tobruk in the process. By May, Rommel was ready to try again and hurled his largely recovered force at the British, forcing them to again retire to the east. This time the fortress at Tobruk could not hold out and the Germans captured the city. Rommel would try again to break through the British defences at the Battle of Alam Halfa. It was his turn to dig in as the British Eighth Army amassed new men and material under its new commander, General Bernard Montgomery.

El Alamein

The resulting battle would be pivotal in the North African campaign. Rather than the fight and dash nature of the war in the desert up to this point, Montgomery would rely on his numeric superiority to fight a more plodding battle of attrition. Montgomery's plan was a massed infantry attack supported by massive bombardment. Once his troops had punched a hole in the German defences his massed armour would exploit the breach – a strategy more similar to 1916 than to 1942.

He wanted to inflict such losses on Rommel that he was compelled to withdraw and would thus be too weak to establish a strong position in the rear. The British plan worked. Forbidden by Hitler to retreat, Rommel committed to defend his northern position, weakening his southern position, where the British eventually broke through. Retreat became the only option and the German-Italian forces would not stop until they reached Tripoli in late January 1943.

▲ German soldiers advance toward El Alamein in 1942. What challenges did fighting in the desert pose for the combatants?

ATL Research and thinking skills

1942 is often viewed as the turning point in the war for the Allies. The years and months up to mid-1942 had been marked by Axis success – the conquest of Poland, France and western Europe, western Russia, Hong Kong, Singapore, the 1942 and its consequences

1942 is often viewed as the turning point in the war for the Allies. The years and months up to mid-1942 had been marked by Axis success – the conquest of Poland, France and western Europe, western Russia, Hong Kong, Singapore, the Philippines. Three important battles in 1942, Midway, Stalingrad and El Alamein, stopped Axis progress. From that point the Allies began to push them back.

Complete the following table to explore the consequences of Stalingrad and El Alamein in more detail.

Battle	Effect on Axis troop strength	Effect on Axis material strength	Other short-term consequences	Long-term consequences
El Alamein				
Stalingrad				

Over the course of the next few months, the German-Italian forces would be driven against the anvil of the US army that had landed in Algeria and Morocco, and although they had some successes at places like Kasserine Pass, their acute supply shortages and dwindling manpower meant that it was only a matter of time before they surrendered. The Royal Navy's dominance in the Mediterranean sunk two-thirds of the material needed to sustain the Germans at fighting strength. The last 275 000 of the Axis forces in North Africa surrendered in May 1943.

Sicily and Italy

The invasion of Sicily was aimed at what the British viewed as the "soft underbelly of Europe". It was designed to divert German forces from the eastern front and to foment a revolt against Mussolini's increasingly unpopular regime. Setting off from Tunisia, US and British airborne and amphibious troops, 10 divisions in all, landed in Sicily in July 1943. They faced ineffectual Italian divisions buttressed by two German divisions. The capture of Sicily was the preliminary stroke in the invasion of the Italian peninsula in September. Peninsulas are difficult for attacking forces. Their narrowness makes outflanking manoeuvres difficult and interlocking defence easier. In Italy the peninsula was split by a mountain range that offered obstacles to attacking forces and cover to defending forces. The mountains further forced the Allies moving up the peninsula to divide and advance up the coasts, allowing the Germans to concentrate their forces on their flanks and leave the centre lightly defended. The US command was hesitant about the Sicilian and Italian operations, viewing them as a distraction from the invasion of western Europe into which they would have to commit valuable men and resources. In any event, the Germans would conduct that defence as the Italians signed an armistice with the Allies on 3 September. Allied troops landed on the peninsula on 9 September.

After landing at Salerno, the Allies raced north to capture Naples, but ran into a strong defensive line running the breadth of the peninsula south of Rome, the Gustav Line, where the advance was bogged down. Some of the bitterest fighting of the war took place around the western anchor of the Gustav Line, a strongpoint around the abbey of Monte Cassino. On the eastern flank, British and Canadian forces encountered heavy fighting in places such as Ortona and Sangro. Unable to outflank a line that stretched from shore to shore, the Allies opted to do so through another amphibious landing, this time south of Rome at Anzio in January 1944. Although it achieved strategic surprise, the US commander failed to exploit this success and another Allied advance became bogged down. It would take another five months for the Allies to enter Rome, two days before the landings at Normandy. The German forces retreated to a second prepared defensive line 300 kilometres north of Rome, the Gothic Line, from which they would conduct their defence for the remainder of the war.

Normandy

The grand Allied strategy had, since the entry of the United States, been in one way or another to involve German in a two-front war. The hard-pressed Soviet Union became ever more insistent on this and Stalin complained bitterly when the date for the establishment of this second front was postponed. The invasion of Sicily and Italy was partially designed to force the Germans to divert divisions from the eastern front thereby relieving some pressure on the Red Army. Although the Allied operations in Italy did divert troops and material from the force pressing the Soviets, it was not enough to satisfy Stalin or to make a difference on the battlefield. Regardless, the main second front was not to be Italy, but rather in France – Operation Overlord.

The obstacles to landing in force in France were formidable. A number of these were highlighted by the Dieppe Raid of August 1942. A force of 5,000 Canadians landed at the port city of Dieppe to probe its defences. On the surface it was a disaster. Of the 5,000 Canadians and 1,000 British soldiers that landed, less than half returned. Nevertheless, the raid did teach some hard won lessons that would be employed in the planning of Overlord:

- attack open beaches rather than established ports

- attack sand beaches – tanks could not get traction on the shale beaches at Dieppe

- land the bulk of tanks after the beaches are secure

- absolute air superiority is necessary during amphibious operations

- landing craft had to be improved and operated by the navy.

An operation the size of Overlord would take unprecedented logistical planning and material build-up. The plan seemed simple enough. The United States, British and Canadian armies would attack five beaches – Omaha, Utah, Gold, Sword and Juno respectively – on the coast of France supported by paratroop drops behind German lines, and establish a beachhead into which men and material would flow in the days after the landings. From this beachhead the invasion force would break out and drive north and east, securing the coast and advance on Paris. Such an undertaking would take a level of cooperation and coordination between all three branches of three national armies. The civilian population of Britain would have to be mobilized to support the build-up that would happen there. Contact and coordination with the French resistance was necessary as was the inclusion of the **Free French** leadership. Intelligence including troop dispositions and maps of the objectives would have to be gathered. Huge amounts of material would have to be produced and stored. All of this would have to be kept secret from German intelligence. Any commander overseeing such an operation needed to be adept at logistics, diplomacy and strategy. US General Dwight Eisenhower was chosen as Supreme Commander. The British General Bernard Montgomery was given tactical command during the landings.

The defences were formidable, but troubled. Rommel had been placed in command of the Atlantic Wall (as the German positions were known). He disagreed with his superior, Field Marshall von Rundstedt, on how

Free French
French soldiers and citizens who escaped occupied France and organized themselves into military formations under the leadership of Charles de Gaulle. These formations fought with the Allies against the Axis Powers.

best to defend the long coastline. Rommel favoured a defence that sought to destroy the enemy on the beach while they were exposed and had yet to muster their forces. Rundstedt instead wanted to slow the enemy with the beach defence and destroy them as they moved inland with a mobile armoured force kept in reserve.

Rommel ordered the coastal defences strengthened. A million mines a month were laid and the number of landing obstacles was drastically increased. These obstacles on the Normandy beaches were designed to wreck landing craft. If the invasion force was to avoid them they would have to land at low tide, thereby increasing the distance that the exposed forces would have to cover from the waterline. Nevertheless, the main defensive effort would have to come from armour. Obviously there was not enough to cover the entire 2,600-kilometre front and so some sort of an estimation of where the landings would take place was required. Hitler intervened personally and split the tank forces between the two generals and further ordered that the reserve could not be used against an invasion force without his personal order. This almost guaranteed a delayed and weak response to an Allied landing at Normandy.

The obvious invasion route was where the English Channel was at its narrowest, the Pas de Calais, and the Allied command did everything they could to encourage that belief. The Allies constructed a fake army, complete with empty barracks, wooden tanks and aircraft opposite the Pas de Calais. Deliberately false radio traffic conveyed the notion that this was where the invasion would take place. The deception went on until the last moment when the Allies dropped "dummy" paratroopers ahead of the actual drops in Normandy. The belief was that once the Germans discovered the paratroopers at Normandy were fake they would conclude that the actual drop was going to take place at the Pas de Calais and would move out of Normandy ahead of the real Allied drops. The Allied air forces concentrated more tonnage of bombs in the area around and east of the Pas de Calais than around Normandy.

By the time the Allied invasion force was ready in May of 1944 it was an impressive assembly. From May 1942 to May 1944 the Allies had managed to muster:

- 1.5 million US, British and Canadian soldiers

- 5 million tonnes of supplies

- 12 000 aircraft

- 1,000 locomotives

- 20 000 railroad cars.

The invasion force itself included:

- 2,500 naval craft

- 4,000 landing craft

- 170 000 soldiers, 18 000 paratroopers

- 1,000 paratroop transport aircraft.

▲ General Eisenhower talking with paratroopers before they drop into France ahead of the Normandy landings. What role did the paratroopers play in the D-Day invasion?

The invasion began on 6 June 1944. The night before, three divisions of British and US paratroopers dropped behind enemy lines to secure bridges and other strategic points with mixed success. The drops were helped by the confusion that seemed to grip the defending forces and their slow response. The experiences of the amphibious forces were varied.

- **Utah Beach**: The 23 000 US troops that landed on Utah, a 5-kilometre stretch of sandy beach on the extreme west end of the Normandy landings, met limited resistance, suffering 197 casualties.

- **Omaha Beach**: The experience of the 34 000 US troops that landed at Omaha was considerably different. Confusion and heavy seas conspired to push many landing craft off course. The "swimming" Sherman tanks foundered in the seas. Omaha was also defended by the most experienced of the German troops at Normandy that day. High banks overlooked much of the landing beaches giving the Germans clear fire at the approaching infantry. After a day of heavy fighting the invaders had established a beachhead at a cost of 4,650 casualties.

- **Gold Beach**: Twenty-five thousand British soldiers attacked the 8-kilometre beach at the centre of the Normandy invasions. The airborne drops behind their positions disoriented the inexperienced defenders. Nevertheless one fortified village provided a stout defence causing heavy casualties on some of the attacking units. By the evening the British were moving inland and linking up with the attackers from Sword and Juno beaches. The British suffered close to 400 casualties.

- **Juno Beach**: The Canadians stormed the beaches with 21 000 men and at first met stiff resistance, primarily from pre-sighted killing zones on the beach and landing obstacles that the engineers had been unable to clear. By evening they had moved inland to link up with British forces from Gold Beach. On the day the Canadians suffered some 1,200 casualties with close to 350 dead.

- **Sword Beach**: The 23 000 troops that came ashore at the far east end of the landings encountered little resistance, but once ashore did face a counter-attack by German tank forces. Allied air superiority blunted this attack. In all, the British suffered 600 casualties at Sword.

The Road to Berlin

From the surrender of the German Sixth Army at Stalingrad, the Red Army continued to grow in both men and material. With this growing strength it marched west, reconquering territory that had been occupied by the Germans since June 1941. The devastation and terror that the Germans had meted out during their occupation was becoming more evident as the Russians advanced, fueling their motivation and shaping their own attitudes on occupation.

The Germans, however, were not finished and planned a massive advance around the Soviet city of Kursk. The result was the largest tank battle in history. The Soviets, forewarned of the attack, pounded the German forces with artillery as they mustered for the advance. As the 1,900 German tanks moved forward they were drawn into an elaborate defensive system and destroyed. The ensuing Soviet counter-attack completed the Red Army's victory. Massive engagements such as Kursk only served to drive home the point that the Red Army could suffer higher losses than their opponent and still claim victory. They were dramatically outproducing their enemy. By October the Red Army was pushing west with over 4 million men and 4,000 tanks reaching Warsaw by the end of August 1944.

The western Allies were themselves making strides toward the Reich. Captured channel ports such as Antwerp allowed for easier supply. An attempt to capture the Rhine bridges intact through a coordinated airborne and armoured operation known as Market Garden fell short of its objectives in September 1944 which would mean that the push across the Rhine into the German heartland would have to wait until the spring.

Berlin itself would fall to the Red Army in early May after a methodical advance through the city from all directions. On 2 May the city was in their hands.

The war at sea

Battle of the Atlantic

The Battle of the Atlantic refers to the ongoing effort to bring supplies – food, munitions and men – across the Atlantic from the factories and fields of North America to Britain. The island nation required over a million tonnes of imports each week to survive – half its overall need – and had a massive merchant fleet of over 3,000 ships to do this. For every 14 merchant ships, the Royal Navy had one escort vessel. In 1939 and 1941 this was generally sufficient to deal with the threat provided by the German navy.

Class discussion

How might the Germans have repelled the Normandy invasion?

▲ An Allied tanker burns and sinks after being torpedoed. To what extent was Britain dependent on imports to survive?

The *Kriegsmarine* as it was known saw a concentration on large surface vessels during the rearmament period, a strategy that continued in the early years of the war. Spectacular losses to Germany's surface fleet such as the sinking of the state-of-the-art battleship *Bismarck* and the scuttling of the "pocket" battleship *Scheer*, helped convince the German high command that the more affordable – and more successful – U-boat programme should be expanded in the hope of strangling her island enemy. Germany's U-boat fleet reached a peak of 300 vessels in 1942, which also marked the height of its success. Rather than lone boats hunting and attacking on their own, the U-boat fleet adopted a "Wolf Pack" strategy in which the fleet would stretch out across established shipping lines. Once a U-boat made contact with an Allied convoy they would radio their location to other boats. When sufficient boats, at times reaching 40 vessels, had convened on the convoy they would attack. Multiple attacking vessels made it far more difficult for the escort vessels to protect the entire convoy.

ATL Research skills

The armies that moved across Europe and North Africa during the Second World War consumed enormous amounts of natural resources. At the same time, land and sea operations made the import and export of materials very tenuous. In fact, the need to secure these resources often dictated overall strategy. To get an idea of the needs of the combatants, complete the following table for Germany, Britain, the USSR, the USA and France and answer the questions that follow.

Resource	Source	Strategic implication
Food		
Iron		
Coal		
Oil		

Which country was in the best situation in terms of resources? Which was in the worst?

How does the information in the table help to explain the strategic decisions made by each country during the war?

Over time the Allies defeated the U-boat threat through a combination of production and technology. Once the US shipbuilding industry was mobilized for war and innovations such as the Liberty ship, built in components around the US and shipped to the coast for assembling, were developed the Allies were building shipping tonnage far faster than the U-boats could sink them. The limitations of anti-submarine technology such as ASDIC (a form of sonar) and depth charges were eventually improved. Anti-submarine aircraft steadily increased their range, reaching far out into the Atlantic to give effective air cover to Allied convoys. By the end of 1943 the Allies were sinking U-boats twice as fast as the Germans could replace them. By the end of the war 75% of all German submariners had been killed.

Technology and war: radar

In the mid-1920s experiments had established that it was possible to measure the distance to an object by timing the return of radio waves bounced off the object. The military applications were soon evident. By the time the war broke out, Britain and Germany had developed radar stations to detect incoming aircraft. Radar's accuracy was refined throughout the Second World War as was the scope of its application. Developments such as the cavity magnetron allowed for the reading of higher frequency radio waves, which proved more accurate. Eventually radar was placed on aircraft to find targets at sea. It was placed on ships to discover surfaced submarines. It was used to aim anti-aircraft guns and find bombing targets through cloud cover.

As with all military technology, each advance in radar prompted the development of countermeasures. Artillery shells that burst in the air releasing fragments of aluminium presented multiple reflective surfaces for the radar to bounce off thus confusing it. Radar detectors mounted on aircraft could alert crews as to when they were being hit with radio waves directing anti-aircraft fire.

Technology and war: anti-submarine warfare

Anti-submarine warfare can be divided into detection/defensive technology and offensive technology. The Allies had discovered the defensive benefits of the convoy system during the First World War. It allowed a comparatively small escort force to protect a greater number of ships. By the end of the war, Allied convoys in the Atlantic grew to over 150 ships. The move by Allied navies toward larger convoys came from the statistical analysis that suggested the number of sinkings in a convoy attack depended on the number of U-boats attacking rather than the size of the convoy, theoretically allowing for larger convoys.

Submarine detection initially relied on ASDIC or sonar developed during the First World War. Although ASDIC was relatively successful in detecting submerged submarines, it could not do so with surfaced U-boats. Escort vessels were eventually equipped with maritime radar sets, which made this easier. Hydrophones were listening devices that could pick up faint sound waves emitted from submerged U-boats. Anti-submarine aircraft used advanced technology such as magnetic anomaly detectors that could detect the change in magnetic fields caused by a submarine hull to find their prey.

Once detected, escort vessels would launch an attack on the submerged U-boat. The primary weapon used by the Allied navies was the depth charge, a waterproof explosive charge detonated by a pressure fuse. Early in the war depth charges were dropped off the stern of ships or thrown by single charge launchers, requiring the attacking ship to pass over the submarine several times in order to either sink it or force it to the surface. The Hedgehog was an improvement in that it fired 24 projectiles 80 metres ahead of the ship and detonated on contact. This meant that the U-boat had far less time to escape once its own hydrophone heard the approaching ship.

Long-range aircraft, which could spot and attack U-boats, were highly effective in protecting convoys. As the war progressed the range of aircraft such as the Sunderland Flying Boat and the PBY Catalina increased, as did their ability to attack U-boats. Devices such as the absolute altimeter meant that aircraft could fly at far lower altitudes with safety, increasing the accuracy of their attacks.

The air war

Battle of Britain

When France surrendered to Germany in June 1940, the German high command expected Britain to ask for terms of peace. Churchill, now the Prime Minister, would hear none of this. To say that Britain was alone does a disservice to Canada, Australia and New Zealand who stood by her. Nevertheless, the fact that Britain would not negotiate meant that a military solution to her resistance would have to be found. That solution became known as Operation Sealion.

Sealion planned Germany's amphibious invasion of Britain. To call it a plan is generous; Sealion lacked the meticulous planning that Germany's other operations had entailed. Even had it been given the attention required, Germany did not have the naval resources to control the channel long enough to get an invasion force across. Hitler and Goering did, however, believe that they had the resources to control the airspace over the islands and the channel, also a prerequisite to invasion. The Luftwaffe was given the mammoth task of destroying Britain's coastal defences, eliminating the RAF's ability to operate, and preventing the ability of ground forces to operate once the invasion was underway. This attempt would become the Battle of Britain.

From the beginning the RAF enjoyed certain advantages over the Luftwaffe.

- British radar installations could detect incoming aircraft.

- The Luftwaffe had suffered greater losses in the Battle of France than the RAF.

- The British Spitfire, though fewer in number than the Hurricane, was equal, if not superior, to the German Bf 109 Messerschmitt.

- The Hurricane, although an inferior fighter, could be produced in large numbers quickly. In all the British outproduced the Germans in fighter aircraft at a rate of 25:7.

- As much of the aerial combat took place over or close to Britain, salvage of damaged aircraft and recovery of pilots was easier than it was for the Luftwaffe.

- Germany had no heavy bombers suited to destroying large urban centres or industrial facilities. The Luftwaffe would rely on medium-sized level flight bombers designed to support ground forces – the "flying artillery" of *Blitzkrieg*.

▲ German Bf 109 Messerschmitts over England in 1940. How did rearming after Germany give Britain a technological advantage?

▲ An RAF Spitfire. What was the relationship between quality and quantity in British aircraft production?

- Because the Luftwaffe was operating far from its bases in France, the amount of time her fighters could stay over the target area to protect her bomber fleets was limited to 15 minutes, leaving these aircraft unprotected for a portion of each operation.

- British Intelligence could decipher Luftwaffe radio transmissions.

The Germans first attempted to eliminate the coastal radar installations during July and early August. Although achieving some success, they abandoned this part of the operation before it was complete, leaving the important early warning system functional throughout the battle. The exchange rate during this part of the battle was telling. The Germans lost 180 aircraft and the British lost 70.

On 13 August the Luftwaffe began to attack RAF airfields, sea ports and other strategic targets. This pattern would continue through to 7 September, and although German losses were always greater than British losses in terms of total aircraft, it was unclear how long the RAF could continue to resist the onslaught against its airfields. It was beginning to lose fighters faster than they were producing them. On 7 September Hitler ordered the focus of attack to shift to London in an effort to break British morale and bomb them to the conference table. Shifting the attacks to London allowed the RAF to recover and rebuild, but it also placed the burden of the battle on the shoulders of the citizens of London. It pushed the RAF hard and on 15 September it committed all its reserves to repulsing a massive raid against the capital. The attack was met and defeated. Daylight bombing raids continued into October, causing damage that was far outweighed by the cost to the Luftwaffe. Germany's air war against Britain would now focus on a terror bombing campaign of urban centres.

Class discussion

These weapons were in part designed to spread terror as well as destruction. How effective is terror bombing as a strategy? To what extent does its effectiveness depend on whether the target country is a liberal democracy or a dictatorship?

Technology and war: pilotless weapons

The Germans had been working on pilotless aircraft, specifically rocket technology, throughout the 1930s. By the end of the decade the programme had grown to the point where a permanent test facility was developed, however, it was not until 1942 that a rocket was successfully tested. The test facility was severely damaged in an air raid in 1943, further delaying the deployment of an operational weapon.

V1 bombs were flying bombs that carried about 900 kg of explosives, could travel about 300 km, and were powered by a jet engine. They could be launched from aircraft or from the ground. Once the preset distance had been covered, the engine would stop and the bomb would fall out of the sky. This meant that it was not a very accurate weapon. The Luftwaffe fired 8,500 V1s, about half of which were destroyed before they landed.

The V2 was a ballistic missile that carried the same explosive power as the V1, but because it was propelled by a rocket, it could travel six times faster than the V1 and was thus more difficult to defend against. About 1,300 V2s landed in London, their primary target, killing 2,400 civilians and wounding many more.

The Blitz

The Blitz refers to the sustained bombing on urban centres and industrial targets between September 1940 and May 1941. German goals throughout the Blitz were twofold. The first goal was to crush civilian morale such that Churchill and his government would have to negotiate an end to the war. Failing that, the raids were designed to impede British war production. On both counts, the campaign was a failure, but at a terrible cost.

The fate of Warsaw had given ample warning to British civilians of what high explosive aerial bombing could do. From September 1939 civil defence authorities in Britain began to make preparations. Many types and sizes of shelters were built or adapted from existing structures, sometimes without direction from the government, the most famous being the London underground. A fear that the enemy might use aerial bombs filled with poison gas prompted authorities to issue as many gas masks as they could. Blackout regulations were enforced in an attempt to make finding targets more difficult.

For eight months the campaign was unrelenting. At one point London endured 57 consecutive nights of bombing. British propagandists turned the suffering into a rallying point. Churchill made a point of being seen out surveying damage and talking to victims. The royal family even toured bombing sites. More than 40 000 civilians were killed during the Blitz.

Strategic bombing

Strategic bombing refers to the aerial bombing of targets of strategic importance to the enemy's war effort. In general, this fell into two categories. Area bombing was the indiscriminant bombing of all the structures in an area, regardless of strategic value. Precision bombing was designed to limit the damage, and thereby concentrate it, on smaller target areas such as industrial sectors, railway lines and ports.

The Luftwaffe, designed to support ground force action, never developed the machines to carry out heavy bombing deep into enemy territory. They would never have this ability, although their night fighters initially inflicted heavy losses on British Bomber Command.

Technology and war: long-range bombers

When the German Luftwaffe switched from attacking radar installations and airfields during the Battle of Britain it did so without the basic requirement of strategic bombing: long-range, level flight heavy bombers. The Allies, being more committed to long-range strategic bombing, devoted more resources into developing models capable of delivering large payloads of explosives to Germany's industrial heartland, delivered by the British RAF and the US Army Air Corps by night.

The British hit upon its most durable design in 1942 with the mass production of the Avro Lancaster. Its range was 4,000 km and was manned by a crew of seven. Its bomb capacity was 14 standard 1,000 lb bombs. It was very versatile in terms of possible payloads with a bomb bay that could be easily converted to carry a wide range of ordinance, including the "bouncing bombs" of the Dam Raids and the 22 000 lb. "Grand Slam". Navigational aids such as the "Gee" system and later "Oboe" allowed for precise navigating at night, essential for the British bombing strategy.

The Boeing Corporation designed a series of very effective long-range bombers for US forces in both Europe and the Pacific. Initially developed in 1937, the B17 was used in large numbers in both theatres, with a number of models produced by a variety of companies. Eventually over 12 000 B17s were produced. Nicknamed the Flying Fortress, the B17 had a range of 3,000 km and could carry between 2,000 kg and 3,600 kg of bombs depending on distance to target. Equipped with the precise Norden bombsight, the B17 dropped approximately 40% of all aerial bombs dropped by the US during the war. The B24 Liberator was designed to replace the B17 and was produced in greater numbers than any other bomber in the war. The B17 was still preferable to aircrew and the B24 augmented rather than replaced the B17 even though it carried a larger payload. The B29 Superfortress only saw action in the Pacific. Its range, ceiling, speed and ordinance all made it the most advanced long-range bomber when it first flew.

The Allied strategic bombing campaign made use of many types and sizes of bombs. The type of target generally determined the type of bomb used. All-purpose demolition bombs ranged in size from 45 to 1,350 kg and were used against industrial targets, railroads and cities. Fragmentation bombs were generally used against ground troops and defences. Incendiary bombs were designed to start fires and were used against cities in both European and Pacific theatres.

Class discussion

Is there an ethical difference between fire-bombing cities with incendiary bombs and demolition bombing cities with high explosive bombs?

▲ A B17 Flying Fortress. What role did strategic bombing play in the Allied victory?

British operational doctrine advocated night bombing missions deep into enemy territory. The cover of night was partially to overcome the fact that the British had no long-distance fighters that could offer protection to its bomber fleets. As the size, number and range of Bomber Command's aircraft increased, it was able to inflict ever-greater damage on German cities in area bombing missions. For example in May 1942, 1,000 British bombers attacked the German city of Cologne,

setting 600 acres of the city ablaze. This highlighted a new tactic of the commander of Bomber Command, Arthur "Bomber" Harris. Incendiary bombs would be salted in among high explosive bombs to ensure that what was not blasted would be burned.

TOK discussion

For each of the following targets write arguments for and against attacking it with aerial bombs during a time of war. In groups of three or four discuss your arguments and make the decision whether or not the target should be bombed.

- Ball bearing factories
- Munitions factories
- Ports
- Cities
- Railroads

1   On what basis did you make the arguments for and against aerial bombing? What were the most important factors in coming to a decision?

2   To what extent did your decision differ from the decision made during the Second World War? How do you account for any difference?

Bomber production		
Bomber	Country	Number produced
B17 Flying Fortress	USA	12 730
B29 Superfortress	USA	3970
Avro Lancaster	Britain	7377
Dornier Do 217	Germany	1900
Heinkel He 111	Germany	6400
Junker Ju 88	Germany	15 000

The arrival of the United States Eighth Air Force in 1942 brought a different approach to strategic bombing. The US bombers were fitted with an excellent daylight bombsight that allowed for more targeting precision. These B17s were heavily armed so that they could fight their way deep into enemy airspace, drop their payloads and fight their way out without fighter protection. This proved disastrous and the Eighth Air Force would limit its deep missions until long-range fighter escorts were available. The US daylight precision bombing was seen as complementing the British night-time area bombing, but its lack of protection limited it to attacking targets in France, Belgium and the Netherlands. By 1944 the United States Army Air Force (USAAF) was equipped with the excellent P-51 Mustang fighter which could operate far into Germany and outmatched any Luftwaffe fighter.

6.5 Effects of the Second World War

Conceptual understanding

Key questions

→ How did the end of the Second World War compare to the end of the First World War?

→ To what extent did the Allies hold the Axis Powers responsible for the conduct of the war?

→ To what extent did the global influence of Europe change as a result of the war?

Key concepts

→ Continuity

→ Change

Immediate effects

Taken as a whole, the European, North African and Pacific theatres were won by the USSR and the United States. They emerged as the two global superpowers. If this is the case it means that the war in Europe was not won by a European power insofar as the Soviet Union had been isolated from the events in the rest of Europe for the majority of the inter-war period. The course of European history in the post-war era would be governed by this fact.

The effects of a war so vast in scope are impossible to detail. The devastation was complete – human, cultural, economic; all aspects of European civilization was clubbed by the war. Perhaps the most immediate effect of the war was the human cost.

European war dead		
Country	Military deaths	Civilian deaths
Belgium	12 100	74 000
Czechoslovakia	25 000	320 000
France	217 600	350 000
Germany	5 533 000	1 067 000–3 267 000
Great Britain	383 600	67 100
Netherlands	17 000	284 000
Norway	3 000	6 500
Poland	240 000	5 360 000
USSR	8 800 000–10 700 000	15 200 000–13 300 000

Source: "By the Numbers: World Wide Deaths", *The National World War II Museum* http://www.nationalww2museum.org/learn/education/for-students/ww2-history/ww2-by-the-numbers/world-wide-deaths.html

The damage to the cultural heritage of the continent was immense. Aerial bombing devastated the architecture of cities across the continent. Warsaw endured the destruction of much of its centuries-old buildings at its city centre. German cities such as Dresden were burned out. The 120 hectares of the city centre of the cathedral city of Cologne were leveled in a single air raid while the cathedral itself remained standing, although heavily damaged by several direct hits. The city would suffer over 200 air raids during the war. While St Paul's Cathedral in London, Sir Christopher Wren's masterpiece, survived the war with limited damage, Coventry Cathedral was not so lucky, burning after being hit by incendiary bombs during the Blitz in 1940. Florence lost all but one of her storied bridges, demolished by the retreating German army. It was just this type of damage that prompted first the Danish and then French authorities to surrender their capitals before they could be devastated from above.

Cultural institutions in many European cities went to extraordinary lengths to shelter collections from destruction and hide them from theft. In the weeks before the German invasion, curators from the Louvre and other French museums moved their collections to secret locations in the countryside. British Museum holdings were stashed in remote parts of Wales. This did not, however, save countless works in central and eastern Europe. In addition to the works of art destroyed, either as collateral damage or deliberately destroyed by the war, many thousands more were pilfered by occupying German forces. Add to these pieces of art those that had been systematically stolen by high-ranking Nazis during the seven years before the war began and the cultural devastation of the war broadens immeasurably.

Recovery

One of the many lessons that came out of the flawed settlement to the First World War was the realization that Europe could not be left on its own to recover. The destruction of infrastructure, urban areas and industrial centres was far more widespread than it had been in 1918. The political instability of the inter-war period was seen by many as a product of the weak global economy of the 1920s and 1930s. As early as 1944 at Bretton Woods the Allied leaders planned to re-establish trade and sound currencies as soon as hostilities ceased. The western Allies understood that the global economy depended upon as timely a recovery as possible in Europe, but they also wanted to avoid any long-term dependence on the US economy. The stock market crash of 1929 had proved the folly of that. Nevertheless the US economy emerged from the war, as it had in 1918, as the dominant economy on the globe. It held two-thirds of the world's gold supply and produced over 60% of the world's industrial output. In the immediate post-war period, direct aid in the form of food, fuel and loans poured from the US into western Europe. By 1947 the European economy had regained much of its lost industrial capacity, but the extent to which it could be self-sustaining was in doubt.

It was to answer this pressing issue and to remove central economic planning or economic nationalism as a potential answer to any resulting economic despair in Europe that the US announced the Marshall Plan in 1947. Aid credits allowing for the improvement of infrastructure and free trade, a condition of Marshall Aid, made recovery more efficient. The United States' economy also benefitted as wartime demand was replaced with European recovery demand. The plan exacerbated deteriorating US/Soviet relations and was a major accelerant in the Cold War.

ATL Research and communication skills

Choose one of the following cities and research the steps taken to rebuild it after the Second World War. What was the extent of the damage? How were historic buildings restored? Were any buildings left as they were? How did the countries pay for the restoration and rebuilding of their cities?

- London
- Berlin
- Hiroshima
- Warsaw
- Dresden
- Tokyo
- Cologne
- Shanghai
- Nagasaki

Illustrate your findings with photographs and present your research to your classmates.

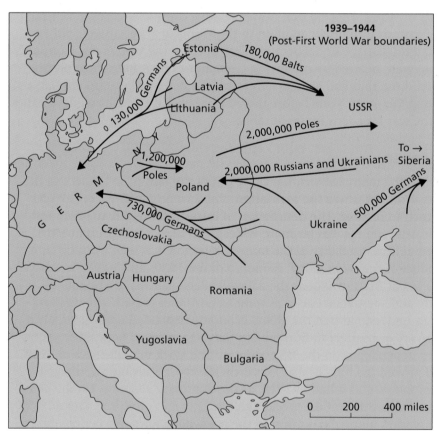

▲ European population migration, 1939–1944. How do you account for the migration patterns in the map?

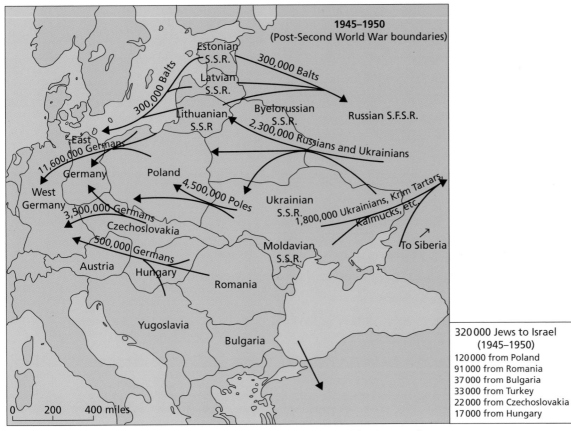

1945–1950
(Post-Second World War boundaries)

Estonian
S.S.R.

300,000 Balts

300,000 Balts

Latvian
S.S.R.

Lithuanian
S.S.R

Byelorussian
S.S.R.

Russian S.F.S.R.

2,300,000 Russians and Ukrainians

East
11,600,000 Germans

Germany

Poland

4,500,000 Poles

Krim Tartars,

West
Germany

3,500,000 Germans

Ukrainian
S.S.R.

1,800,000 Ukrainians, Kalmucks, etc.

Czechoslovakia

500,000 Germans

Austria

Hungary

Moldavian
S.S.R.

To Siberia

Romania

Yugoslavia

Bulgaria

| 0 | 200 | 400 miles |

320 000 Jews to Israel
(1945–1950)
120 000 from Poland
91 000 from Romania
37 000 from Bulgaria
33 000 from Turkey
22 000 from Czechoslovakia
17 000 from Hungary

▲ Post-war European population migration. What effect would this migration have on the opening years of the Cold War?

War crimes

Allied leaders had discussed the issue of holding the German leadership responsible for both the start and the conduct of the war on several occasions. Once Stalin's suggestion of summary execution had been dismissed, it was decided on a tribunal approach in which representatives of the four occupying powers would sit in judgment of the accused. The accused, both individuals as well as collectives such as the SS, were charged with one or more of the following:

- planning an aggressive war
- carrying out an aggressive war
- war crimes
- crimes against humanity.

The main trials were held in Nuremburg, but others were also held around Germany as well as in combatant countries such as France, Belgium and Canada.

The trials continued into 1949, although mostly under the auspices of the United States. The political will to continue the trials dissipated as the Cold War intensified. The trials had never been popular in Germany and with an increasingly aggressive Soviet Union, the United States determined that they needed the support of West Germans more than they needed the convictions of by then minor Nazi officials.

▲ Herman Goering looking bored at his trial for war crimes. What arguments did the accused use in their defence?

War crimes verdicts		
Name	Position	Sentence
Karl Dönitz	Admiral	10 years imprisonment
Wilhelm Frick	Minister of the Interior	Death
Hans Frank	Governor-General of occupied Poland	Death
Hans Fritzsche	Propaganda official	Acquitted
Walther Funk	Minister of Economic Affairs	Life imprisonment
Herman Goering	Commander of the Luftwaffe and Deputy Führer	Death
Alfred Jodl	Chief of German Armed Forces Operations Staff	Death
Rudolph Hess	Deputy Führer until 1941	Life imprisonment
Wilhelm Keitel	Chief of Armed Forces	Death
Kostantin von Neurath	Foreign Minister and later Governor of occupied Bohemia and Moravia	15 years imprisonment
Franz von Papen	Vice chancellor and later Nazi official in Turkey	Acquitted
Joachim von Ribbentrop	Foreign minister	Death
Erich Raeder	Commander-in-Chief of the navy	Life imprisonment
Hjalmar Schacht	Economic minister	Acquitted
Alfred Rosenberg	Minister for the Eastern Territories	Death
Martin Bormann	Head of Party Chancellery	Death
Baldur von Schirach	Leader of the Hitler Youth	20 years imprisonment
Arthur Seys-Inquart	*Reichskommissar* for the Netherlands	Death
Albert Speer	Architect and Minister of Armaments	20 years imprisonment
Julius Streicher	Editor of anti-Semitic magazine *Der Stürmer*	Death

Long-term effects

The Cold War

The Grand Alliance came together for the singular purpose of defeating the Axis Powers. A common enemy was the one thing that held it together. In terms of core values or a shared worldview, the Soviet Union and the United States had nothing in common prior to the United States entering the war against Germany. As the defeat of Germany drew closer the differences between the Allies once again came to the fore. Did the Second World War cause the Cold War? That is far too simplistic. There were, however, aspects of the course of the war that made the Cold War more likely.

- The devastation that the war had visited on the Soviet Union provoked Stalin to take reparations.

- The German invasion of the Soviet Union caused Stalin to look for security in eastern Europe.

- Stalin interpreted the policy of appeasement as an anti-Soviet policy.

- The US decision to not share nuclear weapon technology with the Allies led to a sense of mistrust and competition.

- Stalin chose to interpret the delays in Operation Overlord as deliberate.

- During the wartime conferences difficult questions regarding the post-war settlement were postponed.

There is little doubt that, in part, the origins of the Cold War lay in the conduct of the Second World War. Nevertheless there were other causes. Ideological differences predated the war, as did a mutual misunderstanding and ignorance of values, goals and motives.

ATL Research and communication skills

Research the role that women played in the war effort of the major combatants. Use the information you discover to create an argument for greater equality for women in the post-war years. Express your argument in one of the following formats:

- Pamphlet
- Speech
- Web page
- Video
- Presentation software

The United Nations

It is a testament to the Allied leaders' vision that they did not view the League of Nations as a failed experiment in collective security and international cooperation. It was understood that the absence of some of the major powers was an important impediment to its operations. On the other hand, why would the Great Powers join if their vote counted the same as smaller powers? Still, it was understood by most that the new organization could not simply be another way for the powers to dominate the room. A balance had to be found. This balance was the Security Council. The veto provided to the four powers in the Security Council persuaded them that their role and influence would be respected. The General Assembly and other organs of the United Nations (UN), which operated under the principle of one country one vote, gave a voice to the less powerful states.

Decolonization

This was the second war in a generation to devastate the European imperial powers. The British and French empires had endured the First World War intact, but weakened. Canada and the other dominions had used their contributions to the victory to gain more autonomy and India and other colonies began to expect similar treatment. In the aftermath of the Second World War India's cries for independence could no longer be ignored by the weakened British and the Algerians accelerated their agitation for independence. Ho Chi Minh spent the war fighting the Japanese with his guerrilla force and drafted a declaration of independence once the Japanese surrendered to the United States. By weakening the old colonial powers to the extent that they could no longer maintain their empires, the Second World War contributed to the wave of decolonization that swept Africa and Asia in the post-war period.

Exam-style questions and further reading

Exam-style questions

1 To what extent was ideology a cause of the Second World War in Europe?

2 Evaluate appeasement as an effective diplomatic policy.

3 Discuss the importance of resources to the German military strategy.

4 Examine the importance of air power to the outcome of the Second World War in Europe.

5 To what extent did Allied industrial capacity determine the outcome of the Second World War in Europe?

6 Evaluate *Blitzkrieg* as an effective military strategy.

7 Compare and contrast Allied and German use of naval power in the Second World War in the Atlantic.

8 Examine the significance of the North African campaign to Allied success in the Second World War.

9 Discuss strengths and weaknesses of German strategy during the battle of Stalingrad.

10 Compare and contrast the German offensive in western Europe and Operation Barbarossa.

Further reading

Beevor, Antony. 1998. *Stalingrad: The Fateful Siege, 1942–1943*. Viking. New York, USA.

Gilbert, Martin. 1989. *Second World War*. Stoddart. Toronto, Canada.

Haslop, Dennis. 2013. *Britain, Germany and the Battle of the Atlantic: A Comparative Study*. Bloomsbury. New York, USA.

Keegan, John. 1990. *The Second World War*. Viking. New York, USA.

Kershaw, Ian. 2011. *The End: The Defiance and Destruction of Hitler's Germany, 1944–45*. Penguin Press. New York, USA.

Overy, Richard. 2014. *The Bombers and the Bombed: Allied Air War Over Europe, 1940–1945*. Viking. New York, USA.

Taylor, AJP. 1961. *The Origins of the Second World War*. Hamish Hamilton. London, UK

7 THE SECOND WORLD WAR IN THE PACIFIC: TOTAL WAR

Global context

As with the Second World War in Europe, the war in the Pacific erupted out of the complex ideological and economic context of the 1930s. The Great Depression affected all countries. Many sought refuge in protectionist trade policies that exacerbated the economic situation and isolated some of the states most adversely affected by the global depression. This isolation caused many of these states to look inward which in turn fostered a sense of defiance, and eventually in some states such as Japan, a form of ultra-nationalism.

The ultra-nationalists saw expansion and a sort of neo-mercantilism as a way out of the economic catastrophe that was the depression. The situation in Asia and the Pacific was further complicated by the existence of European imperial administration, underpinned as they were by racist philosophies. An anti-imperialist sentiment had long been simmering in the region and Japan attempted to manipulate this while at the same time building its own empire at the expense of other Asian nations.

Timeline

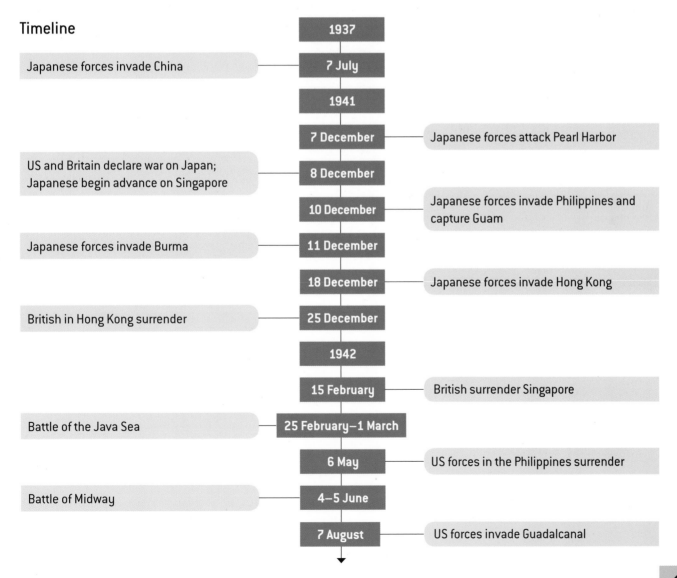

	1937	
Japanese forces invade China	**7 July**	
	1941	
	7 December	Japanese forces attack Pearl Harbor
US and Britain declare war on Japan; Japanese begin advance on Singapore	**8 December**	
	10 December	Japanese forces invade Philippines and capture Guam
Japanese forces invade Burma	**11 December**	
	18 December	Japanese forces invade Hong Kong
British in Hong Kong surrender	**25 December**	
	1942	
	15 February	British surrender Singapore
Battle of the Java Sea	**25 February–1 March**	
	6 May	US forces in the Philippines surrender
Battle of Midway	**4–5 June**	
	7 August	US forces invade Guadalcanal

1943

Japanese forces begin withdrawal from Guadalcanal — **1 February**

18 April — Japanese commander Admiral Yamamoto is killed

US invades Bougainville — **1 November**

20–23 November — Battle of Tarawa

1944

Allied air forces begin aerial bombing campaign — **June**

15 June–9 July — Battle of Saipan

US invades Guam — **19 July**

24 July — US invades Tinian

US forces land in Philippines — **20 October**

1945

19 February–26 March — Battle of Iwo Jima

Allies recapture Manila — **3 March**

9 March — Allies fire bomb Tokyo

Battle of Okinawa — **1 April–22 June**

5 July — Philippines recapture is completed

Atomic bomb successfully tested — **16 July**

6 August — Atomic bomb dropped on Hiroshima

USSR declares war on Japan — **8 August**

9 August — Atomic bomb dropped on Nagasaki

British re-occupy Hong Kong — **30 August**

2 September — Japan surrenders to Allied forces

Key questions

→ To what extent was Japanese foreign policy driven by economic and nationalistic concerns?

→ To what extent could diplomacy have avoided a war in the Pacific?

→ To what extent were the issues in the Pacific linked to the European tensions?

Key concepts

→ Cause

→ Consequence

Long-term causes

The First World War

Although Japan provided aid to the Allies during the First World War, the country was busy expanding her markets at the expense of the western powers, occupied as they were with the war. Imports and exports increased by 300% during the war. Japan had expanded her influence by occupying German colonies in the Pacific and gave China an ultimatum of 21 demands for concessions within its territory. They became the key importer of raw materials and exporter of manufactured goods throughout eastern Asia. However, as the global economy began to recover and switch back to civilian production after the war, Japanese manufacturers suffered from renewed competition. Likewise, her agricultural sector, still mostly small scale, could not compete with the more efficient farming of the West and the falling commodity prices of the mid-1920s. Foreshadowing US policy in the 1920s and 1930s, China erected tariff barriers in attempts to protect their own fledgling industrialization against the cheaper Japanese products. This would set Japan and China on a collision course.

Like those of its future Axis partners, the Japanese delegation to the Paris Peace Conference was to be disappointed with the eventual settlement. She claimed the right to all the German possessions in the Pacific, but was "awarded" the League of Nations mandates to those north of the equator, this despite a pledge from Britain to support such claims. Japan had also hoped to claim all of the extra-territorial trading concessions Germany had enjoyed in China prior to the war, while China had argued that all such concessions should be abolished. The conference gave half of these concessions to the Japanese thereby satisfying neither side. Likewise Japan was frustrated in her attempts to enshrine racial equality in the covenant of the League of Nations, demonstrating to her that as far as the western powers were concerned Asia was to be treated as a retainer at the imperial table rather than an equal partner.

Washington Naval Conference

In an effort to avert a naval arms race between the United States, Britain and Japan in the Pacific, the US invited nine nations involved with Far East concerns to Washington in 1921. The treaties signed at Washington made significant inroads in naval disarmament and limiting the future growth of navies. The US, Britain, and Japan destroyed over 60 ships between them. The Five Power Treaty signed in Washington established the ratio of capital ship tonnage that each of these powers could possess at 5:5:3 and re-established the status quo in terms of naval fortifications in the Pacific for the duration of the treaty. The Nine Power Treaty, also signed at Washington, guaranteed China's sovereignty. While these agreements were important steps toward establishing a working peace in the Pacific, it froze the inequities established at Versailles in place. As the influence of militarists and nationalists grew, Japan increasingly bridled under these restrictions. When Japan argued that the ratio should be equal, Britain and the US refused and Japan did not renew the treaty in 1936.

Ultra-nationalism

On the surface Japan was a liberal democracy overseen by a divine emperor. There was, however, no mechanism for responsible government. In reality a number of large families along with the navy and the army exercised a great deal of political and economic influence. This influence was linked closely to the economic health of the country, which was in turn linked closely to an expanding empire, an empire necessary to provide raw materials and markets for finished goods.

As the Japanese economy began to falter in the 1920s, a fundamentalist movement grew in importance preaching a return to the ways of the Samurai and pre-Meiji Japan. Ultra-nationalism and anti-western sentiments were an important part of this "new" doctrine. This movement found adherents in the army and the army was politically powerful. After the Wall Street Crash of 1929 bit hard into the already frail Japanese economy, civilian influence in the government evaporated and the serving military officers who also held important government ministries argued that expansion was the only answer to the problem of shrinking markets and China was to be the target. The ultra-nationalism that was at the heart of this revival and subsequent expansion saw Japan as the natural leader in East Asia. It envisioned a periphery, rich in oil and other resources, serving an industrialized centre – Japan – and in turn buying its finished product. This relationship would later find expression in the vague organization called the Greater East Asia Co-Prosperity Sphere – in fact a tool of imperial control.

Class discussion

To what extent was Japanese ultra-nationalism similar to fascism?

Short-term causes

Great Depression

As the Great Depression began to spread around the world and tariff walls grew higher, the Japanese government responded with **deficit financing**. The ultra-nationalists and militarists in the government demanded that much of this borrowed money go to rearming the military, which they would then argue was the tool by which the economic crisis could be solved. When Prime Minister Takahashi tried to curtail this spending, he was assassinated. By 1937 over two-thirds of Japanese government expenditure was on armaments. This radical expansion of the military had to be fed and the lands of China appeared to be the source in a sort of neo-mercantilism.

Japanese expansion

The lack of civilian control of the military and, indeed, the government began to tell in the early 1930s. The alleged murder of a Japanese officer in the Chinese city of Mukden and the staged explosion on a nearby Japanese-owned rail line gave the Japanese military a pretext to occupy Manchuria. The reality is that far from an act of Chinese aggression, it was the act of a rogue Japanese military unit. Nevertheless Tokyo supported the expansion and by 1932 had set up a protectorate called Manchukuo under the puppet Chinese emperor **Pu Yi**.

The Chinese government complained bitterly to the League of Nations. While there seemed a political will on the part of the smaller members of the League to act, they had little means to do so. The US urged the League to enforce the Kellogg-Briand Pact to which both China and Japan had been signatories. Unwilling to commit any troops to Manchuria, the League sent the Lytton Commission to investigate and compile a report. The report placed blame on both the Chinese and the Japanese. It also found, however, the resulting territory of Manchukuo to be illegitimate and in violation of the Nine Power Treaty. As a result of the report the Japanese withdrew from the League.

The League had clearly failed its first major test. Collective security had failed to prevent a state from using force to expand at the expense of a weaker neighbour. Economic sanctions were unpalatable to the powers given the fragile state of the global economy. Garnering support for a military adventure to defend a remote part of China only 12 years after the last war and given the economic state of the powers was likewise an impossibility. Understanding the essential weakness of the League, the Japanese government went further, issuing the **Amau Doctrine** declaring China to be within the Japanese sphere of influence and calling on all other countries to remove themselves from all Chinese economic and political affairs. This was a clear rejection of both the "Open Door" policy and the US Stimson Doctrine of 1932, which stated that the US would not recognize any treaty that infringed on US commercial rights in the region.

The Japanese invasion of Manchuria and the West's inability to stop it was illustrative and set the stage for international relations for the rest of the 1930s. Agreements and treaties were only useful insofar as countries were willing to back them up with force. In the difficult economic times of the 1930s, states would choose to protect trade at the expense of

---

deficit financing
Government spending that is dependent on loans, thus pushing the government's budget into a deficit.

Pu Yi
The last emperor of the Manchu dynasty in China. Pu Yi came to the throne in 1908 at the age of three and was emperor until he abdicated in 1912. After the Japanese invaded Manchuria in 1931 they installed him as the emperor of a territory renamed Manchukuo.

Amau Doctrine
A doctrine of 1930s Japanese foreign policy that reserved the right of Japan to act unilaterally to preserve "order" in East Asia.

national self-determination. It was a lesson learned by the future Axis Powers, but not the future Allied Powers. It also illuminated the degree to which US and Japanese policy in the region was contradictory. Should each of these countries continue along its foreign policy path, it was hard to see how they would not come into some sort of conflict.

Sino-Japanese War and US reaction

In February of 1936 a group of junior officers in the Imperial Japanese Army attempted to overthrow the civilian government and assassinate Prime Minister Okado. The coup failed and a number of the perpetrators were executed. This incident, however, had the strange consequence of causing the military to tighten its control of the government, which helped ensure that military solutions to foreign policy issues would take precedence over diplomatic answers.

This ascendance of the military to ever-greater political control prompted the Japanese to pressure the Chinese government for more concessions. When Nanjing refused further concessions, a dispute on the Marco Polo Bridge in Beijing was used as a pretext for a full invasion. The Japanese army made short work of Jiang Jieshi's forces, forcing him out of the capital of Nanjing, and killing some 250 000 civilians in the weeks after the city fell. Within a year the Japanese army had captured much of the Chinese coast and close to its entire north-east. This aggression clearly threatened US interests in the region and they extended loans to Jiang's government. US businesses also traded oil and steel with the Japanese, which the invaders ate up in larger and larger quantities. Eventually the war with China would cost the Japanese government over $5 million a day. This dependence on US resources would prove to be a serious and strategic liability, one that would propel the Japanese government to war with the US.

In essence, the Japanese determined that they needed to expand in order to keep what they had. This expansion would eventually threaten US, British and Dutch holdings in south-east China. Any resources the Japanese could take from the region would be threatened on their journey back to the home islands by the US protectorate in the Philippines. Something would eventually have to give.

War plans

There is competition between the branches of any military and Japan's was no exception. The army's reputation had been sullied by the attempted coup of 1936, but it was still politically very powerful. The navy, the more conservative branch, had never really taken to the rabid nationalism of the army. All branches of the military want to demonstrate that it is the more vital to the national interest and thus claim a greater influence and share in the distribution of resources. The Japanese army thus argued for a solution that emphasized land operations against the Soviets. This plan, known as the "north programme" was tested in the late summer of 1939 when a Japanese division engaged a Soviet force under the command of Georgi Zhukov on the Mongolian border. The Japanese were overwhelmed and withdrew. From that point, the "south programme" which would push the search for resources and hegemony into Indo-China was dominant. The "south programme" gave more strategic planning influence to the navy. It would also likely clash with western interests in the region.

The fall of France in June 1940 and the signing of the **Tripartite Pact** with Italy and Germany seemed to open the way for the expansion of Japanese influence into the French colony in Indo-China. With her right flank protected by a non-aggression pact with the Soviets, Japan had by the summer of 1941 occupied the entire colony.

Pearl Harbor

The months leading up to the attack on the US naval base in the Hawaiian Islands saw a flurry of diplomatic wrangling between the United States and Japan. The US was determined that Chinese territorial integrity be restored and free trade be reopened. The Japanese were just as determined to not forfeit their recent gains, nor to have their strategic plans be subject to western approval.

In July 1941 the Japanese army occupied all of Indo-China and Roosevelt learned, through radio intercepts, that the Japanese were developing military plans at the same time as they claimed to be negotiating in good faith. Roosevelt ordered an embargo, supported by the British and Dutch, on all trade with Japan. This cut the Japanese military off from over 80% of its oil and much of its steel and had the effect of putting the negotiations with the US on the clock. Japan's oil reserves were low and if war with the US was coming, the faster the better, before fuel shortages made combat impossible. This was the view of the commander of the Japanese Imperial Navy and chief military planner, Admiral Isoroku Yamamoto. Yamamoto had studied in the US and understood its awesome industrial strength and military potential; he hoped that his government could avoid a war with the United States. In the event that such a war did come he believed that the Japanese could be reasonably successful for six months to a year. Should the war continue beyond that, Yamamoto had little confidence that they could win. This formed the outline of Japanese strategic thinking in the fall of 1941. Should war be necessary, they would act quickly, expanding their empire's defensive perimeter from which they could negotiate from a position of strength.

Yamamoto was tasked with developing the attack plan. It would contain three assaults. The Japanese army would land and overpower the US outposts on Guam and Wake Islands. A larger force would land in the Philippines. The main focus of the operation was a surprise aerial attack on the US naval base at Pearl Harbor. Waves of torpedo and dive bombers would launch from aircraft carriers that had snuck across the Pacific. The goal was to damage the US fleet to such an extent that it could not carry on operations in the Pacific, thereby giving Japan a free hand to consolidate its gains. Surprise was vital for this operation. The ongoing negotiations in Washington and the US Pacific Fleet's tradition of standing down on Sundays gave the Japanese the confidence that this surprise could be achieved.

> **Tripartite Pact**
> An agreement signed on 27 September 1940 by Japan, Germany and Italy. The pact pledged its signatories to mutual aid should any of them be attacked by a country not then at war.

The US Pacific Fleet was indeed surprised. Over two-thirds of the available anti-aircraft guns went unmanned and there was precious little ammunition for those that were. It took a little over an hour for two waves of bombers to sink four battleships and heavily damage three others. Twelve other vessels of varying sizes were also damaged and 200 aircraft were destroyed, most of them on the ground. By the end of the day the US had suffered 2,700 casualties of which just over 2,000 were dead.

▲ Ships of the United States navy burn at Pearl Harbor. What are the moral implications of attacking before a formal declaration of war? To what extent are such declarations anachronisms?

While the damage caused by the raid was stunning, it was far from the unqualified success the Japanese needed it to be. Despite what was hit during the raid, it is perhaps more significant to consider what was not hit on 7 December 1941. The US aircraft carriers had not been in Pearl Harbor that morning and their survival meant that the US could regain the initiative in the Pacific in short order. The dockyards and huge oil tanks were not heavily damaged, ensuring that Pearl Harbor was still very much an operational base, able to fuel vessels and repair those that had been damaged. Indeed it is a testament to the industrial strength of the US that of the four battleships sunk at Pearl Harbor that morning two were raised and repaired within two and a half years.

Class discussion

What role did luck play in the events of 7 December 1941?

7.2 Combatants

Allied forces

In 1939 the Australian navy was incredibly small given the amount of coastline it had to defend. Its largest vessels were six cruisers of varying sizes. The army had a tiny permanent force of 3,000 men and another 80 000 potential reservists of various levels of training. The air force consisted of 250 machines. By the end of the war, Australia's armed forces numbered 1 million men. This force had served in all major theatres of war, suffering 50 000 casualties.

The British forces in the Pacific theatre initially were concentrated in India, Burma and Singapore, with garrisons in Hong Kong and other smaller holdings. Royal Navy assets were concentrated in the Atlantic and Mediterranean after the outbreak of war in Europe as these were the vital supply lines for the British Isles. The bulk of the British forces defending Burma were made up of units of its Indian army, eventually some 30 000 strong, though poorly supported and trained. Only about 17 000 survived the retreat back to India. Like those troops defending Burma, the British garrison at Singapore was mostly made up of Indian army units. Eventually this force would number over 130 000. Of these over 80 000 would be captured in Singapore after General Percival's surrender.

Jiang Jieshi's Chinese nationalist forces as well as Mao Zedong's communist army fought close to 2 million Japanese soldiers throughout the war. Jiang's forces consisted of about 230 000 effective troops with another 300 weak, under-equipped, and poorly led and trained divisions spread around the country. Mao's army grew to about 400 000 troops in both regular and guerrilla formations during the war.

The United States army would deploy 20 divisions to Pacific operations during the war. The Marine Corps grew to six divisions and 485 000 men during the war and had its own air corps. The US Pacific Fleet stood at 3 aircraft carriers, 9 battleships, 8 cruisers and 40 destroyers in October 1941. By the end of the war, the US Pacific Fleet had grown to 23 battleships, 65 cruisers, and 26 fleet carriers.

Japanese forces

When the Japanese army invaded China in 1937 it had about 24 divisions and about 5,000 aircraft. Conscription and indoctrination swelled this to 50 divisions by 1941. The army and navy combined had 130 squadrons of between 12–24 aircraft. On the eve of the attack on Pearl Harbor the Japanese military had access to over 3 million men who had received varying levels of training. By 1939 Japan was producing over 4,400 aircraft a year. This was nearly twice as many as the US produced in the same period. The problem was that the Japanese aircraft industry had only increased marginally by the time of the attack on Pearl Harbor, whereas the United States was producing over 26 000 by 1941, buoyed by wartime demand from the Allies. By the war's end Japanese aircraft production had risen to 11 000 per year, while the United States was pushing out close to 50 000 aircraft a year. The differential is misleading, but only slightly as US aircraft production had to be divided between the various theatres in which its forces were fighting whereas the Japanese aircraft could be concentrated in the Pacific. The Japanese forces were nonetheless spread thin throughout the war. The political influence of the army ensured that the war in China received the lion's share of reinforcement personnel and replacement equipment. By 1945 the Japanese army had 1.8 million men in China, but far fewer in any position to offer resistance to the Allied forces moving toward the home islands.

Class discussion

Did Japan overreach its military capabilities?

Japanese war plans

Understanding the industrial might and thus military potential of the US, Japanese strategists developed essentially a defensive strategy. An initial period of offensive operations would extend the strategic perimeter of island bases eastward into the Pacific and southward into Malaya and Indonesia. The latter would require the army to force the British and Dutch forces out of strongholds such as Singapore and Hong Kong, thus widening the war. A period of fortification would follow during which the Japanese would reinforce the bases running from the Kurile Islands (in the north) south through the Marshall Islands, west through New Guinea, around the East Indies and then north again to Burma. According to the strategists this perimeter would enclose the resources needed to sustain the empire. It would also necessarily widen the war still further by drawing Australia and probably New Zealand into the conflict. Should the US still be fighting by that point, a war of attrition was planned, eventually forcing the US to the negotiating table. As the Allied war effort gained momentum, the initial perimeter could not be maintained and by mid-1943 had to be re-evaluated and, in fact, shrunk. By spring of 1945 the perimeter that the Japanese high command thought that it could realistically – in its opinion – defend was reduced further to a line narrowly drawn around the islands immediately surrounding the home islands.

Such a plan would require close cooperation between the Japanese army and navy. This coordination had been part of the Japanese operational doctrine for some time and joint training was common. The relatively new technology of the aircraft carrier, however, would make the war in the Pacific like no other naval conflict in history. The Japanese were early adopters. Admiral Yamamoto saw in the aircraft carrier and its planes a long-range extension of the fleet's firepower. The aircraft carriers and their crew were the elite of the Imperial Japanese Navy and considerable time and resources had been poured into their construction and into refining their operation. By 7 December 1941 the operational distance for carrier-borne aircraft was about 300 kilometres. Aircraft navigation was still rudimentary in the first years of the war for one- and two-seat planes, limiting safe long-range operations to relatively clear days.

After their initial successes in the first six months after Pearl Harbor the Japanese land forces were primarily involved in defensive operations. The longer they had to strengthen these defences the stronger they became. Concrete pillboxes covered beach approaches. Islands such as Iwo Jima were a warren of tunnels and bunkers. In the later stages of the war these defences would be defended until no defenders were left. These tactics were inspired by fierce loyalty and often, as on Saipan, included suicide attacks on US units.

US strategy: Island Hopping

Yamamoto's predicted year of success lasted only six months. After a strategic defeat at Coral Sea and a crushing defeat at Midway, the Japanese would now sit behind their defensive perimeter while the offensive initiative went over to the US. The US now had some decisions to make. Which route would it take toward the Japanese home islands? Should they move directly across the central Pacific populated with small garrisoned islands, or through the south-west Pacific with its larger islands? Each route had its advantages and drawbacks. Domestic and inter-service politics would also play a role in the US decision. Choosing the central Pacific route would make the navy the vital service, but it lacked enough land forces in 1942 to conquer and occupy the many little islands across the central Pacific. The army had sufficient manpower but it did not get along with the navy, which would have to play at least some role should the south-west route be chosen. General Douglas MacArthur was the senior US military officer in the Pacific. The fact that he was politically connected with Roosevelt's opponents prompted the President to leave him in the Pacific. The navy, however, was not interested in handing over command of its forces, which included the Marine Corps, to an army officer, especially one with MacArthur's ego. The decision was therefore taken to split the Pacific into two theatres of war.

Command of the central Pacific theatre was given to Admiral Chester Nimitz while MacArthur was given command of the south-west Pacific theatre. By 1943, Nimitz was given command of the entire Pacific. Together they adopted a strategy that played on US strength, air and sea power, while minimizing Japanese strength, strong defensive positions and a willingness to defend them to the last man. This strategy would become known as "Island Hopping". US invasion forces would bypass islands with stronger defences and capture smaller islands. On these islands they would build airstrips that would then allow them to bring air power to bear on the next island. This system of overlapping air cover was to eventually get the US forces close enough that heavy land-based bombers could initiate a strategic bombing campaign against the Japanese home islands. The garrisoned islands that the Allies bypassed were of no strategic value without naval or air support.

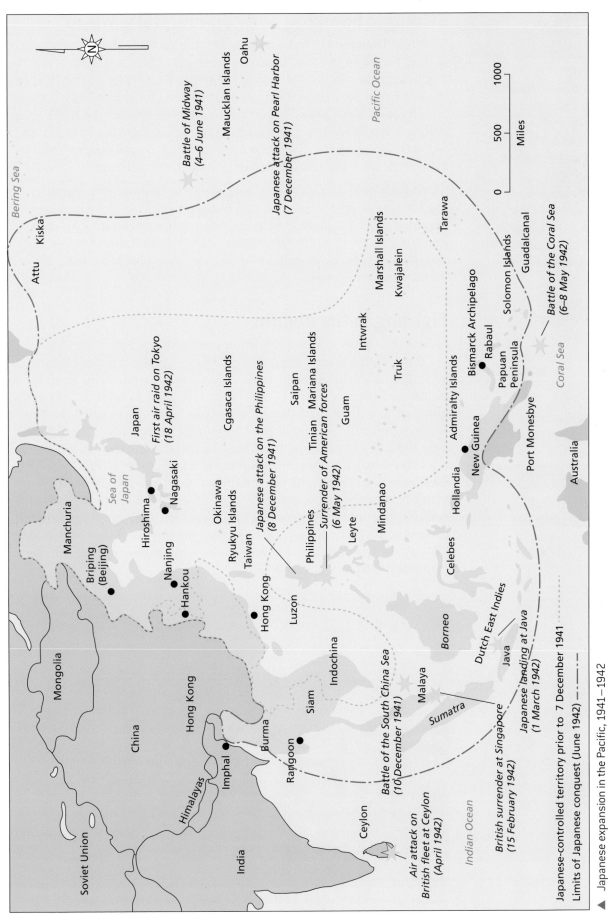

▲ Japanese expansion in the Pacific, 1941–1942

Japanese-controlled territory prior to 7 December 1941 ·············

Limits of Japanese conquest (June 1942) ——·——·——

Strategic bombing and commercial warfare

By 9 July 1944 the US was able to begin putting the second component of their Pacific strategy into action. The capture of Saipan brought the Japanese home islands within range of the newest US long-range bomber, the B-29 Superfortress. Two months earlier the Philippines had come within range of the heavy bombers. The US believed that the B-29s could reduce much of Japan's urban areas, built as they were out of wood. To reduce these cities, the US would use incendiary bombs designed to start fires rather than high explosives designed to blast buildings.

Along with devastating the Japanese ability to produce war material, the US navy sought to interrupt their shipping lines along which they imported their resources. A submarine campaign savaged Japan's merchant shipping, taking advantage of the fact that the Japanese had no coherent plan for its defence in the way the Allies protected their Atlantic shipping lanes.

Fighting in the Pacific

The Pacific Ocean is over 160 million square kilometres in size. To say that locating enemy ships in such a vast expanse is a challenge is an understatement of the first order. Naval warfare until this point in history had been confined to areas relatively close to landfall. This had much to do with the fact that for much of the history of naval warfare, enemies generally occupied the same continent, and when they did not, as in the case of Rome and Carthage, the intervening body of water was relatively small and congested. Not so the Pacific. This is the reason that the aircraft carrier became the indispensable weapon in the Pacific war. While battleships had to generally get within 20 kilometres of each other before they could start pounding each other with their big guns, aircraft carriers could carry on operations against the enemy at distances of 200 kilometres. The vast distances also placed a premium on reliable long-rage reconnaissance aircraft.

▲ A US Lockheed Lightning. To what extent did the Allies have a technological advantage over the Japanese in the Pacific war?

Any land operations undertaken by either Japan or the Allies would entail amphibious landings. Amphibious landings were notoriously difficult enterprises. Landing troops were incredibly vulnerable until they landed and then moderately so until they established a secure beachhead. Command of the air was essential for a successful amphibious operation. The supply ships and troop transports were exposed to attack while they supported the landings and while supplying the offensive as it moved inland.

Technology and war: aircraft carriers

Early in the 1920s militaries around the world were experimenting with aircraft taking off from and landing on a ship. The first aircraft carriers were converted cruisers and other vessels with flight decks built on the existing hull. By the 1930s all the major maritime powers had some form of purpose-built aircraft carriers.

The aircraft carrier made imminent sense in naval warfare. Aircraft dramatically increased the combat effectiveness of surface fleets to the extent that the Battle of Coral Sea, early in the Pacific war, became the first battle in history in which the opposing surface fleets never laid eyes on each other. Nevertheless, adopting the new technology did not come easily to senior staff who had been trained to believe that the battleship was the king of the sea and whose tactical training and experience had been moulded in this tradition. Likewise the air arm had to learn new and dangerous skills, namely taking off and landing from a tiny, bobbing speck in the middle of a vast ocean, not to mention navigating to and from targets with initially rudimentary instruments, the whole time judging fuel consumption to ensure there was enough to return to the carrier.

Nevertheless, the effectiveness of the aircraft carrier was demonstrated early in the war with the British Royal Navy attack on the Italian fleet at Taranto in 1940 and the Japanese attack on Pearl Harbor. From that point carrier production and tactics evolved quickly. An aircraft carrier was only as effective as its aircraft. The Japanese started the war with one of the best carrier-borne fighters of the war, the Mitsubishi A6M Zero. By 1942 the US navy had the Grumman Hellcat which was itself an excellent carrier-borne fighter. Throughout the war most nations created smaller aircraft carriers, escort carriers, designed to protect invasion flotilla and be generally more manoeuvrable.

The increased importance of aircraft carriers placed a greater emphasis on their protection. Fleet carriers were accompanied by a wide range of escort vessels and were armed with the latest in anti-aircraft weapons to keep attacking planes at bay. Inventions such as the proximity fuse, which detonated an anti-aircraft shell when it was near an airplane, rather than requiring a direct hit, improved aircraft carrier defences immensely.

Conceptual understanding

Key questions

→ What role did industrial production play in the war?

→ What factors led to the halt of the Japanese advance?

→ How did land, naval, and air forces coordinate their actions?

→ What role did technology play in the outcome of the war?

Key concepts

→ Continuity

→ Change

→ Consequence

Japanese advance – Philippines, Singapore, Hong Kong

The attack on Pearl Harbor was but one of the operations initiated in December 1941, albeit the most significant. While the attack on the Hawaiian Islands was designed to debilitate the US Pacific Fleet, the assault on Malaya was one of conquest. The resources of the region were desperately needed by the Japanese to fuel its war machine.

The British presence in the East Indies was centred on the garrison of Singapore. In terms of men and material, the British High Command prioritized its operations in North Africa and its need to defend the home islands. This priority was based in part on strategy and part on racist generalizations. British military planners gave little weight to the fighting ability, be it on land, sea or air, of the Japanese. The British felt that the defences at Singapore and the size of the garrison there would be more than enough to hold the Japanese at bay. A naval task force led by the HMS *Prince of Wales* and HMS *Repulse* was dispatched to shore up the naval defences in Malaya. Critically no air power of note was dispatched and the garrison had no armour. Three days after the attack on Pearl Harbor, Japanese torpedo bombers descended on the two ships and sank them.

The British defence of Singapore was conducted with singular incompetence. They outnumbered their enemy in troops and were defending a peninsula, giving them a decided advantage had they extended their flanks into the jungles. As a result of this neglect the Japanese turned the British flanks. Falling back before fighting, the British defenders forfeited much of the peninsula that, had it been defended vigorously, would have forestalled the Japanese advance before it reached Singapore. By the end of January the defenders had been pushed onto the island of Singapore. These defences soon crumbled as well and the city's water supply fell into Japanese hands. The British commander was faced with defending a city of over a million people with no water. In February General Percival surrendered over 80 000 British, Indian and Australian troops and Singapore to the Japanese.

On 8 December the Japanese attacked the British colony of Hong Kong, which held out until 25 December. Likewise the islands of Wake, Guam and Tarawa fell to the Japanese onslaught by the end of December. The British army was also pushed out of Burma. The Dutch surrendered their holdings in the East Indies after the Battle of Java Sea, a classic surface vessel struggle of gunnery.

The presence of the US forces based in the Philippines had loomed large in the overall strategic planning of the Japanese government. Any resources extracted from the East Indies would have to run the gauntlet of the South China Sea if it was to get to the home islands and the right flank of this gauntlet was dominated by the Philippines. All of their East Asian conquests would be for nothing if the Philippines remained in US hands. As important as the islands were, they were defended by a meager force of 30 000 Filipino and US troops, 150 aircraft, 108 tanks and 45 naval vessels of varying sizes. The Japanese deployed two battle-hardened divisions, well supported by carrier-borne aircraft and heavy surface vessels to dislodge them.

The Japanese landings were heralded by the destruction of close to all US aircraft on the ground on 8 December 1941. Within two days they had landed on the main island of Luzon. Another major landing on 22 December forced MacArthur to his defensive fallback on the Bataan Peninsula. The defenders were pushed to the tip of the peninsula and soon were enduring siege conditions. By April the troops in Bataan had surrendered. The last US forces, crowded onto the island of Corregidor surrendered on 6 May 1942.

Guadalcanal

With the defeat of the Japanese carrier fleet at Midway, the initiative passed over to the United States. They chose as their first target the re-conquest of Guadalcanal, an island in the Solomons, which provided an important air base for operations in the region. As Guadalcanal was in the central Pacific theatre, the task fell to Nimitz with the navy and the 1st Marine Division. The choice of target allowed for staging from New Zealand, but made resupply of the troops once ashore, the responsibility of the navy, more difficult. The initial assault against the 2,000 Japanese troops garrisoned on the island was successful, but the Japanese counter-attacked both against the support fleet off the island and the marines on the island, committing another 30 000 troops over the next six months. The result was a six-month brawl in which the United States army and Marine Corps lost about 2,000 men to the Japanese 20 000. Off the coast of the island several important naval engagements were fought. The Japanese navy was trying to run supplies and reinforcements past the US blockade. Over the course of six months the US lost five cruisers, several destroyers and a carrier; the Japanese lost a carrier, two battleships, four cruisers and several destroyers.

▲ US dive bombers head toward Guadalcanal. To what extent did both US and Japanese land operations depend on air power?

The victory at Guadalcanal paved the way for a two-pronged advance against the Japanese stronghold at Rabaul. MacArthur and the US and Australian armies drove at it through New Guinea and New Britain while the navy, under Admiral William Halsey, drove through the Solomons. The US forces made steady, if slow, progress. Since Guadalcanal the Japanese had strengthened their positions and defended these with a fanatical intensity. Throughout this campaign air combat was essential to Allied success. Allied forces constructed countless airstrips that were then used in support of forward operations against both Japanese naval units and land defences. Rabaul and its garrison were captured in March 1944.

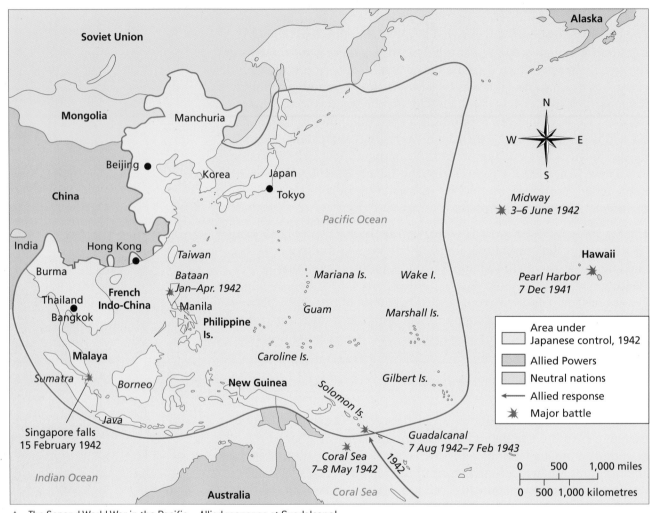

▲ The Second World War in the Pacific – Allied response at Guadalcanal

The Gilbert and Caroline Islands

The amount of material streaming out of US factories allowed the Allies to move through the Gilbert and Caroline Islands in the central Pacific at the same time as Halsey and MacArthur were driving toward Rabaul in the southern Pacific. This offensive would open up the route to recapturing the Philippines and attacking the Japanese home islands with large, land-based B-29 bombers. The campaign opened up in November 1943 with the US Marine Corps assault on the island of Tarawa with 18 000 troops. The fight was desperate and after two days the Marines had suffered 3,000 casualties, 1,000 of them dead, in capturing the island. The Japanese had lost over 4,000 defending it.

The Marshall and Marianas Islands

In January, Nimitz turned his attention to the Marshall Islands, capturing Eniwetok and Kwajalein. In the south, MacArthur moved against Biak, which would put the Philippines within range of the B-29s. Once the Marshalls were under Allied control, they advanced against Saipan in the Marianas island group. Another desperate struggle ensued, in which the US suffered 14 000 casualties. After a bitter defence and air battle in which the Japanese lost two-thirds of their aircraft and one of their remaining two fleet carriers, the remaining 5,000 survivors of the Japanese garrison committed suicide, bringing their death toll to 30 000.

Technology and war: amphibious and landing craft

Amphibious landings are incredibly dangerous for attacking forces. The landing troops are exposed to fire as they approach the beach and once they are on the beach. Amphibious landings were attempted in most major theatres of the war, North Africa, Sicily, Italy and Normandy. It was in the Pacific, however, that they became a regular feature of combat. Developing a durable landing craft that protected soldiers until they were released on to the beach became a vital priority for the US military. Landing craft varied widely in size and construction, carrying from 25–200 men. Some were armed. Perhaps the most versatile was the Higgins Boat. Developed in New Orleans and named for its creator. The Higgins Boat was 11 m long, could carry 36 soldiers and travel at 22 kmh. It was designed with a long ramp at the bow that offered some protection to the troops and when dropped served as a disembarkation ramp.

Other vehicles, such as the US DUKW or Alligator, were designed to travel from the water up onto the beach and continue toward the defences. Others such as the DD Tanks (Duplex Drive) were tanks modified to "swim" to shore. These met with varied success throughout the war as they were easily damaged by high seas.

The Philippines

The Japanese defended the Philippines with about 250 000 troops spread out throughout the complex of islands. On the smaller island of Lyete, where the initial US landings would occur, they had only 15 000. In October the US forces landed and the Japanese reinforced their forces on the small island. The fighting raged for a month and cost the US 15 000 casualties and the Japanese 70 000. In January 1945, the US troops moved to the main island of Luzon and by the end of February the capital, Manila, had been recaptured. It would, however, take until July to defeat the last of the Japanese troops in the islands.

▲ US General MacArthur wades ashore in the Philippines. To what extent were the Philippine Islands strategically significant to the Allies?

Burma

It is important to remember that while the US carried on the bulk of the fighting in the Central Pacific, the Australian army played a vital role in the fighting on New Guinea and in other parts of the southern sector. Meanwhile the British were fighting the Japanese in Burma. Burma had been defended weakly by a single division, poorly trained and with no air support. In the spring of 1942 this force completed the arduous retreat to the relative safety of British India.

The Allied forces that would attempt to retake Burma consisted of British, East and West African troops from the west, while General "Vinegar Joe" Stilwell would thrust into Burma from China in an effort to reopen the supply route into China known as the Burma Road. These attempts were thrown back in November 1942 and February 1943. In March, the Japanese went on the offensive and invaded India with over 85 000 soldiers. Less than a quarter of that returned to Burma after three months of fierce fighting. Starting in late 1944, General William Slim's Allied forces would push into Burma and liberate Mandalay and Rangoon.

▲ Australian soldiers advance in New Guinea. What challenges did island fighting pose for soldiers?

Iwo Jima and Okinawa

With aerial bombing of the home islands intensifying, the US decided to capture the 20-square-kilometre island of Iwo Jima to provide damaged bombers returning from raids with a place to ditch as well as a base from which short-range fighters could support the bombing missions. The Japanese were dug deeply into the rocky terrain and had supported these positions with concrete emplacements. Although the Marines would capture the island's high ground, Mount Suribachi, within four days of the invasion, it would take another month to finish the campaign, costing the US 25 000 casualties, 6,800 of them dead. The Japanese suffered over 19 000 dead.

The next step toward Japan was the heavily fortified island of Okinawa. Okinawa was defended by 70 000 troops well dug in, a number that would swell to over 100 000. Desperate, the Japanese unleashed airborne suicide attacks against the invasion force. The **kamikaze** attacks sank over 30 ships in the invasion force. The US armada pounded the defences for a week ahead of the 50 000 invasion force that landed on 1 April 1945, a prelude to the 200 000 that the US would place on the island during the course of the struggle which continued until 22 June. In the end the US suffered 65 000 casualties, 7,000 of them dead. Unwilling to surrender, 110 000 Japanese soldiers died in the failed defence of the island. As strategically important as Okinawa was to continued US operations, sitting as it did only 550 kilometres from the Japanese islands, it also played an important psychological role in future US decisions. To US strategic thinking Okinawa provided a taste of what awaited them in the invasion of the home islands – kamikaze attacks, suicidal defences and monstrous casualties. This vision coloured all talks of whether or not and how to use atomic weapons.

kamikaze
Literally "divine wind" in Japanese. Kamikaze attacks were suicide attacks by Japanese aircraft on enemy ships during the Second World War.

▲ US Marines inspect a destroyed pillbox on Iwo Jima. What was the military significance of small islands such as Iwo Jima?

The war at sea

Coral Sea

In April 1942 the US Magic programme decoded Japanese transmissions indicating they were manoeuvring for an attack on southern New Guinea. Nimitz sent the aircraft carriers USS *Lexington* and USS *Yorktown* to intercept the Japanese invasion force. The resulting battle was the first naval battle in history in which the surface fleets never laid eyes on each other. Over four days in May 1942 carrier-borne planes traversed the 280 kilometres between the fleets and struggled to deliver crippling blows on the enemy's ships. By the end of the Battle of the Coral Sea, as the encounter has come to be known, the US had lost the USS *Lexington* and the USS *Yorktown* had been damaged. The Japanese had lost one light carrier and had a heavy carrier damaged. The US lost 70 aircraft to the Japanese 90. While numerically the Battle of the Coral Sea was a draw, it was a strategic victory for the US as it had prevented the Japanese landings in New Guinea.

Midway

After preventing the Japanese invasion of southern New Guinea at Coral Sea, an increase in Japanese radio traffic, decoded through the Magic programme, convinced the US navy that another major Japanese offensive was imminent, but the exact place of the attack was unknown. Politicians in Washington were worried about an attack on the continental US, San Francisco perhaps, and encouraged Nimitz to withdraw his carriers east to a position from which such an attack could be repelled. Nimitz, however, was tempted by the opportunity to destroy a major Japanese carrier force if he could find them before the attack. For their part, the Japanese wanted their capture of Midway to lure the US aircraft carriers into a decisive battle where they could finish what they had started at Pearl Harbor. A clever deciphering trick confirmed for the US that the Japanese would attack the US base at Midway Island.

Nimitz dispatched a task force with one carrier and a second with two carriers to a position north-east of Midway to seek out the Japanese fleet and surprise them. The presence of the US carriers would indeed be a surprise to the Japanese, as they believed they were still in Hawaii. A lone US long-range reconnaissance plane found the Japanese fleet, with four carriers steaming toward Midway. The first US torpedo and dive-bomber squadrons to attack the Japanese were repulsed, but a late arriving dive-bomber squadron from the USS *Enterprise* discovered the four Japanese carriers with their flight decks littered with refueling bombers preparing to strike the US carriers. The Japanese fighter cover was at too low an altitude to defend against torpedo bombers. Within five minutes three of the four Japanese carriers were ablaze, the fourth would sink later in the day. The Japanese managed to launch an attack that claimed one US carrier, the USS *Yorktown*. Within seven months of the Japanese attack on Pearl Harbor the US had succeeded in evening the odds in the Pacific. From this point the industrial juggernaut of the US would overwhelm the Japanese in the Pacific. In this sense, the Battle of Midway can be seen as changing the course of the war against Japan in the same way that Stalingrad and El Alamein later that same year would mark the turn of the tide in the war against Germany.

ATL
Research and thinking skills

Find the perspective of three different sources on the following question. Analyse each perspective and come to a conclusion of your own. Be sure to cite the bibliographic details for each source.

To what extent was the US victory at Midway the key event in the defeat of Japan?

▲ The USS *Yorktown* lists heavily before sinking after the Battle of Midway. To what extent were aircraft carriers vulnerable targets?

Leyte Gulf

In an effort to stop the US landing in the Philippines the Japanese fleet launched an attack on the naval force supporting the landings. What was left of the Japanese carrier force approached from the north, attempting to lure the larger US vessels into a fight. Meanwhile the rest of the Japanese battle group fought their way to the lightly defended invasion force. The US ships, though outgunned, fought the Japanese to a standstill from which they withdrew, leaving the invasion troops unmolested.

Technology and war: Magic, cryptology and the code talkers

Magic refers to the information decoded from Japanese diplomatic communications from 1940. In 1939, the Japanese diplomatic corps began using a new machine to code their communications. In 1940 the US Signal Intelligence Service deciphered the codes and built their own version of the Japanese encryption device. The resulting intelligence was codenamed Magic while the Japanese navy's code was named JN-25. The Japanese would periodically change the code requiring US cryptographers to start again with decryption. Intelligence from Magic and the JN-25 code helped lead to important information such as the location of the attack on Port Moseby in May 1942 and on Midway Island in June 1942.

In their own search for an unbreakable code, the United States Marine Corps looked to the Navajo nation of the south-western United States. The Navajo language is unwritten with no symbols, and is extremely complex with multiple dialects. Navajo "code talkers" could code, transmit by wireless or telephone and decode a message in 20 seconds when it would take machines 30 minutes. About 400 Navajo code talkers served with the US Marines in the Pacific. They were assigned to each of the six marine divisions and took place in all major operations. The Japanese never broke their code.

The air war

Bombing campaign

Once the US had captured Saipan and other islands in the Marianas group, the Japanese home islands were within range of US B-29s. This bombing campaign began in earnest in the spring of 1945. Rather than subject the cities to high explosives, the US Army Air Force decided to set them ablaze and attacked at low level with incendiary bombs. The devastated Japanese air force had no answer. By the summer civilian deaths approached 300 000 and over half of the country's urban centres

TOK discussion

To what extent do you agree that the true history of the Second World War will not be written until after the last veteran of the war has passed away?

had burned. On the one hand, although the human toll was terrible, the raids did little to damage Japanese industrial capacity, dispersed as it had been throughout the country. On the other hand, the Japanese industrial economy had precious little capacity left.

Manhattan Project

The conquest of Okinawa had cost the US 65 000 casualties, 35% of those it committed. It had been the first time the US forces in the Pacific had faced a Japanese army in strength in topography similar to the Japanese home islands. The projections for the invasion of the home islands were then in the range of over 250 000 men. The only alternative to invasion, put forth by the navy, was the total isolation of the home islands combined with a concentrated strategic bombing campaign against Japan's urban centres. The efficacy of this plan was called into question when the intensive fire bombing campaign unleashed against the largely wooden cities brought the Japanese government no closer to the unconditional surrender demanded by the Allies. On 8 March 1945 a fire bombing raid against Tokyo killed over 80 000 civilians.

There was another alternative. After receiving word from Albert Einstein that there were scientists left in Germany capable of deciphering how to initiate the chain reaction of nuclear fission and harnessing it into a weapon, President Truman set in motion a programme that would assemble the greatest minds in physics and chemistry. The British had begun their own weapon project, but fused it with the US project in 1942. The scientific efforts were directed by Dr Robert Oppenheimer and included such luminaries as Niels Bohr, Hans Bethe, Enrico Fermi, James Franck, Richard Feynman and Leo Szilard. While the efforts to weaponize the fission process was centred in Los Alamos, New Mexico, the project had elements working from Tennessee to British Columbia to London, employing over 125 000 people from clerks to miners to some of the greatest scientific minds of the time.

By summer 1945 the programme had a prototype they could test and they successfully did so in the New Mexico desert. Truman was told of the successful test while attending the Potsdam Conference. Discussions had been going on for some time as to how to use the weapon to best effect. Should they warn the Japanese before they used it, giving them time to consider surrender? Some advocated summoning the Japanese to a demonstration and then demanding their surrender. Others saw this as a weapon that differed from other weapons only in the scope of its destructive capacity, rather than in the nature of the weapon itself, and as such should be deployed as any other weapon, with no warning and with maximum lethal effect. Seventy of the scientists that helped develop the weapon petitioned Truman to give the Japanese the opportunity to surrender before they were attacked with the weapon. When Oppenheimer told Truman that he felt he had blood on his hands, the President dismissed him as a "cry baby scientist". Truman decided to use the weapon as he would any weapon, without warning and to maximum effect.

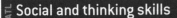

Social and thinking skills

Choose one of the following positions on whether or not to drop the atomic bomb on Japan. Write an argument in support of your position. Be sure to support it with detailed evidence. Exchange arguments with someone who has chosen the other position. After reading it, write a rebuttal to their argument and they will do the same for your argument. Once you have exchanged rebuttals, discuss the strengths and weaknesses of each argument.

To what extent does your knowledge of post-war history affect your outlook on the question?

Position 1: The United States was right to drop the atomic bombs on Hiroshima and Nagasaki in 1945.

Position 2: The United States should have not dropped the bombs on Hiroshima and Nagasaki in 1945.

The targeting committee had settled on a number of industrial centres as the possible targets, but omitted Tokyo and the imperial city of Kyoto in order to maintain a government structure capable of surrendering. After the capture of Saipan in July 1944 the US Navy Construction Battalions built four runways on neighbouring Tinian Island. The runways were reinforced and lengthened to accommodate the potential for B-29s with heavier payloads to lift off. Those heavier payloads would eventually be two atomic bombs, nicknamed Fat Man and Little Boy. On 6 August a B-29 dropped the first bomb on Hiroshima, a city of 370 000 people. After the bomb detonated 580 metres above the city, 80 000 of its inhabitants were dead in an instant with another 50 000 succumbing to their wounds in the weeks following the attack. Three days later, when no surrender was forthcoming, another bomb was dropped on the city of Nagasaki, killing 30 000 instantly with the death toll climbing to nearly 50 000 in the following days. The Japanese Emperor then ordered a general surrender, which was formalized on 2 September 1945. Active units of the Japanese army continued surrendering to Allied forces throughout September and October.

◄ A post-war model of "Little Boy", the atomic bomb that exploded over Hiroshima, Japan, at the end of the Second World War

▲ The devastated city of Hiroshima after the dropping of the atomic bomb. Were there viable alternatives to dropping the bombs?

Technology and war: nuclear weapons

In October 1939 President Roosevelt received a letter signed by Albert Einstein, Eugene Wigner and Leo Szilard, all eminent physicists. They alerted the President to the possibility of using nuclear fission to create a weapon and that the expertise to do so was present in Germany. In fact all of the major combatants, the USSR, Britain, Japan and Germany, had teams exploring the creation of nuclear weapons. Nuclear fission was first achieved in Germany in 1938. In an effort to stymie this effort the Allies helped remove Norway's stocks of heavy water, necessary for managing the reaction, before the German invasion of March 1940.

Once the US was at war, the task of developing a nuclear weapon in the US was turned over to the Army Corps of Engineers. General Leslie Groves assembled a team of physicists who were eventually concentrated at Los Alamos, New Mexico. While the project as a whole was under the control of the army, the scientific activity was conducted primarily by civilians headed by the physicist Robert Oppenheimer. Security was incredibly strict, but this did not stop the Soviets from placing a spy, the physicist Hans Fuchs, deep within the project. Facilities were created in Oak Ridge, Tennessee and Hanford, Washington to manufacture the material required for the explosion. Columbia University, Berkeley and the University of Chicago all conducted research as part of the Manhattan Project. Eventually two types of weapon were developed, one using uranium 235 and the other using plutonium. The uranium bomb was detonated by firing a radioactive piece at the critical mass of uranium. Using TNT to implode on the fissionable material detonated the plutonium bomb.

In the summer of 1945 the team assembled a tower at the test site in Alamogordo, New Mexico from which to drop a prototype of the plutonium bomb.

7.5 Effects of the Second World War on the Pacific

Conceptual understanding

Key questions

→ What practical issues did the Allies face in the wake of Japan's defeat?

→ What role did the dropping of the atomic bombs have on the post-war situation?

Key concepts

→ Continuity

→ Change

Democratization of Japan and US occupation

Unlike Germany, Japan was defeated primarily by the United States and thus its occupation fell to the US and its appointed governor General MacArthur. The US goals for Japan were to see it develop as a liberal democracy with an economy based on free market principles. Specifically the terms of the occupation were:

- punishment of war criminals

- disbanding the military and disarmament

- a ban on former military officers from holding political office

- disbanding the large corporations called "zaibatsu"

- the emperor had to renounce his divinity and accept a figurehead role in government

- land reform that broke up large holdings in favour of smallhold tenants

- the US was permitted to maintain military bases on Okinawa and in Japan.

Between 1945 and 1950 US aid poured into Japan, but it was not until the heightened spending of the Korean War and Japan's resulting strategic location that the capital required for economic take off really flowed into the country. In 1952 the US occupation of Japan formally ended although the terms of the peace did not and Japan remained a demilitarized parliamentary democracy with a flourishing market economy.

Cold War

The US was the sole occupying power in Japan and thus the rehabilitation and political direction of the country was largely determined by the US. Japanese imperial holdings, however, were divided among the Allied Powers including China, which received Taiwan. The USSR took control of the north half of Korea, Sakhalin

Island and the Kurile Islands. Britain recovered control of Hong Kong. Outside of the home islands the United States took control of the south half of Korea below the 38th parallel, and assorted smaller islands.

The Soviet Union had honoured the pledge it made at Yalta to enter the war with Japan. Its declaration and simultaneous invasion of Mongolia happened on 7 August 1945, the day after the atomic bombing of Hiroshima. The two events are related. Part of the decision to drop the bomb had hinged on the US reluctance to accept Soviet help in defeating Japan and with it a share in the occupation. Stalin certainly saw the bombing as an effort to keep the Soviets out of the conflict. This might also explain the precipitous dropping of the second bomb. An earlier occupation plan had divided Japan much as Germany had been divided, but this was when Allied help seemed essential to defeat Japan with conventional arms. With the advent of the atomic bomb, the US no longer need its allies' help. Britain and China were in no position economically to occupy Japan, especially given Britain's occupation responsibilities in Germany. Likewise France had no appetite for the occupation of Japan. This left the Soviets. Truman's growing distrust of Stalin and his policies precluded them, in Truman's mind, from any place in the peace they had not earned by force of arms.

The US occupation of Japan provided an important base for US and United Nations (UN) operations during the Korean War. In fact, the escalation of the Cold War that came with the Korean War accelerated the rehabilitation of both Japan and West Germany.

Imperialism and decolonization

The cost of the Second World War in both Europe and the Pacific reduced Britain and France to second-rate powers, eclipsed by the two global superpowers in military strength, economic power and political influence. Yet both France and Britain still had, or had recently regained, global empires. The events of 1940–1942 illustrated to the British the difficulty in trying to defend such geographically scattered holdings. When this difficulty was combined with the cost of the war and the ascendance of Clement Attlee's Labour government in 1945, there grew in Britain a political will to begin contemplating the independence of some colonial holdings such as India. Eventually the Allied commander responsible for western Asia during the war, Lord Louis Mountbatten, would be dispatched to negotiate the independence of British India. Other British colonial holdings such as Hong Kong reverted to the British. The Philippines became independent in July 1946.

The war's effect on French colonial holdings in Asia proceeded differently. Because of the nature of the war's end in Asia, coming as it did with two nuclear explosions, a large number of active Japanese army units were still in the field and there had been no provisions made for their surrender. The result was a haphazard demobilization of the Japanese army. In Manchuria some surrendered to the Soviet Red Army after a brief but vicious fight in which the Soviets lost 8,000 and the Japanese 40 000 dead, their weapons being left for Jiang Jieshi's nationalist forces rather than Mao's communist fighters in some cases. The Chinese Civil War would erupt again after the interruption of the

Second World War. The Soviets also occupied the Kurile Islands. In Indo-China units surrendered to undermanned British units who in turn used the Japanese forces to maintain order. Unlike the British in India, and much to the annoyance of Ho Chi Minh, who had seized portions of northern Indo-China, the French assumed they would regain control of Indo-China and resume its imperial activities as it had in the pre-war years and this lead to nine years of revolutionary warfare between the Viet Minh and French forces.

ATL Thinking skills

Complete the following table comparing the war in the Pacific with the war in North Africa and Europe. Once you have done that develop two generalizations about the nature of warfare in the Second World War.

Importance of . . .	Europe and North Africa	Pacific
Naval power		
Air power		
Land forces		
Technology		
Generalization 1:		
Generalization 2:		

Source skills

The Franck Report

The following is from the summary section of the Report of the Committee on Political and Social Problems, Manhattan Project "Metallurgical Laboratory", University of Chicago, 11 June 1945 (The Franck Report).

Members of the Committee:

James Franck (Chairman)
Donald J Hughes
JJ Nickson
Eugene Rabinowitch
Glenn T Seaborg
JC Stearns
Leo Szilard

Nuclear bombs cannot possibly remain a "secret weapon" at the exclusive disposal of this country, for more than a few years. The scientific facts on which their construction is based are well known to scientists of other countries. Unless an effective international control of nuclear explosives is instituted, a race of nuclear armaments is certain to ensue following the first revelation of our possession of nuclear weapons to the world. Within ten years other countries may have nuclear bombs, each of which, weighing less than a ton, could destroy an urban area of more than five square miles. In the war to which such an armaments race is likely to lead, the United States, with its agglomeration of population and industry in comparatively few metropolitan districts, will be at a disadvantage compared to the nations whose population and industry are scattered over large areas.

Questions

1   What do the authors mean by "an armaments race"?

2   What does this source tell us about the relationship of science and international relations?

3   With reference to its origin, purpose and content, what are the strengths and weaknesses of the source for historians studying the US decision to drop atomic bombs on Japan in 1945?

Exam-style questions and further reading

Exam-style questions

1   Examine the Japanese decision to go to war with the United States in 1941.

2   Compare and contrast the Allied forces in the Pacific with the Japanese forces in the Pacific.

3   Discuss the significance of the Battle of Midway to the outcome of the war in the Pacific.

4   Evaluate the US decision to drop atomic bombs on Hiroshima and Nagasaki.

5   Compare and contrast the significance of sea and land power in the Pacific.

6   Examine the causes of Japanese success in the first six months of the Pacific war.

7   To what extent did the Second World War affect Japanese society?

Further reading

Costello, John. 1985. *The Pacific War, 1941–1945.* Harper Perennial. New York, USA.

Gilbert, Martin. 1989. *Second World War.* Stoddart. Toronto, Canada.

Keegan, John. 1990. *The Second World War.* Viking, New York, USA.

Kelly, Cynthia C and Rhodes, Richard. 2009. *The Manhattan Project: The Birth of the Atomic Bomb in the Words of Its Creators, Eyewitnesses, and Historians.* Black Dog and Leventhal. New York, USA.

Stille, Mark. 2014. *The Imperial Japanese Navy in the Pacific War.* Osprey. Oxford, UK.

Using the markbands

It is important to understand the assessment criteria that examiners will use to evaluate your work. IB assessments use criteria-based marking, which means that your work is judged against a set of criteria describing levels of achievement. For Paper 2 this is a set of graduated markbands with a maximum mark of 15.

For a detailed break-down of markbands for Paper 2, see page 1, Your guide to Paper 2.

If we look closely at the markbands, we can find information that will be useful for writing a successful essay. Each markband is divided into four sections:

1   Understanding and addressing the question; structure

2   Historical knowledge and concepts

3   Use of examples

4   Level of analysis

Since you must explicitly include all these areas in your essay, you should use these elements as the basis for your outline. Each of the four sections has a set of descriptors across the markbands and these are what determine the characteristics of successful essays.

1 Understanding and addressing the question; structure

Important descriptors in this section include clarity, coherence, lack of repetition, and focus. The demands of the question are understood. This means that the command term is understood. You must answer all elements of the question.

2 Historical knowledge and concepts

The descriptors in this section focus on the accuracy and relevance of your historical knowledge. Accuracy improves with detail, so be as detailed as you can. It is difficult to achieve the higher markbands without including some discussion of the pertinent historical concepts, so make sure you clearly identify them and make sure they are relevant.

3 Use of examples

While the previous section deals with accuracy of your historical knowledge, this section focuses on how well you use your examples and evidence to support your answer to the question. Strong links between examples, where appropriate, and to the question are key to doing well on this aspect of the markbands.

4 Level of analysis

Level of analysis examines the extent to which you have gone beyond a simple recounting of events. Essays that are primarily narrative have difficulty reaching the higher markbands, where the emphasis is on using these events to answer the question.

Historiography and perspectives

Historiography is an important part of the study of history. Understanding the debates, issues, schools of thought and positions of influential historians can foster a deeper appreciation of the discipline of history. In terms of the markbands, however, a discussion of historiography is not necessary to be successful. More important is the concept of *perspectives*. The ability to examine history from multiple perspectives is essential to a balanced understanding of the past and this is what is reflected in the markbands. Some of these perspectives can be traditional historiography, but can also include the perspectives of participants in the historic events.

For example, when addressing a question on the causes of the First World War, it is appropriate to examine the position of the German historian Fritz Fischer or the Marxist historian Eric Hobsbawm. It is equally appropriate to discuss the perspectives of the German foreign ministry or the French Socialist Jean Jaurès. Either approach could help address the descriptor "There is evaluation of different perspectives" from the markbands.

Conclusion: putting it all together

While the IB history course is focused on the comparative and interpretive elements of the discipline, the world history topics are specifically designed to be approached in a comparative fashion. This is the reason why you are required to study multiple regions in each of the topics. One of the reasons we study history is to develop an understanding of humans across the globe and a comparative approach is an important means to this end.

The world history topics are assessed in Paper 2 of your external assessment. It therefore follows that a number of the questions on this examination paper are going to require some form of comparison. In reality, compare and contrast questions will be found on all three external assessments – Papers 1, 2 and 3. Paper 2, however, emphasizes a global approach to history. To help structure this global approach, the IB has divided the world into various regions for the purpose of Paper 2.

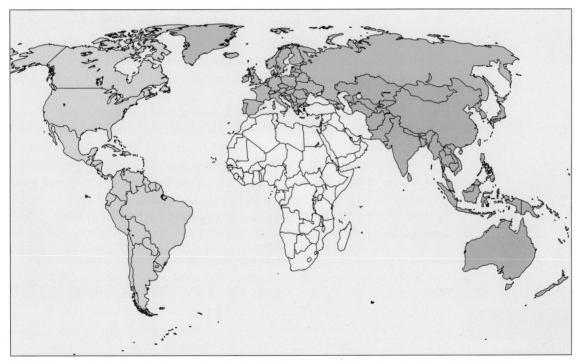

▲ Outline map indicating the four regions for the IB history course. Note that the Second World War is a multi-region war and can be used as such when answering Paper 2 questions.

We discussed the command terms that the IB uses for its assessments in the introduction to this book. In those command terms the concept of "comparison" is detailed as "compare and contrast" to delineate between similarities and differences or, on occasion, one or the other. Before we discuss "compare and contrast" in detail, perhaps we should look at it in broader terms.

At its heart the tasks of comparing and contrasting are activities of analysis. We can think of analysis as the process of breaking down an idea, event or concept into its component parts so that we can not only think more deeply about those components, but also so we can investigate the relationships between them and their individual effects on the whole. In that way we can see how the idea, event or concept is structured and how this informs key historic concepts such as causation and consequence. For example, if we are asked to analyse the leadership of General Giap in the Battle of Dien Bien Phu during the Indo-China War, we would need to pull apart elements of his leadership, his preparation, clarity of commands and strategy to see how they fit together and thereby develop a deeper understanding of what made him the military leader that he was. Analysing the causes of the First World War would require us to separate out the various causes to see the relationship of each to the other and how they combined to trigger the war.

If we look at analysis this way we can see that it forms the basis for a number of other activities such as "evaluation". Before we can evaluate an event, concept or idea – that is, to appraise it against a criteria or objective, weighing its strengths and weaknesses – it makes sense to pull it apart to see how each component contributed to the event, concept or idea. For example, before we can evaluate the FLN's military decisions during the Algerian War, we first need to separate out elements of these decisions so that we can make a thorough and deep appraisal.

This idea of breaking an idea, concept or event into its components, analysing, is a vital element in a comparative approach to history and tackling compare and contrast questions. This is because for a comparison to be meaningful it must be carried out across common components. Simply comparing the Japanese and Italian war efforts in the Second World War will lead to an unfocused description of the two things being compared, in this case Japan and Italy in the Second World War. For the comparison to be meaningful and intellectually fruitful, we must first decide across which common components we are going to conduct our comparison. In the case of Japan and Italy in the Second World War these components could be aircraft production, naval strength and overall strategy.

The structure of the chapters in this book is designed to help with this comparative approach. Each chapter, focusing on a single conflict, is broken into the same elements – causes, combatants, strategy and tactics, operations and effects. These elements can form the basis of commonalities across which we can compare these conflicts. The structure of the entire IB history course likewise lends itself to this essential structure, using as its common elements the concepts of:

- cause
- consequence
- change
- continuity
- significance
- perspective.

The cognitive skill of analysis is an important element in the "thinking skills" component of the IB's approaches to learning (ATL). It also plays a role in the other ATL components such as research skills and self-management skills. The following ATL activities are designed to help you develop your ability to analyse and think of 20th-century wars in a comparative fashion.

ATL **Thinking skills**

Compare and contrast the significance of the factors below in determining the outcome of the Second World War in Europe and the Pacific.

- strategy
- industrial production
- technology

ATL **Thinking skills**

Broadly speaking a thesis or thesis statement is your position on a given topic or answer to a question. While there are a number of ways to write one, strong thesis statements all have some things in common. A thesis statement should contain the following.

- **Your position/answer to the question**: indicates a focus on the task.

- **Any qualification to that position/answer**: because few historical issues/ questions have a straightforward "yes" or "no" answer, some qualification is generally required. A qualifier also indicates that you are thinking deeply about the task. A qualifier is particularly important in responding to a task involving the idea of "to what extent".

- **An indication of how you will support your position/answer**: this provides structure to your response and an indication to the reader of the direction the response will take.

In terms of a compare and contrast essay a thesis might look like this:

QuestionCompare and contrast the role of technology in the Algerian War and the Falklands/Malvinas War.

Thesis statement: Technology played an important role in transporting troops and materials in the Algerian War and Falklands/Malvinas Wars, but had limited effect on land combat.

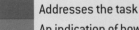 Addresses the task

An indication of how the position will be supported

A qualification to the position

Write a potential thesis statement for each of the following questions.

- Compare and contrast the causes of the Indo-China War and the Algerian War.
- Evaluate the Allied strategy in the Pacific theatre of the Second World War.
- To what extent did militarism and nationalism cause the First World War?

Index